The Greatest Story Ever Retold

ENVISIONING JESUS NARRATIVES FROM GOSPELS TO FILM

John Anthony Dunne
and Jeannine K. Brown

Baker Academic
a division of Baker Publishing Group
Grand Rapids, Michigan

Published by Baker Academic
a division of Baker Publishing Group
Grand Rapids, Michigan
BakerAcademic.com

Printed in the United States of America

Library of Congress Cataloging-in-Publication Data
Names: Dunne, John Anthony, 1986– author | Brown, Jeannine K., 1961– author
Title: The greatest story ever retold : envisioning Jesus narratives from gospels to film / John Anthony Dunne and Jeannine K. Brown.
Description: Grand Rapids, Michigan : Baker Academic, a division of Baker Publishing Group, [2026] | Includes bibliographical references and index.
Identifiers: LCCN 2025029629 | ISBN 9781540967145 paperback | ISBN 9781540969958 casebound | ISBN 9781493453078 ebook | ISBN 9781493453085 pdf
Subjects: LCSH: Jesus Christ—Biography—History and criticism | Bible. Gospels—Criticism, interpretation, etc.
Classification: LCC BT301.9 .D86 2026
LC record available at https://lccn.loc.gov/2025029629

Baker Publishing Group publications use paper produced from sustainable forestry practices and postconsumer waste whenever possible.

26 27 28 29 30 31 32 7 6 5 4 3 2 1

"So much has been written about Jesus movies over the past three decades that it might seem impossible to approach these films from a fresh perspective. Yet Dunne and Brown have done exactly that—by stressing that readers of the Gospels are doing what filmmakers do: visualizing the characters, scripting the scenes, and composing the soundtracks. Dunne and Brown provide an engaging interplay between the Gospels and the Jesus movies, addressing matters of genre, characterization, and themes all while keeping the reader/viewer at the center of the hermeneutical enterprise. A wonderful addition to the library of books on Jesus in the Gospels and on the screen."

—**Adele Reinhartz**, University of Ottawa; author of *Jesus of Hollywood*

"Dunne and Brown have produced a volume that is deeply engaged with the depiction of Jesus and the Gospels in film but is also wonderfully engaging for anyone who has read a Gospel or watched a film about one. Drawing examples from a wide range of films, the authors show with admirable clarity how Jesus films inevitably depend on and reflect a myriad of interpretive decisions. What is so unique and exciting about Dunne and Brown's approach is that they invite us to consider how every reading of the gospel is truly an act of imagination."

—**David J. Shepherd**, Trinity College Dublin; author of *The Bible on Silent Film: Spectacle, Story and Scripture in the Early Cinema*

"*The Greatest Story Ever Retold* is a valuable contribution to the study of Bible and visual culture. Unlike previous works, which tend to prioritize film over textual analysis, Dunne and Brown pay attention to the interpretation of both modern and ancient media without privileging either. Their skillful exploration of over two hundred Jesus films produces surprising insights into traditional topics, such as the synoptic problem, the Gospel genre, and narrative criticism. More importantly, the authors invite readers to recognize their own assumptions about the Jesus story and develop a deeper appreciation for the art of biblical interpretation. They present the interpretive nature of the Gospels and Jesus films not as a problem to be solved but as a reality to be acknowledged and studied. This volume is sure to help readers engage biblical literature and Jesus films more thoughtfully and with a clearer understanding of their own roles as interpreters."

—**Rhonda Burnette-Bletsch**, Eastern University

"If you're searching for an excellent way of thinking about how the stories of Jesus have been transformed in early writings, Jesus films, and our own imaginations, then this book might be what you're looking for. Dunne and Brown track the development of harmonization, invention, and characterization in portrayals of Jesus and his supporting cast, urging us to consider more deeply the creative task underpinning the original Gospels, Jesus movies, and our own mental images."

—**Matthew Page**, author of *100 Bible Films*

"Dunne and Brown invite readers to share both their fascination with Jesus films and their humble recognition of interpretation's inevitability, which empowers readers to reflect on their own evaluative standards for Jesus films—and their own preexisting internal Jesus 'films.' Such humble curiosity is particularly recommended for anyone creating Jesus films/stories. An additional benefit is the authors' extended attention to the most popular Jesus films and series, particularly *The Chosen*, as it has received so little academic attention."

—**Richard Walsh**, Methodist University (emeritus)

For all the storytellers
who have captured our imaginations

Contents

Preface

This book started as a course: Jesus, Now Playing: Ancient and Contemporary Tellings of the Jesus Story. We offered this online elective at Bethel Seminary, where we both teach, in 2022 and were surprised when almost fifty students joined. After exploring the fascinating connections between ancient and modern stories about Jesus, we are no longer surprised by that interest. We ourselves have been drawn more deeply into these varied and vivid narrative retellings.

From the beginning, we were interested in the hermeneutical (interpretive) questions that swirled around the use of Gospels—both canonical and noncanonical—in Jesus films. In this book, as in the class, we explore patterns of use that extend across the centuries—patterns such as harmonizing Gospel accounts, filling in gaps about parts of Jesus's life that get less airtime in the New Testament, and going deeper and wider with the captivating characters that populate the Gospels. We have also become more convinced than ever that, as readers and viewers, we interact with the Gospels and Jesus films with our own "directors" in our minds. That is, we are directors of our own Jesus films, having *envisioned* the story already in our mind's eye from our encounters with the Gospels.

We have found researching and writing this book a delightful experience, not least because the entire process has been brimming with stories. We have read and reread stories about Jesus and watched and rewatched stories about Jesus—and we have had the opportunity to rehearse many parts of these stories throughout the book. Like with a good novel that is hard to put down, we hope you will have moments of being caught up in these retold stories.

We have also enjoyed writing this book *together*. In the course we taught, much of the division of labor fell along lines of specialty and interest. Jeannine provided input from and narrative analysis of the Gospels,[1] while John took on the momentous task of analyzing a portion of the over two hundred Jesus films we have now cataloged in these pages.[2] As the work continued, each of us learned from what the other was researching. And we thought together—over numerous coffees, lunches, and Zoom meetings—about ways the Jesus story has inspired fresh retellings and what these retellings reveal about filmmakers *and* about ourselves as viewers, as well as what they reveal about the Gospels themselves. This book is truly a collaboration, and many versions of each chapter have been passed back and forth between us.

We want to thank Baker Academic, and Bryan Dyer in particular, for publishing the book and for providing such able editorial guidance all along the way. We are also indebted to an amazing cadre of New Testament scholars who have paved the way for studying Jesus films in conversation with the Gospels. These include Mark Goodacre, Adele Reinhartz, W. Barnes Tatum, and Richard Walsh, among others, as well as Matthew Page, who has done incredible work on his *Bible Films Blog* and elsewhere. We are grateful to the Bethel Alumni Association for a grant that allowed us to invite experts in the Gospels and in film to our online course, and we thank these experts for enriching the conversations: Helen Bond, Nicholas Perrin, Mark Goodacre, and Chris Hewett (book and film critic at *The Minnesota Star Tribune*). Thanks are also due to the guests who joined John on *The Two Cities* podcast for a short series on Bible films and Jesus films (episodes 130–37 from the summer of 2022), including, in order of appearance, Matthew Page, Richard Walsh, Mark Goodacre, Siobhán Jolley, Katie Turner, Adele Reinhartz, Robert Derrenbacker, and Michelle Fletcher. A final word of thanks goes to Josh Johnson, a student at Bethel Seminary and videographer for our university, for editing the lectures for our Jesus film course and for reading the manuscript for this book and providing such helpful input.

Our hope is that this book will ignite a passion for returning to the Gospel narratives and for venturing further into the Jesus stories that have been inspired by them, whether on page or in film. And we hope you'll get a fresh glimpse of the Jesus story you hold in your own mind's eye as you contemplate *the greatest story ever retold*.

1. Brown, *Gospels as Stories*; Brown and Roberts, *Matthew*.

2. This is part of his scholarly attention to pop cultural reception of biblical texts (Dunne, *Esther and Her Elusive God*) as well as theological engagement with contemporary TV and film (e.g., Bowen and Dunne, *Theology and Black Mirror*; Dunne and Song, *Theology, Religion, and Twin Peaks*).

Abbreviations

Apocryphal, Pseudepigraphic, and Gnostic Texts

1–4 Macc.	1–4 Maccabees
Acts John	Acts of John
Ep. Apos.	Epistle to the Apostles
Gos. Barn.	Gospel of Barnabas
Gos. Jud.	Gospel of Judas
Gos. Mary	Gospel of Mary
Gos. Nic.	Gospel of Nicodemus
Gos. Pet.	Gospel of Peter
Gos. Phil.	Gospel of Philip
Inf. Gos. Thom.	Infancy Gospel of Thomas
NHC	Nag Hammadi Codex
Prot. Jas.	Protevangelium of James

Josephus

Ant.	*Jewish Antiquities*

Rabbinic Sources

b.	Babylonian Talmud
Lev. Rab.	Leviticus Rabbah
m.	Mishnah
Mikv.	Mikva'ot
Neg.	Nega'im
Nid.	Niddah
Shabb.	Shabbat
Sheqal.	Sheqalim
t.	Tosefta
Tehar.	Teharot
Zavim	Zavim

Apostolic and Patristic Writings

Augustine, *Cons.*	Augustine, *De consensu evangelistarum* (*Harmony of the Gospels*)
Irenaeus, *Haer.*	Irenaeus, *Adversus haereses* (*Against Heresies*)
Origen, *Cels.*	Origen, *Contra Celsum* (*Against Celsus*)
Tertullian, *Apol.*	Tertullian, *Apologeticus* (*Apology*)

Bible Versions

CSB	Christian Standard Bible

ESV	English Standard Version
GNB	Good News Bible
Message	*The Message*. Edited by Eugene Peterson. Colorado Springs: NavPress, 2018
NASB	New American Standard Bible
NA^{28}	*Novum Testamentum Graece*. 28th ed. Edited by Barbara Aland et al. Stuttgart: Deutsche Bibelgesellschaft, 2012
NET	New English Translation
NIV	New International Version
NKJV	New King James Version
NLT	New Living Translation
NRSVue	New Revised Standard Version Updated Edition
RSV	Revised Standard Version

Secondary Sources

BDAG	Danker, Frederick W., Walter Bauer, William F. Arndt, and F. Wilbur Gingrich. *Greek-English Lexicon of the New Testament and Other Early Christian Literature*. 3rd ed. Chicago: University of Chicago Press, 2000
TSAJ	Texte und Studien zum antiken Judentum
WUNT	Wissenschaftliche Untersuchungen zum Neuen Testament

Introduction

Whenever we read a narrative, we visualize the story in our own unique way. How we engage with a great novel, for example, will be distinct from how others do. The way someone envisions a story cannot be fully duplicated by anyone else. Each person's imagination leads them to picture how characters look and to conjure up the world in which the story takes place. In this sense, we are like directors who get to call the shots for the films projected in our mind's eye as we read.[1]

We suggest that the same is true of biblical narratives, including the Gospels. This means, then, that the process of reading the Gospels has cinematic analogies. Because we each "direct" our own Jesus story as we read, actual Jesus films can be valuable for understanding the Gospels. And, given this same internal dynamic, Jesus films can also help us understand the ways we each visualize the narrative as we interpret it. In this book, we are interested in analyzing the work of Jesus film directors like Alice Guy, Cecil B. DeMille, Pier Paolo Pasolini, Martin Scorsese, Mel Gibson, and Dallas Jenkins. But the film director that we are most interested in is you. You are the director of an original Jesus film each time you read the Gospels.

Envisioning the Stories of Jesus

As we read the Gospels, each of us makes subtle decisions that resemble the kinds of choices filmmakers make. We imagine the scenery, the characters,

1. Some people aren't able to visualize in their mind's eye as often or as easily as others, and those with a rare condition called aphantasia aren't able to do it all. See, e.g., the podcast episode "Aphantasia" by *Radiolab* (Lulu Miller and Latif Nasser, hosts, WNYC Studios, June 14, 2024, https://radiolab.org/podcast/aphantasia).

and the action. Some of us may not be prone to strong direction; we may be reticent to stray too far from the "script" (the Gospels). Yet all films are adaptations of scripts, just as the film in our mind's eye is an adaptation. Staying close to the script is just one possible directorial decision. Others will do it differently, whether in their minds or on-screen.

When we evaluate a Jesus film, we are often comparing our own "direction" with the film's direction. A common critique of film adaptations is something akin to "That's not how I imagined it," which is another way of saying, "I'd direct the story differently." Or, more accurately, "I *have directed it differently* in my previous readings." Consider a pastor preaching a sermon on a Gospel text this way: "I imagine it went like this . . ." and then proceeding to renarrate the story with additions and modifications. The pastor is directing the scene and asking the congregation to imagine it similarly. As with a Jesus film, the audience is given a new way to visualize the biblical scene.

Now, visualization occurs with any kind of story, but the stakes are higher with Jesus films. They build on stories from sacred texts about a religious figure whom Christians believe is God incarnate. And the difference between "I don't imagine it that way," when it comes to fiction, and "It didn't happen that way," when it comes to history, raises the stakes further. The Gospels, however, are not modern histories or news reports that record everything that happened. The Gospels are fundamentally narratives, and narrative texts inevitably prompt our minds to fill in gaps to imagine a fuller story.

Since Jesus films externalize what we already perform internally when we read or hear the Gospels, they confront us with the role that visualization plays in interpretation. This is true of any variety of reading—not least the practice of visualization made popular by Ignatius of Loyola (fifteenth–sixteenth century CE) in which readers prayerfully imagine scenes from the Gospels so thoroughly that they place themselves within the story. Regardless of the kinds of visualization, however, films inevitably differ from our imagined depictions. But they can help us identify our assumptions about the Jesus story. Jesus films might not necessarily be more accurate than our own conceptions of the story, but they showcase that our visualization is only one among many possibilities. They press us to reckon with questions about the text that often go unaddressed and reveal that we typically take our own visualizations for granted.

Let's consider a specific example. How do you envision Jesus's triumphal entry into Jerusalem on Palm Sunday? Undoubtedly, the answer will depend in part on your familiarity with the relevant Gospel texts (cf. Matt. 21:1–11; Mark 11:1–11; Luke 19:28–44; John 12:12–36), but your visualization may also take into account your encounters with artistic representations of the

See-Saw Films / Porchlight Films / Universal Pictures International Production

Promotional photo for *Mary Magdalene* (2018)

event, including paintings and film, as well as sermons and other liturgical elements from your church experiences. Yet other influences could also be in play, such as experiences of riding a donkey (or horse), being in a large crowd, or visiting Jerusalem. A feature likely to be common among visualizations of this scene (confirmed in Jesus films) is that all eyes are on Jesus. He is the center of gravity, so to speak. In what might be its most compelling moment, *Mary Magdalene* (2018) goes against this trend of centering Jesus.

This film portrays Jesus arriving in Jerusalem amid a flurry of activity already occurring in the city and at the massive temple complex before the start of Passover later that week. The disciples do their best to turn the crowd's attention to Jesus, but the people hardly notice—their attention is drawn in many different directions. Depicting a well-known story in such an unusual way can unsettle the viewer's assumptions. This version isn't necessarily more accurate (it might be entirely wrong), but viewers are compelled to interrogate their own assumptions about this Gospel event and consider whether there might be other ways of imagining the episode, akin to a commentary or sermon introducing us to new ways of thinking about a passage.

Cognitive psychology has studied the active role of readers (or hearers or viewers) in narrative interpretation. A narrative's audience plays an integral, even participatory, role alongside the author(s). Keith Oatley suggests that fiction "is a guided dream, a model that we readers and viewers construct in collaboration with the writer."[2] Although Oatley is referring primarily to literary fiction, his analysis is applicable to reading any narrative, including biblical ones. In addition to the metaphor of dreams, Oatley compares narratives to the technological image of simulations, which "run not on computers but on minds."[3] From the standpoint of cognitive psychology, narratives are a kind of cocreation between the writer and the audience. Oatley writes further: "The dream model when it is externalized into text, or when it is realized in performance of actors on a stage, exists in an intermediate place, half-way between the world and the mind. When we as readers or as audience members take up this intermediate object we construct from it our own mental performance, based on our own mental models. We connect what goes in the model to aspects of our own selves, to our own memories, to our own concerns."[4] When we encounter a story, we bring our full selves to it, and the story is brought out of that "intermediate place" that Oatley mentions. Indeed, we are brought into the story *in neurological ways*, since when we read about certain actions, there is corresponding brain activity "in the areas concerned with making the same actions ourselves."[5] The reader's role in constructing the world of the story along with the writer is also apparent in our retelling of stories, which we do in *our own words*, emphasizing aspects that stand out to us.[6]

Every encounter with a story, therefore, is unique to the individual.[7] Virtual reality (VR) Jesus films confirm and illustrate this phenomenon. Currently there are two major VR Jesus films, *7 Miracles* (2018) and *Jesus VR* (2016). Because of the interactive nature of this medium, these films underscore how reading and visualizing the Jesus story invite choices of emphases in the mind's eye. Quite a few VR features are predetermined in these films, including casting, direction, blocking, and the selection and sequence of events as the viewer is led linearly through the storyline. Yet the viewer-participant experiences more freedom than in a standard film or TV show since the singular gaze of the camera is decentralized. Though limited, this dynamic quality of VR further illuminates the collaborative nature of storytelling, with the viewer engaging in their own "mental performance" of the story (Oatley's term).

2. Oatley, *Such Stuff as Dreams*, ix.
3. Oatley, *Such Stuff as Dreams*, 17.
4. Oatley, *Such Stuff as Dreams*, 19.
5. Oatley, *Such Stuff as Dreams*, 20; cf. 34, 77.
6. This is even true of short stories, as demonstrated through experimental studies going back to 1932 (Oatley, *Such Stuff as Dreams*, 58–63).
7. Dancygier, *Language of Stories*, 57.

Some Jesus films accent individual encounters with the Jesus story by focusing on a particular character and developing their role within the story more fully. In effect, this focal character offers the viewer a fresh point of view (POV) for considering Jesus, as Steven Greydanus observes.[8] For example, in *The Cross* (2001) viewers witness the events of the passion (Jesus's suffering and death) from Jesus's own POV. While everyone has a distinct engagement with stories, stories do have an ability to constrain our imaginations since texts have certain boundaries.[9] Yet as Barbara Dancygier notes, "The emergence of the story relies to a comparable degree on the frames evoked in the reader's mind."[10] Stories, then, involve both a text of some kind and what readers, hearers, or viewers bring to that text. In this book, we consider the value of Jesus films for engaging the Gospels, especially as we all are already directors of our own Jesus stories. Whether we love Jesus films or hate them (or fall somewhere in between), all readers of the Gospels are engaged in their own imaginative "filmmaking."

What Exactly Is a Jesus Film?

A label like "Jesus film" probably seems intuitive. Surely these are films that tell a historically rooted story about the life of Jesus based on one or more of the canonical Gospels. But the boundaries of this category can be difficult to determine, so which films fit and which do not are open questions. How much verisimilitude with the past is required for a work to "count" as a Jesus film? Do Jesus films need to tell the story of Jesus's life from birth to resurrection, or is narrating one portion of his life adequate? Is it a Jesus film if Jesus isn't the main character? If a film revolves around a "Christ figure," is it a Jesus film? These questions highlight the complexity of the label. Complicating the matter even further, people debate whether the category of "Jesus film" constitutes a genre designation or whether it refers to a broad collection of films with many subgenres.

The Cinematic Scope of Jesus Films

We begin with the "film" side of the "Jesus film" question. To state the obvious, Jesus films are forms of recorded audiovisual media. It is possible to limit the designation of Jesus films to feature-length movies released in

8. Greydanus, "Through Other Eyes," 78.
9. Stockwell, *Cognitive Poetics*, 155.
10. Dancygier, *Language of Stories*, 56; cf. 195.

cinemas by major production companies, and many do. But this excludes made-for-TV films, so-called straight to VHS/DVD movies, TV or streaming series, and recordings of live theatrical performances (e.g., passion plays). We know that there's a risk in placing these distinct media under a single umbrella of "film," such that their respective integrities might not be recognized. But given our emphasis on visualizing the text, and especially considering today's media ecosystem and its plethora of celluloid Jesuses, we see more upside in broadening the conversation. For our purposes, we understand Jesus films to include a wide range of visual productions and recordings.

The Genre of Jesus Films

The genre of Jesus films is not easily defined and so needs clarification. What distinguishes these films, and do they constitute a distinctive and discrete genre?

As a Subset of "Bible Films"

To begin to answer the question of genre, we can first acknowledge that Jesus films are themselves a subset of "Bible films." The broader category of Bible films can help us understand the history of cinema, as Matthew Page contends, not least because of their prominence within the story of film—their origins coinciding with the birth of film itself.[11] Specifically, Jesus films routinely belong to the type of Bible films that Adele Reinhartz calls "the Bible on film" as opposed to "the Bible in film."[12] Reinhartz further narrows the categorization of Jesus films to *biopics*, since they focus on the life of a historical figure.[13] Yet this Bible film category does not help much to identify the actual genre of Jesus films. While a number of Jesus films can comfortably fit within this designation (e.g., *Jesus of Nazareth* [1977]; *Jesus* [1999]), many more do not (e.g., *Godspell* [1973]; *Io Sono Con Te* [*Let It Be*, 2010]). In the end, an overly essentialist definition of Jesus films based on genre does not do justice to the diversity of the films commonly designated with that label.

Jesus Films as a Discrete Genre (Mixed with Other Genres)

This is our perspective on what Jesus films are and which films fit the category: *Jesus films are their own genre, and Jesus films can also participate in other genres at the same time*. That Jesus films are their own genre can be

11. Page, *100 Bible Films*, 3.

12. Reinhartz (*Bible and Cinema: An Introduction*) reserves "the Bible in film" for films that contain allusions and parallels to biblical stories rather than retellings of those stories.

13. See, e.g., Reinhartz, "Jesus and Christ-Figures," 424–26.

seen in the conventions and tropes of these films that are passed on and perpetuated with each new generation. This line of inheritance highlights a key feature of what constitutes a genre—namely, *imitation*. Jesus films and their filmmakers seem to recognize their participation in the "Jesus film" genre as they imitate as well as adapt Jesus films that have come before.

Jesus films can also readily participate in other film genres. In Andrew Judd's helpful exploration of genre theory, he contends that genres are "relatively stable conventions" that people routinely use and adapt[14] and that texts can participate in multiple genres at once.[15] Judd's insights apply to film genres as well, which are never hermetically sealed. Movies, like written texts, can be hybrids of multiple genres. For example, Tim Burton's *Sweeney Todd* (2004) is a musical but also fits the genre of horror, and *Shaun of the Dead* (2004) and *Zombieland* (2009) are horror films but are at the same time comedies. In the same way, Jesus films can both be their own genre ("Jesus films") and participate in other film genres. Some are also musicals, such as the first four Jesus film musicals, all of which dropped in 1973: *Jesus Christ Superstar*, *Godspell*, Johnny Cash's *The Gospel Road: A Story of Jesus*, and *Jesus*, an Indian film with Bollywood influences. In addition to musicals and biopics, Jesus films can also participate in the genres of epics, parodies, documentaries, and horror.

Jesus Films as Cinematic Gospels

So far, we have focused our discussion of genre on formal characteristics (what a film *looks like*). But genres are also bound up with their aims or purposes (what a film *does*). To discern what a Jesus film aims to do, we find it helpful to view Jesus films as "cinematic Gospels." This perspective gets to the heart of the *Jesus* side of the "Jesus film" label. Jesus films aim to retell the story of Jesus in a distinct way, just as early Gospels purposed to do. Viewing these films as cinematic Gospels is productive for a few reasons. First, this understanding taps into a genre category of the early Christian movement that includes many examples. While most Christians understandably focus primarily or solely on the canonical Gospels from the first century (Matthew, Mark, Luke, and John), quite a few noncanonical Gospels were produced in subsequent centuries.[16] Many stories about events in the life of Jesus were

14. Judd, *Modern Genre Theory*, xv, 24–29.

15. Judd, *Modern Genre Theory*, 19–24. Thus, Reinhartz is not wrong to say that Jesus films are biopics, with certain films acknowledged as outliers. Those outliers participate in other genres.

16. For many Christians, the question will naturally arise whether films designated as Jesus films can only take so many liberties before they become something else—before they stop

being told by different communities in these early centuries. Viewing Jesus films as a contemporary exercise in Gospel production can open new avenues for thinking about Jesus films.[17]

Second, while early Christians did not, of course, have access to film as a medium, each of the four Gospels seems to follow a distinct kind of media, as Nicholas Elder has argued.[18] If so, the use of film can be understood as another expansion of the story of Jesus into a new medium intended for audiences to engage in a distinct way. Matthew, Mark, Luke, and John all participate in the genre of Gospel (which is a kind of Greco-Roman biography). Yet Elder proposes they are self-consciously different media: Mark is "good news" (Mark 1:1), Matthew is a "book" (Matt. 1:1), Luke is an "account" (Luke 1:1), and John is a "document" (John 20:30), with each meant to be experienced in distinct ways. Elder states, "If each gospel is a different kind of text and different kinds of texts make for different kinds of reading events, then we should not expect that the gospels were read or experienced the exact same way."[19] As the Jesus story moved into the medium of film, its cinematic retellings inevitably began engaging audiences in ways distinct from the Gospels they build on.

Third, viewing Jesus films as cinematic Gospels emphasizes that these films *are stories in their own right*. They are not a derivative art form but unique stories about Jesus, just as the four Gospels themselves are discrete stories with their own unique emphases.[20] Jesus films involve many storytelling decisions like those evident in both canonical and extracanonical Gospels—decisions we will explore throughout the book. For example, the decision of some Jesus films to focus only on Jesus's birth or youth (e.g., *La Sacra Famiglia* [*The Holy Family*, 2006]) resembles certain apocryphal Gospels. And as some noncanonical Gospels focus on Jesus's passion, some Jesus films do the same (e.g., *The Passion of the Christ* [2004]).[21] The canonical Gospels provide the broader scope of Jesus's life, ministry, death, and

being about the Jesus revealed in the four canonical Gospels. While this is a fair question for evaluating Jesus films, our focus in this book includes the analysis of any film that tells a story about Jesus in some way.

17. Viewing Jesus films as cinematic Gospels does not preclude other frameworks or analogies—e.g., "rewritten Bible" texts, Rabbinic midrash, or even modern fan fiction—that could be fruitfully developed. For a positive appraisal of ancient apocryphal writings as akin to modern fan fiction, see de Bruin, *Fan Fiction and Early Christian Writings*. For a dismissal of the category of "rewritten Bible," see Mroczek, *Literary Imagination in Jewish Antiquity*, 8–9, 119–20, 140–41, 187.

18. Elder, *Gospel Media*.

19. Elder, *Gospel Media*, 83.

20. See Brown, *Gospels as Stories*.

21. Staley, "First Seventy Years of Jesus Films," 89.

resurrection—something we see especially in Jesus films participating in the biopic genre. Another kind of example involves the choice—evident in both some apocryphal Gospels and some Jesus films—to focus on underdeveloped characters from the Gospels.[22] (These films are sometimes designated as "Jesus adjacent films" because of the prominence of other characters besides Jesus.) When readers engage such apocryphal Gospels and encounter characters with whom they are familiar from the canonical Gospels, they will find that their characterizations may have been enhanced and adapted. Whether they are consciously aware of this or not, readers inevitably bring their mental models of those characters into their readings of the apocryphal text—a phenomenon known as character *migration* in cognitive psychology.[23] A similar process occurs when viewers watching Jesus films engage a character whose portrait has been expanded.

Jesus Films as Gospel Interpretations

As unique cinematic stories of Jesus that can participate in multiple genres, Jesus films are not simply artistic *illustrations* of the Gospels but rather *interpretations* of the Gospels, regardless of the theological standpoints of the filmmakers. In fact, Christian art has always functioned in an interpretive manner. From its origins, Christians did not make art simply to illustrate the Bible. Instead, Christian artists offered "visual exegeses"[24] of biblical texts and made "meaning in its own right"[25]—something true of all kinds of artistic expressions, whether icons or stained glass, mosaics or sculptures, illustrated Bibles or children's picture books, or passion plays. Additionally, Jesus films are not merely *influenced by* the Gospels; they also exert their interpretive power on viewers by *influencing* how the Gospels are read and interpreted, a mutual influence Larry Kreitzer has explored in his work on the use of

22. E.g., films focused on (1) Mary of Nazareth (*Reina de Reinas: La Virgen María* [*Queen of Queens: The Virgin Mary*, 1948]; *Mater Dei* [*Mother of God*, 1950]; *Je Vous Salue, Marie* [*Hail Mary*, 1985]; *Marie de Nazareth* [*Mary of Nazareth*, 1995]; *Mary, Mother of Jesus* [1999]; *Maria, Figlia del Suo Figlio* [*Mary, Daughter of Her Son*, 2000]; *Maryam Moghadas* [*Saint Mary*, 2002]; *Io Sono Con Te* [*Let It Be*, 2010]; *Maria di Nazaret* [*Mary of Nazareth*, 2012]; *My Son, My Savior* [2015]; *Full of Grace* [2015]; *Mary* [2024]); (2) Peter (*The Big Fisherman* [1959]; *Apostle Peter and the Last Supper* [2012]; *The Apostle Peter: Redemption* [2016]; cf. *Quo Vadis?* [1913]; *Quo Vadis?* [1924]; *Quo Vadis* [1951]; *Quo Vadis?* [1985]); (3) Thomas (*Thomasleeha* [*Saint Thomas*, 1975]; *Gli Amici di Gesú: Tommaso* [*The Friends of Jesus: Thomas*, 2001]); (4) Barabbas (*Barabbas* [1953]; *Barabbas* [1961]; *Barabbas* [2012]; *Barabbas* [2019]); and (5) Salome (*Salomé* [1918]; *Salome* [1953]); and (6) Roman soldiers involved in the passion (*The Robe* [1953]; *Risen* [2016]; *The Christ Slayer* [2019]).

23. Rüggemeier and Shively, "Introduction," 419.

24. Hornik et al., introduction to *Art of Biblical Interpretation*, 1.

25. Jensen, *Understanding Early Christian Art*, 5; cf. 24–26.

the Bible in fiction and film.[26] In a similar vein, Mark Goodacre has argued that the way Jesus films edit their source materials, as well as rearrange and redistribute scenes and sayings, can teach us something about the way that ancient Gospels operated with respect to the synoptic problem.[27]

The interpretive power of Jesus films shines a spotlight on the importance of considering the role of our imaginations in envisioning the Gospel stories. We contend that Jesus films deserve our attention as readers of the Gospels because these films can illuminate the storytelling techniques found within ancient Gospels and because Jesus films are able to uncover our own hermeneutical processes of engaging and visualizing the stories of Jesus, in whatever form and medium we experience them.

Situating and Surveying *The Greatest Story Ever Retold*

Previous scholarship on Jesus films has been wide-ranging. Some volumes offer a guide to the full scope of Jesus films.[28] Others provide encyclopedic information, with deeper analyses of select films from across the industry.[29] Many other resources opt for depth of evaluation instead of breadth—for example, focusing in detail on a single Jesus film[30] or a single era of Jesus films (e.g., the silent era).[31] Other works investigate niche issues across multiple Jesus films[32] or examine character representations in detail.[33] Offering a particularly creative approach, Richard Walsh selects films, juxtaposes each with one of the four Gospels, and "reads" them together.[34] Many more noteworthy journal articles and book chapters could be mentioned, but this brief summary provides a

26. Kreitzer, *New Testament in Fiction and Film*; Kreitzer, *Old Testament in Fiction and Film*; Kreitzer, *Pauline Images in Fiction and Film*; Kreitzer, *Gospel Images in Fiction and Film*.

27. E.g., Goodacre ("Synoptic Jesus and the Celluloid Christ") argues that the way that some Jesus films break up Matthew's Sermon on the Mount can provide a response for at least one argument against the Farrer-Goulder Hypothesis—namely, that Luke couldn't have used Matthew because it's unlikely that Luke would have adjusted and altered Matthew's lengthy sermon.

28. See esp. Malone, *Screen Jesus*. For a brief overview of many Jesus films from within the construct of Bible films, see, e.g., Page, *100 Bible Films*; Reinhartz, *Bible and Cinema: Fifty Key Films*. Other studies include Jesus films within a broader engagement with Bible films via themes; e.g., Burnette-Bletsch, *Bible in Motion*; Reinhartz, *Bible and Cinema: An Introduction*.

29. See, e.g., Stern et al., *Savior on the Silver Screen*; Walsh and Staley, *Jesus, the Gospels, and Cinematic Imagination*; Baugh, *Imaging the Divine*; Tatum, *Jesus at the Movies*.

30. Taylor, *Jesus and Brian*; Corley and Webb, *Jesus and Mel Gibson's "The Passion of the Christ"*; Garcia et al., *Watching "The Chosen."*

31. See Shepherd, *Silents of Jesus in the Cinema*.

32. E.g., Walsh, *T&T Clark Handbook of Jesus and Film*; Turner, "Representation of New Testament Figures"; Turner, *Costuming Christ*.

33. E.g., Reinhartz, *Jesus of Hollywood*; Hebron, *Judas Iscariot*.

34. Walsh, "Reading the Gospels in the Dark."

sense of both the major contributions to Jesus film scholarship and the kinds of analyses that have been undertaken.

In the present volume, our central goal is to highlight the hermeneutical value of Jesus films for underscoring the interpretive nature of our mental visualizations of the Jesus stories told in the Gospels. Our contention is not simply that Jesus films can help us understand the Gospels better, though insights can certainly come from engaging a Jesus film. Our larger aim is to bring to the surface the implicit comparison a viewer inevitably makes between a Jesus film and their own visualization of the Jesus story derived from their reading of the Gospels (and other inputs). By uncovering our own ways of visualizing the Jesus story, we can more thoughtfully compare our perspectives with the way the story is told in a Jesus film. This process of conscious comparison can help us stay in inquiry mode rather than jumping quickly to evaluation mode, something that is easy to do with Jesus films. If you've had the experience of watching a Jesus film and finding yourself frustrated and critical of the filmmaker's choices, you understand the quick rush to judgment that Jesus films often engender, especially for those who take Jesus and his portrayal seriously (as we ourselves do). Yet staying in inquiry mode, in analysis, before moving to evaluation, can lead us to engage both the Gospels and the films more sensitively. Nevertheless, evaluation is appropriate and even important—all viewers ought to watch Jesus films critically, even their favorites. If any film is appropriated uncritically, that film could virtually replace our own visualizing work the next time we read the Gospels. Our hope for you who read this book is that, by increasing your awareness of the role you play as director of the Jesus story in your own mind, your engagement with Jesus films will become more perceptive, more curious, and more critically attentive.

We would suggest that, with this approach, our book offers something distinctive among Jesus film studies. We do not try to provide a history, an encyclopedic guide, or a close analysis of the core "canonical" films.[35] While we do cast a wide net for what constitutes a "Jesus film," we do not intend to be exhaustive. Instead, our investigation illustrates and represents patterns of storytelling common to many Jesus films. Given our contention that Jesus films should heuristically be considered as *cinematic Gospels*, throughout the

35. By "canonical" we mean that certain films tend to receive more attention than others in books and syllabi about Jesus and film. A representative sampling includes: *The King of Kings* (1927); *Ben-Hur* (1959); *King of Kings* (1961); *Il Vangelo Secondo Matteo* (*The Gospel According to St. Matthew*, 1964); *The Greatest Story Ever Told* (1965); *Jesus Christ Superstar* (1973); *Godspell* (1973); *Jesus of Nazareth* (1977); *Life of Brian* (1979); *Jesus* (1979); *The Last Temptation of Christ* (1988); *Jésus de Montréal* (*Jesus of Montreal*, 1989); *Jesus* (1999); *The Passion of the Christ* (2004); *Jezile* (*Son of Man*, 2006).

volume we highlight certain tropes, trends, and trajectories that begin within the four Gospels themselves and are extended further in the apocryphal Gospels before they make their way to film. As we follow these trajectories, we will discover the indebtedness of Jesus films to ancient literary Gospels. And we will see how Jesus films develop familiar content to tell their own unique stories of Jesus that make sense of a film's cultural and temporal context (its "second horizon").

In chapter 1, we begin exploring the hermeneutical impact of Jesus films by addressing the question of faithfulness, specifically whether Jesus films ought to or can be faithful to the Gospels. As we will see, deciphering what exactly such faithfulness means is difficult to determine, since even a film that purports to be a "visual translation" of a single Gospel necessarily requires numerous interpretive decisions as it moves from text to screen. The result? No Jesus film is truly able to "give it to you straight." This reality then reshapes the question of what faithfulness looks like, since these visualizations of the Jesus story are inevitably interpretations of it.

As readers of the four Gospels know, it is not always easy to remember which story or saying comes from which Gospel; it is far easier to conflate multiple versions into a composite in our minds—to harmonize the Gospel accounts. Chapter 2 addresses the ways most Jesus films harmonize the four Gospels to create a single story about Jesus. In chapter 3, we explore story gaps in the Gospels, such as the gap in narrating Jesus's life between the ages of twelve and thirty. Interested readers often wish to know more about what happened in such gaps. When films fill in these kinds of holes in our knowledge, they are often doing nothing more speculative than what readers do when imagining what happened by reading "between the lines" of the Gospels.

Readers of the Gospels naturally seek to encounter relatable and lifelike characters, desiring to understand the motivations that drive the characters' words and actions. In fact, we often read stories for their characters. This keen interest in characters fuels chapters 4–6, which focus on characterization in Gospels and films. Jesus films have the potential to develop characters much more fully than the New Testament does, and we often do the same kind of character expansion in our minds as we read. To understand better how characters function, we examine the concept of characterization and offer examples of how minor characters, like Thomas and Mary Magdalene, are developed in film beyond their Gospel depictions (chap. 4). Then we turn to the central protagonist, Jesus himself, looking at the challenges associated with portraying him in film, especially with respect to his physical appearance and personality (chap. 5). To round out these chapters on characterization, we survey the most prominent characters or groups typically identified as the villains of the Jesus story—namely, Judas, Pilate, the Jewish leaders, and the Jewish people—with sensitivity to how the treatment of each of these characters has contributed to the problem of antisemitism (chap. 6).

Chapter 7 addresses themes woven into Jesus stories. As the Jesus story is retold in ancient literary and modern cinematic Gospels, new themes emerge that shape and fashion it. Themes are often key to discerning how any kind of retelling is a discrete Jesus story in its own right, regardless of how dependent it is on earlier sources. As readers of the Gospels may be impressed by certain themes that they detect, so, too, filmmakers may choose to focus on particular themes that stand out for their own sense of Jesus's significance.

In chapter 8, we introduce and explore the "two horizons" present in any Jesus story or film. Every retelling or recollection of the story of Jesus is not about the past alone ("the first horizon"). It also reflects the moment in which that story is recalled or told ("the second horizon"). Just as readers of the Gospels bring their own experiences and backgrounds to the process of reading about the life of Jesus, each new Jesus story brings a second horizon alongside the first. In our analysis, we identify specific ways Jesus films relate the two horizons, recognizing that all films inevitably signal their cultural and temporal locations.

Finally, we round out the book with a brief conclusion, reflecting on the hermeneutical implications of our study. As you turn the page to engage our work, we invite you to take in the richness of Jesus films and to consider how they might help us all better understand what takes place in our heads as we visualize and direct our encounters with the Gospels. Remember, each of us is the director of our own Jesus film, and these internal reels visualizing the Jesus story are the films we are ultimately most interested in illuminating.

The Question of Faithfulness

Perhaps the metric that most moviegoers use to evaluate Jesus films is fidelity to the canonical Gospels. Many of the most common questions asked about Jesus films reveal this underlying concern. How closely does the film follow the Gospels? Does the film take too many liberties? Do the filmmakers have a theological or political bias? Questions like these are appropriate and significant, yet they can also overlook the complexities involved in adapting, or indeed "translating," the biblical texts to the medium of film, as well as ignore the variety of reasons filmmakers could have for making a Jesus film. Moreover, if we recognize that Jesus films externalize the sort of internal visualization of the story of Jesus that we set in motion when we read the Gospels, we will also need to reckon with the degree of faithfulness our own visualizations achieve.

In this chapter, we address the matter of faithfulness directly and problematize it as a criterion for discerning whether a Jesus film is a "good" movie or even worth watching. After doing so, we explore drawbacks of a "faithfulness" approach for assessing Jesus films by analyzing films that stick closely to the text of a single Gospel—films we refer to as "visual translations." Even these films required many interpretive decisions to bring Jesus into view. Thus, a visual translation is, in fact, an interpretation.

Problematizing the Criterion of Faithfulness

The core problem with using faithfulness as an evaluative criterion for Jesus films is that it masks the degree to which all Jesus films, indeed all retellings of the Jesus story, are interpretations that involve creative reflection and adaptation for intended audiences. Jesus films "must be analyzed both *as films* and *as readings of biblical texts*, neither of which can be ideologically neutral."[1] Yet it can be difficult for viewers to separate the intake of a film as a film, on its own terms, from perceptions of faithfulness or unfaithfulness to Scripture. In this book, we invite you to distinguish these two categories—your experience of a film and your assessment of its faithfulness—so that you can ask a wider set of questions about Jesus films.

When tied to Scripture, faithfulness as a criterion is also problematic because it tends to imply that "the text has one single correct meaning to which the director should adhere and must faithfully reproduce."[2] Yet between narrative ambiguity and narrative's lack of overt argumentation, there is an openness to meaning that allows for more than one interpretation, and often quite a few legitimate (textually allowable) interpretations. In this light, claims of "faithfulness" can simply become code for "my own personal interpretation." Jesus films are inevitably interpretive (see introduction), and the mere fact that a film's interpretation differs from our own is no guarantee that the film has been *unfaithful* to the Gospels.

Metrics of Faithfulness

As we consider how the criterion of faithfulness is often leveraged to evaluate Jesus films, a few common metrics emerge. These metrics are not always clearly articulated in assessments of Jesus films, since viewer evaluation often happens implicitly and at a "gut level." We hope to show that these metrics have layers of complexity that complicate assessment of particular Jesus films as faithful or unfaithful to the Gospels.

Faithfulness as Not Adding Anything to the Bible

For some viewers, claims of unfaithfulness can be a result of a film "adding to the Bible." Yet if the measure of faithfulness is *not adding anything*, then all Jesus films will fail, since, even if the dialogue and narrative plotline come directly from the text, the visuals and sound have to be added to create a *film*. Consider the audiovisual factors germane to—even required of—filmmaking that inevitably add to the story even if the text is left unaltered:

1. Burnette-Bletsch, "Bible and Its Cinematic Adaptations," 156 (emphasis original), referring to all Bible films.

2. Doughty and Etherington-Wright, *Understanding Film Theory*, 24. Brown (*Scripture as Communication*, 74–75) problematizes the notion of a "singular meaning," even from the perspective of determinate meaning, by stressing the complexity of meaning and by pointing to the whole-book context for meaning; e.g., all of Matthew.

casting, costuming, location, set design, character blocking, everything visible on-screen (mise-en-scène), musical arrangement, camera angles, and editing. Each of these involves decisions with interpretive implications. Moreover, even if dialogue is taken directly from a reputable translation of the Gospels, decisions still must be made regarding intonation, hand gestures, and the people to whom speech is directed. If we're honest, we already add some of these interpretive contours in our minds as we read the Gospels. And certainly, if the Gospels are read aloud, as in church contexts, the reader makes interpretive decisions of tone, pace, and register. For example, the interpretive nature of reading aloud is clearly demonstrated in David Rhoads's performative recital of Mark's Gospel ("A Dramatic Presentation of the Gospel of Mark" [1992]). All to say, when the Gospels are visualized in film (or even when they are read, internally or aloud), interpretation is happening before any other content is added. Strict faithfulness, if defined as not adding a thing, is an elusive goal, an impossibility. As Martin Scorsese said in response to criticism of *The Last Temptation of Christ* (1988), "Ultimately, it was all a choice between my wrong version, and your wrong version, and somebody else's wrong version."[3]

Faithfulness as Being True to History: Verisimilitude

Another metric of faithfulness is verisimilitude, or how well a film represents the history it purports to tell. Viewers are usually assuaged on this count with a basic attempt at verisimilitude with the past. Yet what is perceived as authentic or historical in a Jesus film may instead be anachronistic, rooted more in medieval, renaissance, or Victorian art than in history, or based on an orientalization that paints figures from the Gospels with brushstrokes from contemporary Middle Eastern stereotypes.[4] Because our historical perceptions are often colored by anachronisms, if a truly historical portrait, rooted in archaeology and the study of material culture, were incorporated into film, we could ironically deem what is historical as unhistorical and thus *unfaithful*![5]

It might come as a surprise that some films that aren't known for their verisimilitude are truer to the Gospels in ways that surpass their more "faithful" counterparts. For example, Goodacre notes that *Jesus Christ Superstar* (1973), a film less historical than *Jesus of Nazareth* (1977), *The Greatest Story Ever Told* (1965), and *King of Kings* (1961), was nevertheless the only one filmed in Israel.[6] Similarly, we may not expect *Monty Python's Life of Brian* (1979), a parody film aimed at spoofing the entire Jesus film genre, to be at all concerned

3. Chattaway, "Jesus in the Movies," 45.
4. McGeough, "'False Syllogism' of Archaeological Authenticity in Jesus Movies."
5. Turner, "Representation of New Testament Figures," 18.
6. Goodacre, "Do You Think You're What They Say You Are?," 11.

Handmade Films / Python (Monty) Pictures

Representative costuming in *Monty Python's Life of Brian* (1979)

with historical fidelity. Yet Katie Turner, an expert on costuming in Jesus films and passion plays, regards *Life of Brian* to have "the most historically accurate costumes of any Jesus film."[7] In this domain, *Life of Brian* follows historical evidence that Jews wore Roman-style tunics and did not dress in ways fundamentally different from anyone else in the Greco-Roman world.[8]

Additionally, verisimilitude is virtually impossible to achieve in Jesus films with respect to the languages used. Most Jesus films we explore in this book, though definitely not all, were made in English. Anything other than Aramaic (with some mix of Greek) would be inauthentic to the historical Jesus.[9] *The Passion of the Christ* (2004) has sometimes been put on a pedestal for faithful verisimilitude because of its unique choice to use only Aramaic and Latin,[10] but even this choice is not fully accurate to the linguistic situation of first-century Galilee and Judea and, in some ways, distracts the viewer

7. Turner, "'Shoe Is the Sign!,'" 234.

8. Cf. Turner, "Representation of New Testament Figures," 29–105. However, she notes that the film does stray from verisimilitude in its overuse of beige and anachronistic use of Middle Eastern head coverings.

9. E.g., Porter, "Did Jesus Ever Teach in Greek?"; Gleaves, *Did Jesus Speak Greek?*

10. Other films use background Aramaic, with a narrator speaking over it in English. See *The New Media Bible: The Gospel According to Luke* (1979); *The Gospel of John* (2014); *The Gospel of Mark* (2015); *The Gospel of Luke* (2015); *The Gospel of Matthew* (2016). In the latter four examples, director David Batty apparently instructed the actors to fake their Aramaic at times. Cf. Walsh, "Reading the Gospel(s) in the Dark," 108.

from the many interpretive decisions made across the film (see chap. 8). The decision to make Jesus films in any modern language (e.g., English, Spanish, Italian) is a concession for the sake of relatability and accessibility (just as Bible translations are) and, in a real sense, compromises exacting verisimilitude. Yet most viewers would not consider such linguistic choices a matter of *unfaithfulness*, since translation is and always has been a necessary and integral part of the transmission of the Jesus story.[11] *Jesus: A Deaf Missions Film* (2024), in American Sign Language (ASL), underscores this reality by using the event of Pentecost as a framing narrative. As the first Jesus film in ASL, it is self-consciously concerned with the expansion of the Jesus story into multiple languages, including modern sign languages.

What If a Film Doesn't Aim for "Faithfulness"?

Some Jesus films decidedly do not aim at the goal of "faithfulness," at least if measured in terms of verisimilitude or staying only with the content of the Gospels. While we can certainly choose to evaluate Jesus films by comparing them with the Gospels and history, we suggest that it is rather unfair to measure them by a criterion that they are not claiming for themselves. Nicholas Wolterstorff offers a critique of three Jesus films from 1973: *Jesus Christ Superstar*, *The Gospel Road: A Story of Jesus*, and *Godspell*. They each "fail," he says, because "they are not *religious* films about Jesus"; they do not inspire faith or force viewers "to face the real possibility that they had been confronted with the transcendent God."[12] Yet the filmmakers of *Jesus Christ Superstar* and *Godspell*, in particular, were clearly not intending to make "*religious* films" in Wolterstorff's sense. We wonder: If they did not achieve a goal their makers didn't set out to reach, can they have failed?[13] This example uncovers the truth that viewers of Jesus films inevitably bring their own metrics for determining faithfulness, whether these metrics are clearly articulated or even consciously held. Asking what a particular Jesus film is trying to accomplish can help us see our predetermined metrics more clearly and provide a potentially more evenhanded appraisal of that film.

Reverence for Jesus and the Gospels might seem an obvious category by which to measure faithfulness. Yet one of the more reverent portrayals of Jesus was not necessarily intended as a "faithful" rendering. Pasolini's *Il Vangelo Secondo Matteo* (*The Gospel According to St. Matthew*, 1964) stays quite

11. The New Testament itself communicates the reality and necessity of translation: Jesus's teachings are recorded in Koine Greek rather than in Aramaic.

12. Wolterstorff, "Three Films About Jesus," 10.

13. Wolterstorff acknowledges this point in the next paragraph, without rescinding his main critique.

close to the text of Matthew's Gospel and is filmed in a reverent tone and register. Yet its filmmaker, Pier Paolo Pasolini, was not aiming for faithfulness in the film; he was, in fact, gay, Marxist, atheist, and critical of institutional forms of religion. He appreciated Matthew for its antiestablishment critique of the Pharisees, which reflected his own feelings toward Catholic leaders, and he chose to make the film in black and white to reinforce the rigidity that he sensed in Matthew (cf. chap. 8).[14] Some Christian viewers might be put off by Pasolini's personal background, but his film is widely regarded as one of the best, if not the best, Jesus film of all time.

Conversely, many Jesus films may stem from a posture of faith, with their filmmakers striving explicitly for faithfulness to the Gospels. Yet, as we've already discussed, all Jesus films are interpretations of the Jesus stories. So what constitutes faithfulness, even for filmmakers committed to that ideal, will always be in the eye of the beholder. What faithfulness looks like in a Jesus film could be different for each person involved in making the film.[15] As we've already suggested, each viewer will inevitably compare their own internalized Jesus film with the externalized film on the screen.

Adaptation as a Complicating Factor

As we think about Jesus films and faithfulness, another complicating factor is the phenomenon of film adaptations. Films are often adapted from literary sources like books and novels, with Bible films being adaptations of the world's most popular book. Technically, every film could be described as a series of adaptations from a screenplay, even if the screenplay is original. Adaptation of any screenplay involves the director, cinematographer, set designers, makeup artists, actors, editors, sound designers, and more. The screenwriter imagines the story a certain way, but it is adapted many times over before the final cut. The countless adjustments made while adapting the source material come about for a host of reasons, only one of which is faithfulness (however conceived). As Matthew Page notes, "Textual fidelity is often in tension with the filmmakers' need to create something that is dramatically engaging, artistically interesting, or financially viable at least."[16] Take, for instance, the original *Hunger Games* book trilogy by Suzanne Collins (2008–10). The series follows Katniss Everdeen, a young woman competing for food and resources for her district in a brutal game. Players fight to the death in hopes of being the last competitor standing. To make the story work on-screen, the

14. Baugh, "Three Revolutionary Gospel Films," 142–43.
15. Doughty and Etherington-Wright, *Understanding Film Theory*, 24.
16. Page, *100 Bible Films*, 10.

films had to move from Katniss's first-person-present perspective in the books to a third-person perspective typical of films. This change allowed the film to portray events that Katniss was not privy to. As adaptations, films based on books require their own aims, aesthetics, and integrity to work well, making at least some adjustments necessary.

People who read the book first are often critical of its film adaptation. "The film wasn't as good as the book" is a common refrain (and we'd affirm this preference). Alternatively, a film might prevent people from ever picking up the book it's based on, with the film acting not as a supplement but rather as a more accessible or entertaining replacement. Consider *The Lord of the Rings* film trilogy (2001–3), for example. This can happen with biblical films as well, such that distinguishing what's in our Bibles from its pop-cultural interpretation can be a challenge.[17] And whether audiences like them or not, film adaptations inevitably bring something new to the original.

Good film adaptations are like cover songs. If a musician merely reproduces another artist's song using the same arrangement, what is the point of the cover? It might be "faithful," but it would be unnecessary. We may as well go back and enjoy the original. A good cover takes a well-known song and transforms it in some way, whether bringing it into a new genre or adding new features to create a fresh expression and interpretation. Whether it's Leonard Cohen's "Hallelujah" in the hands of Jeff Buckley, Bob Dylan's "Knockin' on Heaven's Door" taken up by Eric Clapton or Guns N' Roses, or Whitney Houston's meteoric rendering of Dolly Parton's tender "I Will Always Love You," a cover is valued because it offers us a new experience of an old favorite. Great covers inevitably bring something new to the original.

As adaptations, Jesus films bring something new as well. If we're not fully comfortable with this idea, the Gospels themselves press us to consider the interpretive layers of adaptation that they themselves contain. According to the majority of Gospel scholars, Matthew and Luke are dependent on Mark (cf. Luke 1:1–4).[18] Yet their faithfulness to Mark does not mean simply reproducing it. Both Matthew and Luke selectively incorporate portions of Mark's Gospel in their new narratives, rearrange episodes, and add other Jesus stories and teachings to the mix. Even interpreters who do not see literary dependence among the Gospels readily recognize that the evangelists have brought together and adapted the oral traditions about Jesus passed down to them. The Gospels themselves suggest that adaptation can be faithfully done.

17. For this phenomenon, using the story of Esther as an example, see Dunne, *Esther and Her Elusive God*.

18. For a helpful summary of this question, see Strauss, *Four Portraits*, 61–75.

Faithful to What?

As we conclude our discussion of the question of faithfulness in Jesus films, we return to a question raised at the beginning of this chapter: How closely does a film follow the Gospels? At this point, we would like to fine-tune that question, since Jesus films address the Gospels in any number of ways. Is a film "faithful" if it closely follows only one of the Gospels (see next section)? Or, should a film somehow follow all four Gospels? And if so, how should this be done (e.g., through harmonization?; see chap. 2)? Or is the goal of faithfulness to portray "what actually happened" historically—the reality that sits behind the Gospels?[19] Additionally, does the aim of faithfulness require us to follow the trajectory of the history of orthodox Christian faith and the traditions that have been passed down about the Gospels through art and liturgy? Since no one, including filmmakers, can access the Gospels pristinely, apart from the traditions that have mediated them across history, these traditions inevitably affect our individual and collective imaginations about Jesus. Jesus films stand within these traditional theological and artistic streams, and some films draw on these traditions explicitly.

To illustrate how Christian tradition about the Gospels finds its way into Jesus films, we provide two brief examples: the magi who visit the infant Jesus and the Via Dolorosa. Church tradition has shaped how many of us picture the magi of Matthew's Gospel (Matt. 2:1–12). First specified in the Armenian Infancy Gospel from the sixth century CE, the magi are portrayed as three wise men, with the names Melchior, Gaspar, and Balthazzar, who come from three different parts of the world.[20] While Matthew's Gospel provides none of this specificity, artistic depictions of these three figures are ubiquitous in Christian art as well as in Jesus films.[21]

19. In New Testament scholarship this is referred to as the study of the "historical Jesus" (see Strauss, *Four Portraits*, 415–61).

20. Terian, *Armenian Gospel of the Infancy*.

21. Cf., e.g., *La Passion* (*The Passion*, 1898); *La Vie du Christ*, or *La Naissance, La Vie et La Mort du Christ* (*The Birth, the Life and the Death of Christ*, 1906); *La Vie et Passion de Notre Seigneur Jésus-Christ* (*The Life and Passion of Our Lord Jesus Christ*, 1907); *From the Manger to the Cross* (1912); *Ben-Hur: A Tale of the Christ* (1925); *Reina de Reinas: La Virgen María* (*Queen of Queens: The Virgin Mary*, 1948); *Mater Dei* (*Mother of God*, 1950); *The Nativity* (1952); *The Star of Bethlehem* (1956); *The Life of Christ* (*Mysteries of the Rosary* series, 1957); *Ben-Hur* (1959); *The Prince of Peace* (1959); *The Greatest Story Ever Told* (1965); *The Little Drummer Boy* (1968); *Jesús, el Niño Dios* (*Jesus, the Child of God*, 1971); *Jesus* (1973); *Il Messia* (*The Messiah*, 1975); *Jesus of Nazareth* (1977); *Karunamayudu* (*Ocean of Mercy*, 1978); *The Fourth Wise Man* (1985); *Marie de Nazareth* (*Mary of Nazareth*, 1995); *Giuseppe di Nazareth* (*Joseph of Nazareth*, 2000); *Maria, Figlia del Suo Figlio* (*Mary, Daughter of Her Son*, 2000); *Maryam Moghadas* (*Saint Mary*, 2002); *Ben-Hur* (2003); *Santhi Sandesam* (*Message of Peace*, 2004); *Su Re* (*The King*, 2012); *Son of God* (2014); *My Son, My Savior* (2015);

Padmalaya Studios

Saint Veronica holding up the true icon of Christ in *Santhi Sandesam* (*Message of Peace*, 2004).

A second instance of traditional material often woven into Jesus films is the Via Dolorosa—the route Jesus took from Jerusalem to Golgotha carrying the cross (commemorated as the stations of the cross). Though they're not mentioned in the Gospels, many Jesus films incorporate some of these stations, and most notably the tradition of Saint Veronica, who wipes the sweat from Jesus's face after he collapses.[22] The towel Veronica used is believed to

Joseph and Mary (2016); *The Star* (2017); *Chasing the Star* (2017); *The Penitent Thief* (2020); *Journey to Bethlehem* (2023); *Mary* (2024).

22. For depictions of Veronica in cinematic Jesus stories, see, e.g., *María Magdalena, Pecadora de Magdala* (*Mary Magdalene, Sinner of Magdala*, 1946); *Reina de Reinas: La Virgen María* (*Queen of Queens: The Virgin Mary*, 1948); *The Living Christ Series* (1951); *El Mártir del Calvario* (*The Martyr of Calvary*, 1952); *El Beso de Judas* (*Judas' Kiss*, 1954); *The Life of Christ* (*Mysteries of the Rosary* series, 1957); *Snapaka Yohannan* (*John the Baptist*, 1963); *El Proceso de Cristo* (*The Trial of Christ*, 1966); *Jesús, Nuestro Señor* (*Jesus, Our Lord*, 1971); *The Thorn* (*The Greatest Story Overtold / The Divine Mr. J*, 1971); *Jesus* (1973); *Secondo Ponzio Pilato* (*According to Pontius Pilate*, 1987); *Santhi Sandesam* (*Message of Peace*, 2004); *Mulla Kireetam* (*Crown of Thorns*, 2006); *Jesús de Nazaret: El Hijo de Dios* (*Jesus of Nazareth*, 2019). A few films include Veronica but do not reveal the image of Christ on the towel: *I.N.R.I.* (*Crown of Thorns*, 1923); *Maria, Figlia del Suo Figlio* (*Mary, Daughter of Her Son*, 2000); *Das Neue Evangelium* (*The New Gospel*, 2020). In one film, instead of a single print of Jesus's face there are three images side by side (*Kristo* [1996]), which is presumably meant to reflect trinitarian theology. *The Chosen* (2017–present) introduces Veronica as the woman with the

contain an exact imprint of Jesus's face and to be housed in the Vatican as a relic of the church.

We could carry on pointing to many other examples of how Jesus films include homages to famous works of art, like Leonardo da Vinci's painting *The Last Supper*,[23] or prominent representations of Christ's death, such as Mary cradling the body of Jesus after he's been taken down from the cross in Michelangelo's sculpture *Pietà* or Jesus being mourned in Caravaggio's painting *The Entombment of Christ*.[24] Illustrated Bibles by James Tissot and Gustave Doré were also highly influential in the early days of Jesus films for blocking and staging.

Although Jesus films cannot help but draw from the Gospels mediated via art and tradition, some Jesus films work to convey authenticity, and so faithfulness, by integrating the evangelists, *as authors*, into their storylines. This move is strongly implied in *The Chosen* (2017–present). On multiple occasions, both Matthew and John can be seen taking notes, and Matthew even helps Jesus craft his Sermon on the Mount (season 2, episode 8, "Beyond Mountains," 2021). This choice is more overt in films that use the evangelists as *narrators*. John is portrayed as narrator in *Son of God* (2014), and Luke has this role in *The Savior* (2014). Both films do this primarily through framing narratives rather than voice-over narration. Yet despite what the framing narratives could imply, each film deviates from its respective Gospel, omitting scenes and incorporating moments from other Gospels. Even these films that include an evangelist to give veracity to the film's version of the Jesus story are, in the end, interpretations.

---

issue of blood, which is a traditional connection (season 3, episode 4, "Clean: Part 1," 2023; season 3, episode 5, "Clean: Part 2," 2023).

23. Cf., e.g., *I.N.R.I.* (*Crown of Thorns*, 1923); *Ben-Hur: A Tale of the Christ* (1925); *Jesús de Nazareth* (*Jesus of Nazareth*, 1942); *María Magdalena, Pecadora de Magdala* (*Mary Magdalene, Sinner of Magdala*, 1946); *Reina de Reinas: La Virgen María* (*Queen of Queens: The Virgin Mary*, 1948); *The Pilgrimage Play* (1949); *Mater Dei* (*Mother of God*, 1950); *The Greatest Story Ever Told* (1965); *Jesús, Nuestro Señor* (*Jesus, Our Lord*, 1971); *Jesus* (1973); *Das Neue Evangelium* (*The New Gospel*, 2020); *The Book of Clarence* (2023).

24. Cf., e.g., *Christus* (1916); *Reina de Reinas: La Virgen María* (*Queen of Queens: The Virgin Mary*, 1948); *Mater Dei* (*Mother of God*, 1950); *El Mártir del Calvario* (*The Martyr of Calvary*, 1952); *The Life of Christ* (*Mysteries of the Rosary* series, 1957); *Celui Qui Doit Mourir* (*He Who Must Die*, 1957); *Barabbas* (1961); *Il Messia* (*The Messiah*, 1975); *Jesus of Nazareth* (1977); *Jésus de Montréal* (*Jesus of Montreal*, 1989); *Kristo* (1996); *Jesus* (1999); *Maria, Figlia del Suo Figlio* (*Mary, Daughter of Her Son*, 2000); *Judas* (2004); *The Passion of the Christ* (2004); *Mulla Kireetam* (*Crown of Thorns*, 2006); *Maria di Nazaret* (Mary of Nazareth, 2012); *The Gospel of Us* (2012); *La Espina de Dios* (*The Thorn of God*, 2015); *A.D.: The Bible Continues* (season 1, episode 1, "The Tomb Is Open," 2015). For Jesus being held by Mary Magdalene in the form of the *Pietà*, see *The Last Temptation of Christ* (1988).

Faithfulness and Visual Translations

But what about films that stick to the exact language of a Gospel? Wouldn't these "visual translations" be examples of faithfulness in Jesus films? As we'll soon see, even these are interpretations.

Visual Translations: What Are They?

The Jesus films we designate as visual translations are those based on a single Gospel that offer dramatic visual representation of the words of that Gospel.[25] Most Jesus films don't fit the category, given their use of some amount of harmonization. Pasolini's *Il Vangelo Secondo Matteo* (*The Gospel According to St. Matthew*, 1964) was the first attempt at a visual translation, and while it stays close to Matthew's text, it does rearrange material and omit portions of the Gospel. Other visual translations are

- *The New Media Bible: The Gospel According to St. Luke* (1979),
- *The Gospel According to Matthew* (1993),
- *The Gospel of John* (2003),[26] and
- the four films directed by David Batty: *The Gospel of John* (2014); *The Gospel of Mark* (2015); *The Gospel of Luke* (2015); *The Gospel of Matthew* (2016).

The Gospel According to Matthew (1993), like *Son of God* (2014) and *The Savior* (2014) discussed above, presents Matthew as a narrator both in a framing narrative and in moments interspersed here and there, and it uses his voice throughout the film. It also includes the entire text of Matthew (using the NIV), making it a visual translation. This film conveys its authenticity by announcing at the outset, in the initial framing narrative with an elderly Matthew, that what follows is a "word-for-word" account. The bottom right corner of the screen includes running chapter and verse numbers to reinforce that it is a visual translation. The film commits to including every word of the

25. Although the subtitle to *Godspell* (1973) presents itself as *A Musical Based on the Gospel of Matthew*, the parables used in the film are mostly Lukan, so the film doesn't qualify as a visual translation. Similarly, the recording of David Rhoads's oral performance of Mark ("A Dramatic Presentation of the Gospel of Mark" [1992]) is not a visual translation, since it does not aim to "translate" fully to the visual medium, even though there are visual aspects that make up his Markan interpretation.

26. The first two films in this list were made by Visual Bible International; cf. also *Visual Bible: Acts* (1994).

translation so that Jesus's speech is often interrupted by the narrator saying "Jesus said" or "he replied."[27]

The Gospel of John (2003) is another visual translation and opens with three sets of captions. The first two provide historical context for the Roman occupation of Jerusalem and the polemic between Jesus followers and the broader Jewish communities when John was written—two generations after Jesus (providing an interpretive framework).[28] The final caption reads, "This film is a faithful representation of that Gospel."[29] As these additions indicate, even visual translations can offer overt interpretive frameworks to viewers that go beyond the text. This category of Jesus film ostensibly leaves accretions to the side and attempts to deliver the uninterpreted Gospel text. But even visual translations have to interpret that text.

Comparing Visual Translations

Because there are some visual translations for Matthew, Luke, and John, we can compare decisions across films of the same Gospel to explore their interpretive nature, even though they are "visual translations." The interpretive decisions by these films range from the tricky to the trivial. Let's begin with a couple of brief examples from the passion narratives. Fairly inconsequential but still requiring a decision is the placement of Luke's penitent thief on the right or left side of Jesus (and visually, on our right or Jesus's right). Both *The New Media Bible: The Gospel According to St. Luke* (1979) and *The Gospel of Luke* (2015) place the penitent thief to Jesus's right (our left), as do many other films,[30] though not all.[31]

A more complex issue involves how to render the unique and unusual scene in Matthew (already befuddling to interpreters) when Jesus dies and the dead in Jerusalem leave their tombs and enter the city (Matt. 27:52–53). All three visual translations of Matthew visually omit this detail. In both *The Gospel*

27. *The Gospel According to Matthew* also makes numerous decisions to break up Jesus's lengthy discourses *visually* by having Jesus act in various ways while speaking to heighten interest, including dumping water on people's heads, playing with their hair, and many more quirky behaviors. The film is indeed faithful to include every word of the NIV, but choices like these clearly go beyond the text and provide interpretation.

28. Inspired by, e.g., Martyn, *History and Theology in the Fourth Gospel*.

29. For films that open with written statements saying that although their makers take license, they get to the heart of the story, see, e.g., *Mary, Mother of Jesus* (1999); *The Bible* (2013); *The Young Messiah* (2016); *The Chosen* (season 1, episode 1, "I Have Called You by Name," 2019); *Forty-Seven Days with Jesus* (2024). Conversely, the captions that begin *The Last Temptation of Christ* (1988) indicate that the film is *not* based on the Gospels (see chap. 7).

30. E.g., *La Espina de Dios* (*The Thorn of God*, 2015); *Ben-Hur* (2016); *The Penitent Thief* (2020).

31. E.g., *The Judas Project* (1993); *The Two Thieves* (*Once We Were Slaves*, 2014).

According to Matthew (1993) and *The Gospel of Matthew* (2016), viewers hear about this incident with no depiction, while Pasolini's *Il Vangelo Secondo Matteo* does not mention it at all. These choices either belie an unease with the account (whether to interpret it literally, metaphorically, or apocalyptically) or signal the difficulty of depicting it visually.[32]

To analyze such choices more closely, we will explore several examples from the two visual translations of John—*The Gospel of John* (2003) and *The Gospel of John* (2014). Two introductory notes are in order. First, the 2014 film, by David Batty, narrates the text of John from the NIV (with a KJV version available), whereas the 2003 film, by Philip Saville, uses the GNB, and instead of using full narration, the actors dramatically perform direct speech. These differences in narration style and in translation used already affect the storytelling.[33] A second relevant observation involves *The Gospel of John* (2014) specifically. This film was made at the same time as the other Batty visual translations of Matthew, Mark, and Luke. As a result, there are several instances of harmonization and of reuse of common footage. For example, during the narration of John 1:10–11 about "the light," three wise men bring gifts to the infant Jesus (cf. Matt. 2:1–12). This material is irrelevant to John, which has no infancy narrative. Footage from *The Gospel of Matthew* (2016) is used to fill out the John film.[34]

John 1: John the Baptist

For a comparison of these John films, we begin with John the Baptist's testimony in John 1, where the Baptist testifies that he has seen the Spirit descend on Jesus like a dove (1:32–33). Many readers familiar with the Synoptics

32. Only a few Jesus films depict anything related to this scene. *Jesús, Nuestro Señor* (*Jesus, Our Lord*, 1971) offers the most literal account, depicting people physically rising from their graves and leaving their tombs wrapped fully in burial garments. In *Barabbas* (1961), Barabbas meets with one of the resurrected people after the incident as part of the theme of Barabbas (a survivor of a death sentence) meeting with other people who have escaped death (like Lazarus). *The Judas Project* (1993) portrays a spiritual resurrection, with ghostlike figures emerging out of coffins in a cemetery and floating up to heaven, as part of a conflation of this event from Matthew with the harrowing of hell tradition, which is anticipated at a few moments in the film (including in Jesse's [i.e., Jesus's] words to "Pete," James, and John after the transfiguration).

33. All translations are necessarily interpretations. As Michael Gorman suggests, "Every translation is itself an interpretation. Therefore, in a certain sense, every Bible translation is a kind of streamlined exegesis representing innumerable interpretive judgments and decisions" (*Elements of Biblical Exegesis*, 44).

34. Additionally, sometimes in *The Gospel of John* (2014), the narrator describes something that is missing from the footage. In John's Gospel, Jesus makes a whip and uses it in the temple cleansing scene (John 2:15). Yet no whip shows up in this scene in the film, presumably because common footage from the recording of the Synoptics was being used, where a whip is not mentioned.

will interpret this scene as Jesus's baptism (cf. Matt. 3:13–17; Mark 1:9–11; Luke 3:21–22), but here in John's Gospel Jesus's baptism is not narrated. Interestingly, the two films make divergent interpretive decisions. In the 2014 film, John baptizes Jesus as his testimony about Jesus is being narrated, but in the 2003 version, John the Baptist reports what he has seen to his disciples, with Jesus's baptism represented visually in a flashback. So although Jesus's baptism is not mentioned in John 1:29–34, both films understand John's testimony to be about Jesus's baptism and portray that interpretation visually.[35]

John 2: Water to Wine

The turning of water into wine at a wedding (John 2:1–11) provides another more subtle example for comparison. In nearly every film depicting this scene, including the two visual translations from 2003 and 2014, the wine is visibly red and noticeably *not water* before the master of the banquet drinks it.[36] Yet the text does not indicate that this "sign" was noticeable—visibly or otherwise—before being tasted.[37] In other words, John does not suggest that the wine was red—it could have been white.[38] Many people have been conditioned to visualize wine as red, and that assumption has influenced art and film.

John 3: Nicodemus and Jesus

John's episode of Nicodemus meeting with Jesus requires a few significant interpretive decisions to be made when translating it to film. First, filmmakers need to decide to portray Nicodemus as either a sincere seeker or a combative challenger. Both John films (as all others that include Nicodemus) opt for the

35. Although the 2003 film seems to recognize (rightly) that the Baptist does not baptize Jesus within the Gospel of John.

36. Cf., e.g., *Mater Dei* (*Mother of God*, 1950); *The Living Christ Series* (1951); *Jesús, Nuestro Señor* (*Jesus, Our Lord*, 1971); *The Gospel Road: A Story of Jesus* (1973); *Un Bambino di Nome Gesù* (*A Child Called Jesus*, 1987); *Marie de Nazareth* (*Mary of Nazareth*, 1995); *The Revolutionary* (1995); *Mary, Mother of Jesus* (1999); *Maria, Figlia del Suo Figlio* (*Mary, Daughter of Her Son*, 2000); *Mulla Kireetam* (*Crown of Thorns*, 2006); *The Life of Jesus Christ* (2013); *Maria di Nazaret* (*Mary of Nazareth*, 2012); *My Son, My Savior* (2015); *Jesús de Nazaret: El Hijo de Dios* (*Jesus of Nazareth*, 2019). The exceptions simply omit showing the wine to their audiences; e.g., *Intolerance* (1916), *The Prince of Peace* (1959), *The Last Temptation of Christ* (1988), and *Kristo* (1996). In black-and-white films, the wine is often visibly darker than the water; see, e.g., *La Vie et Passion de Notre Seigneur Jésus-Christ* (*The Life and Passion of Our Lord Jesus Christ*, 1907); *From the Manger to the Cross* (1912); *Reina de Reinas: La Virgen María* (*Queen of Queens: The Virgin Mary*, 1948); *El Beso de Judas* (*Judas' Kiss*, 1954).

37. *Reina de Reinas: La Virgen María* (*Queen of Queens: The Virgin Mary*, 1948) is unique in having the master of the banquet's words about the quality of the wine rest solely on the *visual presentation* of the dark wine rather than on tasting it.

38. Cf. Dunne, *Mountains Shall Drip Sweet Wine*, 14–15, 192.

former,[39] but the scene itself does not provide enough information to make a definitive pronouncement on the matter (although see John's additional references to Nicodemus at 7:45–53; 19:38–42). Another key decision involves determining when Jesus stops talking and the evangelist returns to narrating. Jesus responds at length to Nicodemus in 3:10, and certainly by 3:22 (at the latest) John's narration has resumed. In between 3:10 and 3:22, it is unclear where Jesus concludes his response to Nicodemus. The question has higher stakes than one might think, since the famous verse, John 3:16 ("God so loved the world . . ."), could be read as John's narration, not Jesus's words. Bibles using quotation marks (most translations) or red letters for Jesus's words already make this decision in their translation—a reminder that Bibles themselves are forms of visual media,[40] with paragraph units, headings, and other interpretive decisions represented on every page. English translations differ on this issue, with most placing quotation marks to show Jesus responding to Nicodemus through the end of 3:21 (e.g., CSB, ESV, Message, NASB, NKJV, NLT, NRSVue). Others understand Jesus's address to conclude after 3:13 (e.g., GNB) or 3:15 (e.g., NET, NIV, RSV).[41]

What about the visual translations in film? What do they do when Jesus stops speaking and the narrator begins? In the 2014 film, Jesus is still speaking to Nicodemus (in Aramaic, with voice-over) through 3:21, despite the fact that the NIV (the text it uses) indicates that Jesus stops talking at 3:15. By contrast, in the 2003 film, Jesus concludes after 3:15, with the narrator resuming at 3:16—a decision that also goes against the grain of the translation the film is using (GNB), where Jesus concludes already at 3:13. Both films required interpretive decisions, both are at variance with the translations they are using, and only one of them portrays Jesus uttering the words of John 3:16 (*The Gospel of John* [2014]).[42]

John 8: The Woman Caught in Adultery

Both visual translations of John include the scene of the woman caught in adultery (John 7:53–8:11), despite the question of whether it was originally a part of John. Although many Greek manuscripts of John exist from the

39. *The Bible* (season 1, episode 8, "Betrayal," 2013) initially portrays Nicodemus as a challenger, but only until the recorded encounter in John 3 (so he is already sincere in its version of John's account).

40. Robbins, "New Testament Texts," 13.

41. The KJV lacks any markers at all.

42. Other cinematic Jesus stories depict Jesus saying the words of John 3:16 (*Jesus: The Desire of Ages* [2014]; *The Bible* [season 1, episode 8, "Betrayal," 2013]) or signing them in ASL (*Jesus: A Deaf Missions Film* [2024]), and some films include v. 17 (*The Pilgrimage Play* [1949]; *Jesus of Nazareth* [1977]; *Kristo* [1996]; *The Savior* [2014]; *The Chosen* [season 1, episode 7, "Invitation," 2019]).

second century CE and forward, not all (and not the earliest) include this episode. Textual criticism—the evaluative process of sifting through manuscript copies of the New Testament to determine what John wrote—suggests that this episode is a later addition to John and not what he originally composed (see the NIV's notation between John 7 and 8).[43]

This episode also raises interesting issues for visualization. What did Jesus write in the dirt with his finger (twice; John 8:6, 8)? Neither visual translation fills in this detail (neither do most other Jesus films that depict this action),[44] and plenty of films omit the writing part altogether.[45] Both visual translations do portray Jesus writing twice, but the 2003 film shows Jesus writing in two separate locations—first while he is sitting before the scene starts,[46] and then, after he stands to engage with the woman's accusers, Jesus stoops down to write something in another spot. From quick edits that cut between Jesus and the woman and then the crowds, we get only a glimpse of what he writes, though he appears to be writing something different the second time. Alternatively, the 2014 film has Jesus stooping down twice, writing in what appears to be the same place and continuing what he was previously writing.

Viewers of these films will need to tap into their imaginations to fill in the gap of what Jesus wrote. Other Jesus films, however, are more expansive than these visual translations. For example, *Jesus of Nazareth* (1977) and *Jesus* (1999) both depict Jesus drawing an image of a fish, which is both anachronistic (this image did not represent the Christian faith until more than a hundred years after the Christian movement began) and something of a non sequitur. Intriguingly, a few films tie Jesus's writing directly to his confrontation with the Pharisees and scribes and all those willing to stone the woman. *The King of Kings* (1927) visualizes Jesus writing individual words in Hebrew that are quickly "translated" in the dirt into English. The words reveal the primary sin of each man standing nearby, such as "thief," "murderer," and even "adulterer."[47]

43. For an in-depth study of this passage, see esp. Knust and Wasserman, *To Cast the First Stone*.

44. E.g., *Jesus* (1973); *Karunamayudu* (*Ocean of Mercy*, 1978); *Marie de Nazareth* (*Mary of Nazareth*, 1995); *Maria di Nazaret* (*Mary of Nazareth*, 2012); *The Life of Jesus Christ* (2013); *Histoire de Judas* (2015).

45. Cf. *Ben Hur: A Tale of the Christ* (1925); *Jesús, Nuestro Señor* (*Jesus, Our Lord*, 1971); *Il Messia* (*The Messiah*, 1975); *Barabbas* (2012); *Jesús de Nazaret: El Hijo de Dios* (*Jesus of Nazareth*, 2019).

46. Cf. also *Marie de Nazareth* (*Mary of Nazareth*, 1995). In both *Jesus* (1973) and *Jesus of Nazareth* (1977) not only is Jesus sitting before the incident, but he is also writing in the ground beforehand.

47. Although *Jesús, Nuestro Señor* (*Jesus, Our Lord*, 1971) omits Jesus stooping and writing, it seems to carry on this tradition from *The King of Kings* (1927), since Jesus confronts each

DeMille Pictures Corporation

Jesus's writing in the dirt, which names the sins of the crowd in *The King of Kings* (1927).

Salam Media

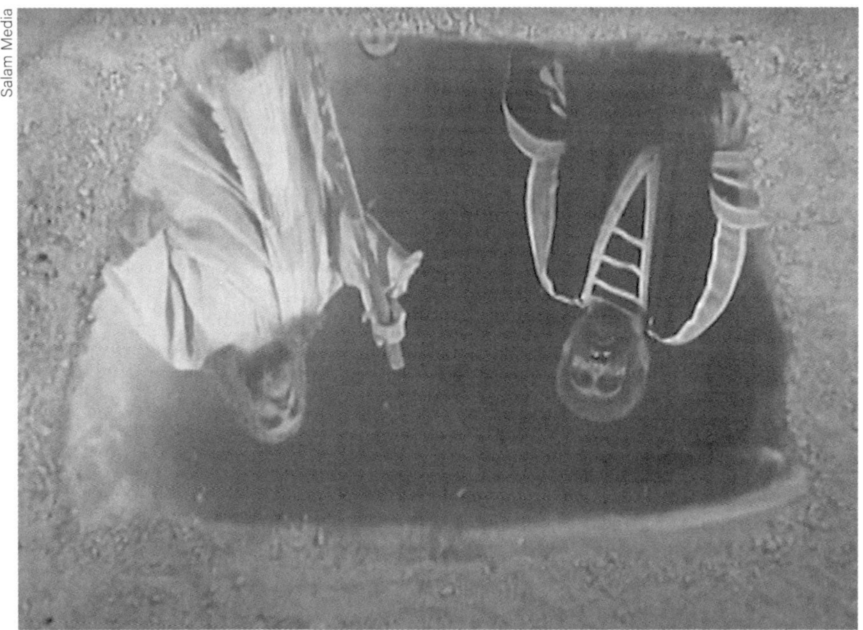

The reflection of Jesus and one of the monstrous men from the crowd in part 6 of *Mesih* (*Jesus, the Spirit of God*, 2010)

In *The Gospel Road: A Story of Jesus* (1973), Johnny Cash narrates this same possibility for what Jesus may have written. In *The Sword and the Cross* (1958), Jesus draws a semicircle around the woman (with his staff), perhaps creating a barrier of protection around her. The Iranian series *Mesih* (*Jesus, the Spirit of God*, 2010) takes the accusatory interpretation of Jesus's drawing even further by showing Jesus draw a circle that miraculously becomes a spiritual mirror revealing how monstrous and demonic the men standing there truly are.

Cleverly, although Jesus does not write in the dirt in *The Greatest Story Ever Told* (1965), Jesus throws the stone in his hand straight to the ground, after extending it outward to anyone who might be without sin, revealing that he alone is the sinless one who, in fact, casts the first stone.[48]

John 13–17: Upper Room Discourse

The Johannine "Upper Room Discourse" (John 13–17) provides these John films a long scene requiring numerous interpretive decisions. Although seemingly set during the same time frame as Jesus's Passover meal with his disciples in the Synoptics, the Upper Room Discourse bears little resemblance to that synoptic meal and bread ("the Lord's Supper"). Other than briefly mentioning a meal (13:2, 26–30), anticipating Judas's betrayal, and predicting Peter's denial, John 13–17 offers quite different material than the Synoptics. And John does not record Jesus's words of institution over the bread and the cup (Matt. 26:26–28; Mark 14:22–25; Luke 22:14–23). Yet both the 2003 and the 2014 John films portray Jesus passing around the bread and wine during this sequence, as in the Synoptics.[49] Additionally, in this portion of John, the "Beloved Disciple" is first mentioned in the text (13:23), although this figure's identity is never revealed (cf. 19:26; 20:2; 21:7; 21:20). Church tradition has identified the Beloved Disciple with John the son of Zebedee, who is likewise considered to be the author of the Fourth Gospel, and following these traditional connections is not unreasonable. Yet neither identification is explicitly indicated in John, and so an interpretive decision is required when visualizing the Beloved Disciple for film. And both films choose to go the conventional route.

In *The Gospel of John* (2003), an unnamed woman is present at this meal along with Jesus and the twelve male disciples. The woman first appears earlier

person individually and in turn with their own particular sin (cf. also *The Last Temptation of Christ* [1988], where Jesus confronts a man for his adultery).

48. Malone, "Who Do You Say That I Am?," 36.

49. While we could suggest that these choices are not exactly faithful to *John*, presumably the filmmakers perceived their changes as being faithful to the four Gospels as a whole, or to the broader Christian tradition.

Jesus speaking the words of John 6:37 to the woman in red in *The Gospel of John* (2003)

in the film wearing a long red dress, but without any formal introduction, and from that point on, she follows Jesus and the disciples. And Jesus has his hand resting on her shoulder when he declares that he will never turn away anyone the Father gives to him (from John 6:37).

The decisions to have Jesus direct these words to the woman, to have him make physical contact, and to portray her in that particular attire, imply that viewers are meant to identify her as a sex worker. She continues to accompany the disciples until Jesus's crucifixion, when she is finally revealed to be Mary Magdalene (cf. John 19:25, where this Mary is first mentioned in John). The filmmakers made the decisions to introduce her earlier and to represent her as a sex worker without any textual prompting from John itself. Indeed, the idea of Mary Magdalene being a reformed sex worker is not reflected in any canonical Gospel, though she is commonly presented this way in Christian art and in Jesus films (see chap. 4).

John 20: Mary Magdalene and Jesus

A final example of interpretive decisions in visual translations of John also involves Mary Magdalene—in this case, how to visualize her encounter with the resurrected Jesus (20:14–17). John writes that Mary Magdalene did not recognize Jesus and instead mistook him for a gardener. Was this a supernatural concealment of Jesus's identity, or is the reason for her confusion more mundane? Most film characterizations provide a naturalistic explanation. In some films, Mary does not recognize Jesus because his face is concealed, whether by a tree, a bush, or a hood that covers his head, or because he is crouched over.[50] The 2003 visual translation opts for a combination of these, which in effect makes Jesus appear to be a gardener.

In other films, Mary Magdalene is inside the tomb and Jesus is outside it, so she can't see him clearly.[51] In another, both are in the tomb, and the darkness shrouds Jesus's face.[52] In a few films, Mary's tears blur her vision, or she is crying directly into her hands,[53] or she is facing away from Jesus.[54] The 2014 John film follows the latter tack, with Mary kneeling and crying while she faces the tomb and Jesus stands behind her. A lone cinematic rendering of this scene draws on a supernatural explanation for Mary Magdalene's confusion. BBC's *The Passion* (2008) replaces Joseph Mawle, who plays Jesus in the rest of the film, with another actor in this scene.[55] By using a distinct actor, *The Passion* (2008) implies that the resurrected Jesus looks discernably different from the Jesus Mary has known—a supernatural transposition of sorts. Jesus films seem clearly more comfortable depicting this scene's resurrected Jesus in natural rather than supernatural ways.

Conclusion

In this chapter, we have explored the question of the faithfulness of Jesus films through a few lenses, including attempts at historical verisimilitude and at sticking close to a single Gospel—what we have called "visual translations." We have concluded, through analyzing many cinematic examples,

50. Cf., e.g., *Jesus* (1999); *Magdalena: Released from Shame* (2007); *Maria di Nazaret* (*Mary of Nazareth*, 2012).

51. E.g., *Son of God* (2014); *A.D.: The Bible Continues* (season 1, episode 2, "The Body Is Gone," 2015).

52. *Kristo* (1996).

53. E.g., *The Pilgrimage Play* (1949); *Jesus: The Desire of Ages* (2014). Cf. *The Cross* (2001), where the film's only scene in third-person perspective switches back to Jesus's POV once Mary finally recognizes Jesus.

54. E.g., *The Prince of Peace* (1959); *The Testaments of One Fold and One Shepherd* (2000).

55. This new actor continues to play Jesus in *The Passion* (2008) until the moment in Luke's account of the road to Emmaus (Luke 24:13–35) when the disciples finally recognize Jesus during a meal. Then it reverts to Joseph Mawle playing Jesus for a brief moment before he disappears; cf. *Color of the Cross 2: The Resurrection* (2008), which also uses another actor for this Lukan scene. Luke's road to Emmaus account offers a phenomenon similar to Mary's lack of recognition of Jesus. The two visual translations of Luke are notable for also interpreting this scene with a naturalistic explanation, since Jesus's face is concealed by the hood he is wearing. See *The New Media Bible: The Gospel According to St. Luke* (1979); *The Gospel of Luke* (2015).

that all Jesus films are interpretive, making faithfulness a much more complicated measure of a film than it might initially seem. Even a film that offers a "straightforward" visual translation of a Gospel requires a host of interpretive decisions along the way. And whether makers of Jesus films claim to be faithful or freely admit to taking liberties, they have to make interpretive choices just to get Jesus on-screen. In the final analysis, there is no such thing as an uninterpreted Jesus film. Yet this does not mean we should abandon Jesus films as a lost cause for people of faith—those who might be particularly interested in faithful representations of Jesus. Rather, as viewers we have the opportunity to discern the variety of interpretations being offered in each film and consider their rationale and plausibility.

Although we've focused on the question of faithfulness in this chapter, we also want to turn our gazes inward, since the Jesus "films" we visualize and direct in our own minds are also activated as we watch and evaluate Jesus films. We, like Jesus films, are interpreters of the Gospels, even as we engage questions of faithfulness on film. By attending to the ways our own interpretive lenses intersect with those in Jesus films, we can cultivate a more capacious approach to these films while also thinking critically about their hermeneutics and our own.

A final note on faithfulness: If we assume a simple binary between films that are faithful and those that are not, we run the risk of uncritically watching films we deem "faithful." And worse, an uncritical stamp of "faithful" on a film could encourage us to substitute viewing the film for reading the Gospels, discouraging us from returning to the Scriptures to deepen our understanding and, in turn, cultivate our facility for critically engaging Jesus films.

Unlike the visual translations we've explored in this chapter, the Jesus films that run in most of our minds do not represent a single Gospel but are rather selective conflations of all four. Such conflation is known as harmonization. The vast majority of Jesus films harmonize, and they do so in spades. In the next chapter, we delve into the lure of harmonization, both for Jesus films and for our own internalized Jesus stories.

2

Harmonization

The Lure of a Single Story

While the four canonical Gospels are discrete stories in their own right, their collection together into the New Testament sometimes has the effect of causing readers to blur the lines between them. When we imagine the story of Jesus in our mind's eye, we might forget whether it was Matthew specifically that included this or that saying of Jesus, or whether Luke alone narrated a particular event in Jesus's life. At the end of the day, distinguishing these details might not seem to matter much for many devout readers because *as long as it's in the Bible, it reflects what Jesus said and did, right?* The collection and circulation of these four Gospels encourage us to read them as a single story, not least because all four focus on Jesus's life. Indeed, the strong similarities among the four Gospels can make it particularly hard to keep them distinct in our minds. Yet their many differences often prompt readers to wonder exactly what Jesus said at certain moments or which chronological ordering of events is historical. Their similarities and differences frequently lead readers to favor a *harmonization* of the four Gospels.

Harmonization is the attempt to bring the various details of the four canonical Gospels into a single, coherent picture. A Gospel harmony is a project that addresses the scope and scale of all the events of the four Gospels. When parallel accounts occur among the Gospels, a harmony will bring together the unique details across the Gospels to create a single episode inclusive of all features from the respective accounts. For example, since Matthew, Mark, Luke, and John include Jesus feeding a crowd of five thousand, a Gospel harmony will bring unique features from the four together into a longer, harmonized version of the episode. On the other hand, if aspects of the parallel accounts are deemed to be too divergent, then a choice could be made to say that *similar* events occurred *multiple* times in Jesus's life. For instance, some Gospel harmonies suggest that Peter denied Jesus six or even nine times, given differences in episode arrangement among the passion narratives, even though each Gospel narrates just three denials by Peter. Yet the harmonizing impulse is not limited to large-scale Gospel harmonies. Readers routinely harmonize the Gospels in implicit ways as they're reading, or in their memories, by conflating details across the four Gospels.

Unlike the visual translations we explored in the previous chapter, most modern retellings of Jesus in film do not follow the structure and content of a single Gospel. Instead, they bring all four Gospels to bear *selectively* in the construction of new cinematic Gospels—making decisions that inevitably involve harmonization. Yet harmonization is not unique to Jesus films or the concerns of modern readers. It can already be seen in the reception of the Gospels in the church's early centuries, and it is even represented within and among the four Gospels themselves. Harmonization is, in fact, a common feature of retelling the Jesus story, beginning with ancient retellings and continuing all the way to stories made for the silver screen (and for TVs and tablets). The present chapter explores the ways in which harmonization is a hallmark of Jesus stories—from the canonical Gospels themselves, to early Gospel harmonies, to contemporary Jesus films.

Harmonization Within the Four Gospels

Harmonization is a feature within the canonical Gospels because each Gospel writer brought together multiple sources. A close reading reveals their awareness of other narratives and Jesus traditions. Luke, for example, begins by acknowledging that other records of Jesus's life had already been produced (Luke 1:1–4),[1] and John concludes by affirming that Jesus did and said much more than what is contained in his Gospel or could be contained in a world full of books (John 20:30; 21:25). These statements point to the

1. Notice that Luke seems to refer to both written narratives (*diēgēsis*, "account," in 1:1) and oral traditions (that which was "handed down to us by those who from the first were eyewitnesses" in 1:2).

evangelists' awareness of Gospel production and the wider circulation of traditions about Jesus, both oral and written. Through a close comparison of the Gospels, a consensus has emerged that Mark was a source for Matthew and Luke, and possibly for John as well.[2] The very fact that the evangelists were aware of and used multiple sources as they composed their Gospels speaks to the tendency to harmonize. One place where this likely occurs is in the overlap between Matthew and Luke that does not derive from their respective access to Mark.[3] A common explanation for this overlap is that Matthew and Luke independently used a common source, referred to by scholars as Q (from the German *Quelle*, meaning "source"). Given the lack of manuscript evidence for Q, other common explanations are that Luke used Matthew, or perhaps that Matthew used Luke. Whatever the solution is to this so-called synoptic problem, any scenario would provide an opportunity for harmonization of sources. Yet harmonization did not preclude the Gospel authors from telling their own stories. Instead, their use of sources reveals something about how they composed their expanded stories about Jesus.

The Longer Ending of Mark (Mark 16:9–20), as it is called, provides a straightforward example of harmonization within the four Gospels.[4] The resurrection appearances from Matthew and Luke have been brought together in this ending in something of a hodgepodge manner. Luke's resurrection narrative is particularly well represented in (1) the description of Mary Magdalene (Mark 16:9; Luke 8:2) and the disciples' disbelief when she announces that Jesus has been raised (Mark 16:11; Luke 24:10–11), (2) the reference to Jesus's appearance to two particular disciples (Mark 16:12–13; Luke 24:13–35), and (3) Jesus's ascension (Mark 16:19; Luke 24:51). Furthermore, the Longer Ending also draws from 1 Corinthians and Acts when it refers to speaking in tongues (cf. Mark 16:17; Acts 2:5–13; 1 Cor. 14) and handling snakes without being harmed (cf. Mark 16:18; Acts 28:1–6). Reflecting awareness of multiple Gospel accounts and offering a composite account of its own, the Longer Ending of Mark is an early example of harmonization that remains codified within the Gospel collection in our modern translations (usually with some typesetting adjustments to indicate its dubious origin).

2. For John's use of Mark, see, e.g., Becker et al., *John's Transformation of Mark*; North, *What John Knew*.

3. Since we do not know precisely what the additional sources were that the evangelists had at their disposal, the specific nature of harmonization cannot be shown definitively.

4. In the next chapter we will address how this Longer Ending does not fit themes of Mark's Gospel but was added by scribes as an attempt to "fill in the gaps" left by Mark's storytelling, which lacks an account of Jesus's resurrection.

Harmonization of the Four Gospels in Early Gospel Harmonies

The oldest preserved Gospel harmony is the Diatessaron and was composed in Syriac (or possibly Greek) by Tatian in the second century.[5] "Diatessaron" (meaning "through four") refers to the project of harmonizing the four canonical Gospels. Tatian wasn't the only person to make a Gospel harmony and might not have been the first. Harmonies and harmonizing projects have been attributed to a handful of people from antiquity and late antiquity. (Some of these projects are no longer extant.) One other notable Gospel harmony comes from Augustine and was produced at the start of the fifth century CE.

We will briefly explore two scenes from the Gospels and their "afterlives" in harmonies to illustrate the kinds of decisions involved in harmonizing: the temple cleansing and Jesus's seven sayings from the cross. Along the way, we will mention briefly what Jesus films do with these scenes before we transition in the following section to look more closely at elements of harmonization in film.

The Temple Cleansing

The Synoptic Gospels place the temple-cleansing incident, when Jesus prophetically rebukes merchants in the temple's outer courts, at the end of Jesus's ministry (Matt. 21:12–17; Mark 11:15–19; Luke 19:45–48), just after his "triumphal entry" into Jerusalem. In the Gospel of John, however, this event occurs at the very beginning of his ministry (John 2:13–22), immediately following the wedding at Cana, where Jesus performs his first sign (John 2:1–12). This difference raises multiple historical questions, including whether Jesus may have cleansed the temple twice—once at the beginning of his ministry and then again at the end. Proposing two cleansings is one way to harmonize the accounts, and this is the solution of Augustine (*Cons.* 2.67), who contends that the details in John's account are different enough to warrant two cleansings. John's unique details include Jesus making and using a whip as he drives out people (and animals, John 2:15) and his claim to be able to rebuild the temple in three days (2:19). Another way to harmonize the episodes is to propose a single temple incident and suggest that John had theological reasons for moving the story forward.

5. The preservation of Tatian's Diatessaron is a complex issue. There are two broad traditional streams that preserve it, the Eastern and Western sources, respectively, but the sources internal to these streams do not agree with one another. It is generally thought, however, that the Arabic sources within the Eastern tradition best preserve Tatian's *sequence* of the Gospel events, although the issue of Tatian's *precise wording* is a separate matter. See Barker, *Tatian's Diatessaron*, 44–58; cf. also Perrin, "Diatessaron."

Some who argue for a single event that falls in the synoptic sequence also merge John's unique features with the synoptic version, providing another kind of harmonization.[6]

The Diatessaron follows the latter option (single event, harmonized details from John and Synoptics) but places the event in the second of the three Passovers celebrated by Jesus in the sequence of John's Gospel (Diatessaron §32).[7] This is something of a via media (i.e., a middle way). John places the temple cleansing in the first of three Jerusalem visits, and although the Synoptics do not record Jesus's participation as an adult in multiple Passover festivals,[8] they place the temple incident in the final week of Jesus's life, during his last visit to Jerusalem.

The various approaches to the accounts of the temple cleansing illustrate that there is no single way to harmonize. Harmonization occurs both when a harmonizer assumes that the differences in detail between multiple accounts mean that multiple events occurred and when a harmonizer conflates multiple accounts into a single event on the basis of their similarities.

Jesus films prefer to depict the temple cleansing as a singular event at the end of Jesus's ministry (as in the Synoptics). In some examples, certain Johannine elements, like the whip, are incorporated into the synoptic timeline.[9] Very few Jesus films follow John and place the temple cleansing at the beginning of Jesus's ministry, though the film *Judas* (2004) is an exception. Some movies put the event in the middle of the story and retain the Johannine whip, resembling the Diatessaron.[10] The only film that goes beyond a single cleansing event is *The Last Temptation of Christ* (1988). In the sequencing of the film, Jesus appears to cleanse the temple twice on consecutive days (rather than three years apart, as in Augustine's harmonization)—yet another distinctive harmonization of this event from the Gospel accounts.

6. E.g., Snodgrass, "Temple Incident."

7. Barker, "Narrative Chronology of Tatian's Diatessaron," 295. Since the section numbers and referencing systems vary across the different versions that preserve the Diatessaron, we are following the conventions in Hope W. Hogg's translation in Roberts and Donaldson, *Ante-Nicene Fathers*.

8. Luke records Jesus participating in Passover with his parents in Jerusalem at the age of twelve (Luke 2:41–42).

9. *From the Manger to the Cross* (1912); *I.N.R.I.* (*Crown of Thorns*, 1923); *The Pilgrimage Play* (1949); *El Mártir del Calvario* (*The Martyr of Calvary*, 1952); *The Prince of Peace* (1959); *The Greatest Story Ever Told* (1965); *Jesús, Nuestro Señor* (*Jesus, Our Lord*, 1971); *The Chosen* (season 4, episode 8, "Humble," 2024).

10. *Reina de Reinas: La Virgen María* (*Queen of Queens: The Virgin Mary*, 1948); *Jesus* (1973); *The Revolutionary* (1995); *Mulla Kireetam* (*Crown of Thorns*, 2006).

The Seven Sayings on the Cross

While the extended accounts of Jesus's crucifixion in the Gospels provide many details that could be harmonized, we would like to highlight the seven sayings of Jesus from the cross. These are a major feature of the Gospel accounts and are highly thematic in each of them.

Luke and John record multiple sayings found only in their individual Gospels, while Matthew and Mark together share one saying: "My God, my God, why have you forsaken me?" (Matt. 27:46; Mark 15:34; cf. Ps. 22:1). Luke includes three sayings: "Father, forgive them, for they do not know what they are doing" (Luke 23:34); "Truly I tell you, today you will be with me in paradise" (23:43); and "Father, into your hands I commit my spirit" (23:46). John also has three unique sayings. The first is Jesus's dual directive to his mother, Mary, and to the Beloved Disciple: "Woman, here is your son" and "Here is your mother" (John 19:26–27). Then John records Jesus saying "I am thirsty" (19:28), and finally, after drinking from the sour wine offered to him, Jesus responds, "It is finished" (19:30).

Harmonizing these sayings involves simply creating a composite account of all seven sayings. This is what we see in the Diatessaron and Augustine's harmony, as well as in many Jesus films. But a complicating question in harmonization relates to the order of the sayings. The Diatessaron (§§51–52) contains the seven sayings in the following order:[11]

1. "Truly I tell you, today you will be with me in paradise" (Luke 23:43).[12]
2. "Woman, here is your son. . . . Here is your mother" (John 19:26–27).
3. "I am thirsty" (John 19:28).
4. "It is finished" (John 19:30).
5. "My God, my God, why have you forsaken me?" (Matt. 27:46; Mark 15:34).
6. "Father, forgive them, for they do not know what they are doing" (Luke 23:34).
7. "Father, into your hands I commit my spirit" (Luke 23:46).

As we might expect, Augustine's order differs from Tatian's. For example, although the Diatessaron and Augustine agree that Luke 23:46 (". . . I commit my spirit") should come last, Augustine places John's "It is finished" immediately before it (*Cons.* 3.18). Jesus films depicting the crucifixion usually

11. We use the NIV to represent the saying and leave aside the project of reconstructing precise Tatianic readings.

12. Notably, the Diatessaron does not even preserve the Lukan order of sayings in this composite sequence but begins with the second Lukan saying.

include a couple of the sayings,[13] and several include most of them,[14] but the films that incorporate all seven sayings do not maintain any kind of consistent ordering (see table 2.1 below).

Table 2.1
The Seven Sayings from the Cross in Jesus Films (Abbreviated)

	A	B	C	D	E	F	G	H	I
1.	Forgive	Forgive	Forgive	Forgive	Forgive	Paradise	Forgive	Forgive	Forgive
2.	Thirst	Mother	Mother	Paradise	Paradise	Forgive	Paradise	Mother	Paradise
3.	Paradise	Paradise	Paradise	Mother	Mother	Mother	Mother	Forsaken	Thirst
4.	Mother	Forsaken	Thirst	Forsaken	Forsaken	Forsaken	Thirst	Thirst	Mother
5.	Forsaken	Thirst	Forsaken	Thirst	Thirst	Thirst	Forsaken	Paradise	Forsaken
6.	Finished	Finished	Finished	Finished	Spirit	Spirit	Spirit	Spirit	Finished
7.	Spirit	Spirit	Spirit	Spirit	Finished	Finished	Finished	Finished	Spirit

*Here we represent the sayings in English shorthand even for the films that word them differently (or are not in English).

A. *Jesús, Nuestro Señor* (*Jesus, Our Lord*, 1971). **B.** *The Pilgrimage Play* (1949); *El Mártir del Calvario* (*The Martyr of Calvary*, 1952); *The Greatest Story Ever Told* (1965). **C.** *El Proceso de Cristo* (*The Trial of Christ*, 1966). **D.** *Jesús de Nazareth* (*Jesus of Nazareth*, 1942); *The Life of Christ* (*Mysteries of the Rosary* series, 1957); *Santhi Sandesam* (*Message of Peace*, 2004); *The Passion of the Christ* (2004); *Son of God* (2014). **E.** *The Living Christ Series* (1951); *I Beheld His Glory* (1953); *Day of Triumph* (1954); *Jesus* (1973). **F.** *The Prince of Peace* (1959). **G.** *María Magdalena, Pecadora de Magdala* (*Mary Magdalene, Sinner of Magdala*, 1946); *Reina de Reinas: La Virgen María* (*Queen of Queens: The Virgin Mary*, 1948). **H.** *The Savior* (2014). **I.** *Kristo* (1996).

As table 2.1 makes clear, "Father, forgive them" is consistently included as the first saying of the seven, except in *The Prince of Peace* (1959). Another consistent feature is that the two sayings "It is finished" and "Father, into your hands" oscillate for the penultimate and final saying, respectively. Even in the ASL film *Jesus: A Deaf Missions Film* (2024)—which does not include all seven sayings since Jesus is unable to sign while his hands are nailed to the cross—this broad pattern is followed. Jesus signs "Father, forgive them" as they are putting him on the cross by ripping his hands away momentarily just before they are pierced. Then before he dies, Jesus loudly yells, "It is finished"—the only spoken English in the entire film.

These examples from ancient and modern harmonies illustrate that, when the Gospels are read in light of one another, harmonization is virtually inevitable but far from clear-cut. Harmonization rarely follows a single process. Instead, particular choices for harmonizing the Gospels create, in a real sense, a "new Gospel." We can see this already in the Diatessaron, which is not a

13. Although some films, like *Il Messia* (*The Messiah*, 1975), do not include any of them.

14. Surprisingly, *Jesus of Nazareth* (1977) only includes six of the seven, leaving out John's "I am thirsty" saying.

Jesus: A Deaf Missions Film (2024) produced by Deaf Missions and GUM Vision Studio

Jesus: A Deaf Missions Film (2024) includes one other "saying," which could be regarded as an interpretation of "Woman, behold your son." When Mary and John come near to the cross, Jesus signs "I love you" with his right hand as it remains firmly pierced to the cross.

mere conflation of the evangelists' stories of Jesus. Rather, as Francis Watson affirms, "Tatian's treatment of his sources is on a continuum with Luke's or Matthew's."[15] In other words, Tatian was making various decisions in the evaluation of the four Gospels to compose a new Gospel. In Jesus films we see similar harmonizing tendencies and creative decisions, some of which go well beyond previous harmonizing endeavors.

As we consider these varied ways of harmonization, we should recall that our own understandings of the Jesus story will play a role in how we interact with these new Gospels. When we reflexively react—whether positively or negatively—to a particular retelling, we are likely encountering our own role as director of the Jesus story as we have come to conceive it (i.e., direct it!). As suggested already, we each have our own internal Jesus film in mind, one that inevitably guides our engagement with other ways of telling the Jesus story. These other tellings make a myriad of decisions, including choices about harmonization, to rehearse the story of Jesus in a *fresh* way (as the Diatessaron was doing). As we turn to explore in more depth the ways Jesus films have harmonized the four Gospels, we want to attend to these fresh messages being conveyed about Jesus in films.

Harmonization in Jesus Films

Strictly speaking, *no* Jesus film is a full-on Gospel harmony, because none attempts to account for a proper chronological ordering of every episode from the Gospels nor tries to synthesize all the divergent details of parallel accounts. Jesus films are highly selective in what they choose to harmonize, but almost

15. Watson, "Towards a Redaction-Critical Reading," 96.

every Jesus film displays some level of harmonization of the four canonical Gospels. In what follows we will look at how simple forms of harmonization go back to the very beginning of Jesus films. Then we will analyze how later films that incorporate many more episodes from the Gospels need to make decisions about the distinctive timelines provided in the Synoptics and in the Gospel of John, respectively.

Harmonization in Early (Silent) Jesus Films

The first examples of cinematic harmonization that we explore are three early silent films. The majority of silent Jesus films use a *tableau vivant* (living picture) style, with the camera positioned statically as the scene unfolds. Scenes often begin with title cards, and occasional intertitles provide Bible references or quick summaries to help the viewer understand what the films are portraying. For many early silent films, the filmmakers could rely on the viewers' familiarity with the stories to connect the dots and fill out details in the unfolding scenes,[16] thus making the viewer a kind of cocreator. It was not until Cecil B. DeMille's silent Jesus film from 1927, *The King of Kings*, that dialogue was incorporated into the intertitles, and the *tableau vivant* style expanded into more dynamic forms of cinematography.[17] In the early years of Jesus films, screenings varied quite a bit depending on whether the director of the film house chose to accompany the film with music, include a brief lecture, or even rearrange the sequence of the tableaux.[18] Thus, not every screening would have been the same. Not only could different "paratextual features" accompany any given screening, but also, as discussed in the introduction with respect to cognitive psychology, each viewer would bring their own unique experience, familiarity, and background knowledge to inform what they were watching. The early silent films especially relied on this dynamic.

La Passion (1898)

The earliest extant Jesus film, *La Passion* (*The Passion*, 1898), is a natural starting place.[19] It is quite short, close to eleven minutes in length. Yet precisely

16. Greydanus, "Through Other Eyes," 77.

17. One exception is D. W. Griffith's film *Intolerance* (1916)—a silent film that did incorporate dialogue. However, there are very few scenes with Jesus in the three-hour film, which narrates three additional interwoven stories across multiple centuries (cf. chap. 8).

18. This dynamic has some fascinating parallels with the early days of oral tradition when the Jesus story first circulated. See Shepherd, "Introduction," 4–5; Boillat and Robert, "*La Vie et Passion*," 24–26.

19. We know of other films that were made previously, but we sadly no longer have access to them. These include *La Passion du Christ* (*The Passion of Christ*, 1897), *The Horitz Passion Play* (1897), and *The Passion Play of Oberammergau* (1898).

because of its brevity, *La Passion* is an intriguing Jesus film to consider. If you were limited to about ten minutes to tell the Jesus story as you understand it, with no ability to incorporate dialogue, what would you include? *La Passion* opens with a Matthean infancy narrative (though a single Lukan shepherd is present with the magi), followed by a singular scene from John when Jesus raises Lazarus from the dead (John 11). Then the story shifts to a few key moments from the canonical passion accounts—from the Last Supper to Jesus's death and resurrection. This short film includes only a single scene from Jesus's ministry, but the miracle of raising someone from the dead thematically anticipates the miracle of Jesus's own resurrection.[20] As succinct as it is, this Jesus film can be understood as the Jesus story retold with a keen focus on death and new life.

La Vie du Christ (1906)

La Vie du Christ, or *La Naissance, La Vie et La Mort du Christ* (*The Birth, the Life and the Death of Christ*, 1906), is just over thirty minutes long. The film opens with a blend of Luke's and Matthew's infancy narratives, although notably omitted is the slaughter of the innocents from Matthew. Instead, we get a novel scene of female angels praying for Jesus while he sleeps. Only three events from Jesus's ministry are incorporated before the film transitions to key episodes from the passion narratives. Intriguingly, those moments are Jesus's interaction with the Samaritan woman, his raising of Jairus's daughter, and Mary Magdalene washing Jesus's feet,[21] highlighting Jesus's connections with women. The film continues with events from the passion accounts, although it is notable that the cleansing of the temple is altogether absent. The minimal narrative tension in this Jesus story (through the omission of scenes like the slaughter of the innocents and the temple cleansing) provides little rationale for Jesus's execution. As the passion events unfold in the film, Veronica appears and wipes the blood and sweat from Jesus's face after he has fallen while carrying his cross. Veronica adds to the film's already prominent focus on women. As a retelling of the Jesus story, *La Vie du Christ* thematizes how Jesus is good news for women.[22] This is especially noteworthy since the director, Alice Guy, is the first female director in cinematic history.[23]

20. Another early silent film by contrast, *The Miracles of Jesus* (1910), depicts several miracles from Jesus's ministry, but without any narrative framing or cohesion.

21. Although Luke does not name this woman in Luke 7:36–50, church tradition (and Jesus films) often conflate Mary Magdalene with other women from the Gospels (cf. chap. 4).

22. As also rightly noted by Shepherd, "*La naissance*," 60–77.

23. Page, *100 Bible Films*, 18.

Société des Etablissements L. Gaumont.

Angels accompany Jesus as he sleeps in *La Vie du Christ* (1906). Thanks to David Shepherd for providing a copy of this image. See Shepherd, "*La naissance*."

La Vie et Passion de Notre Seigneur Jésus-Christ (1907)

La Vie et Passion de Notre Seigneur Jésus-Christ (*The Life and Passion of Our Lord Jesus Christ*, 1907) is another short silent film, just under forty-four minutes in length.[24] The film opens with a birth narrative that draws from both Matthew and Luke. Jesus's birth is one of the most commonly harmonized segments of the Gospel stories within modern Jesus films (and in broader artistic expression). It is only in Luke that we read about Joseph and Mary traveling to Bethlehem, the lack of room to accommodate them,[25] and the shepherds' presence directly after Jesus's birth. Matthew uniquely records the account of the magi who come to Jesus sometime after he is born, Herod's slaughter of the innocents, and the family's flight to Egypt before returning north to Nazareth. Yet even though these stories come from different Gospels with distinct narrative purposes and are not set in the same time frames in Jesus's infancy, they are routinely combined.[26] We see this portrayed clearly in

24. We focus on the 1907 version of the film since it underwent an elaborate evolution containing different shots that were filmed at different times from 1902–5. See, e.g., Boillat and Robert, "*La Vie et Passion*"; Friesen, "*La Vie et Passion*."

25. This was not in a commercial inn or motel of some kind. The Greek term *katalyma*, often rendered as "inn" in English translations, most likely refers to a guest room within an ancient home; see Carlson, "Accommodations of Joseph and Mary." The only Jesus film that seems to go in this direction is *Magdalena: Released from Shame* (2007). *The Nativity* (2010) comes very close by incorporating family drama into the return to Bethlehem, although it still includes an innkeeper with no available rooms.

26. Another aspect of this harmonization involves the way Jesus films address how Joseph first learns about Mary's pregnancy. Most commonly, he finds out when Mary returns pregnant from her trip to visit Elizabeth. See, e.g., *Jesus of Nazareth* (1977); *Per Amore, Solo per Amore*

Christmas nativity sets, with magi and shepherds both surrounding the newborn Jesus (conflating Christmas and Epiphany). This conflation also occurs in Jesus films where shepherds and magi are portrayed together[27] or where they see Jesus during the same night, one after the other.[28] Offering an interesting comparison, Tatian's original sequence in the Diatessaron appears to keep the Lukan and Matthean elements as discrete events (§§2–3). Specifically, the Lukan events are recorded first, including Luke's account of the shepherds at Jesus's birth, his circumcision on the eighth day, and his dedication in the temple, all before the magi begin their journey to Bethlehem.

In the harmonized infancy narrative of *La Vie et Passion de Notre Seigneur Jésus-Christ*, however, the Lukan shepherds see the star just as Matthew's magi do, and they, too, use it as a guide to find the stable.[29] Strangely, in this film Mary does not actually give birth. Instead, the baby Jesus simply *appears* in the manger. So, calling this sequence in the film a birth narrative is something of a misnomer!

When the film shifts to Jesus's ministry, it includes a mixture of synoptic events, such as the healing of Jairus's daughter and the transfiguration, coupled with a few Johannine scenes: the wedding at Cana, the Samaritan woman at the well, and the raising of Lazarus. After this combination of events, the triumphal entry and the incidents surrounding Jesus's passion ensue. Within its relatively short duration, the film harmonizes the Gospel accounts to create its own, new narrative. An intriguing feature involves Jesus's "disappearance" at the film's conclusion. After Jesus is buried, he is depicted

(*For Love, Only for Love*, 1993); *Marie de Nazareth* (*Mary of Nazareth*, 1995); *Giuseppe di Nazareth* (*Joseph of Nazareth*, 2000); *Maria, Figlia del Suo Figlio* (*Mary, Daughter of Her Son*, 2000); *The Nativity Story* (2006); *La Sacra Famiglia* (*The Holy Family*, 2006); *The Nativity* (2010); *Maria di Nazaret* (*Mary of Nazareth*, 2012); *The Star* (2017); *Mary* (2024). Luke does not record a response by Joseph to the news, or that he had a vision of his own. But by delaying the Matthean vision to accommodate the Lukan details, there is an added level of dramatic tension; cf. Prot. Jas. 13–14.

27. E.g., *La Passion* (*The Passion*, 1898); *La Vie du Christ*, or *La Naissance, La Vie et La Mort du Christ* (*The Birth, the Life and the Death of Christ*, 1906); *The Star of Bethlehem* (1912); *Christus* (1916); *I.N.R.I.* (*Crown of Thorns*, 1923); *Reina de Reinas: La Virgen María* (*Queen of Queens: The Virgin Mary*, 1948); *The Nativity* (1952); *Ben-Hur* (1959); *The Life of Christ* (*Mysteries of the Rosary* series, 1957); *The Little Drummer Boy* (1968); *Jesus* (1973); *Santhi Sandesam* (*Message of Peace*, 2004); *The Nativity Story* (2006); *Son of God* (2014); *The Star* (2017); *Journey to Bethlehem* (2023).

28. E.g., *From the Manger to the Cross* (1912); *Ben-Hur: A Tale of the Christ* (1925); *Giuseppe di Nazareth* (*Joseph of Nazareth*, 2000); *The Nativity* (2010).

29. So too in, e.g., *The Star of Bethlehem* (1912); *Ben-Hur: A Tale of the Christ* (1925); *Reina de Reinas: La Virgen María* (*Queen of Queens: The Virgin Mary*, 1948); *The Prince of Peace* (1959); *Herod the Great* (1959); *The Little Drummer Boy* (1968); *My Son, My Savior* (2015); *Mary* (2024); cf. also the Latter-day Saint (Mormon) film *The Testaments of One Fold and One Shepherd* (2000), in which even the Nephites in the Americas are able to see the star.

Mary and Joseph pray to God (left) and the baby Jesus appears in a manger (right) in *La Vie et Passion de Notre Seigneur Jésus-Christ* (1907).

as ascending from the tomb and vanishing, only to appear to his disciples before ascending to God's right hand. Considering this cinematic Gospel as a whole, and its portrait of Christ in particular, Jesus is displayed as not entirely human, with the film bookended by Jesus appearing and vanishing. At the beginning he suddenly appears in the manger, and he abruptly disappears at the film's conclusion.[30]

Extensively Harmonized Dialogue

The silent film era largely harmonized the Jesus story by pulling episodes from the different Gospels into a new storyline and conflating overlapping details. Another kind of harmonization emerged in "sound films" or "talking pictures" as the use of dialogue became prominent. Jesus's words are often a bricolage of multiple sayings from the Gospels and even other biblical passages. This feature is most pronounced in the film *The Greatest Story Ever Told* (1965). Nearly every time that Jesus speaks, his sayings are conflations of statements that appear in very different contexts across the Gospel narratives. One of the more random amalgamations involves the sequence of Jesus's words after the temple cleansing, which turns into an extended time of teaching into the evening.[31] Here is just a sampling (with the wording taken from the film):

- "I desire mercy, not sacrifice" (Matt. 9:13, citing Hosea 6:6), from the call of Matthew.
- "Think not that I have come to destroy the law or the prophets. I have not come to destroy, but to fulfill" (Matt. 5:17), from the Sermon on the Mount.

30. This feature has been called Gnostic by some critics. See Stern et al., *Savior on the Silver Screen*, 291–95; Walsh and Staley, *Jesus, the Gospels, and Cinematic Imagination*, 29.

31. Even apart from the dialogue, the scene is itself a harmonization of the synoptic timeline and the Johannine whip.

- "I have come as a light into the world" (John 8:12), set during the Festival of Booths.
- "Faith, hope, and love abide—these three, but the greatest of these is love" (1 Cor. 13:13), a Pauline statement!
- "Where several gather together in my name, there will I be" (Matt. 18:20), from Matthew's Community Discourse.

None of these sayings have anything to do with the temple incident as portrayed in the Gospels. The net effect of this type of harmonized dialogue is the portrayal of Jesus as a sage—a pithy speaker of wise proverbial sayings—rather than as a storyteller or an apocalyptic prophet.

Selecting the Synoptic or Johannine Outline

As Jesus films grew in length, especially as they were made for TV (and then for streaming) in serialized form, the question of the narrative structure of the film or series became increasingly significant. Typically in Jesus films, Jesus makes a single visit to Jerusalem at the end of his life. Whether because of time constraints or other reasons, such films have essentially chosen a synoptic outline for their Jesus stories. The Synoptics record events in Jesus's northern ministry in Galilee leading up to a single climactic trip to Jerusalem just before his crucifixion. Luke's version is the most geographically focused of the three Synoptics, especially in his extended "travel narrative" from Galilee to Jerusalem (Luke 9:51–19:27), which culminates in Jesus's triumphal entry and passion. The other option for sequencing a harmonized Jesus story is to follow the frame of John's Gospel, with its presentation of a multiyear ministry organized around Jewish festivals, including multiple trips to Jerusalem (see John 2:13; 5:1; 7:10; 12:12). In fact, it is only from John's Gospel that we derive the idea that Jesus had a three-year ministry.[32] In what follows we will briefly look at the sequencing of three film examples: *Jesus of Nazareth* (1977), *Son of God* (2014), and *The Chosen* (2017–present).

***Jesus of Nazareth* (1977)**

Jesus of Nazareth (1977), which was originally a miniseries made for TV, reflects a decision to adopt a broadly synoptic outline and yet retain many of the Johannine episodes that take place in Jerusalem before Holy Week. But the Johannine episodes before Holy Week are shifted. Events from earlier in John are placed after Jesus's triumphal entry into Jerusalem (i.e., his single

32. Based on the presence of (at least) three distinct Passovers in John (2:13; 6:4; 11:55).

trip there), a few days before his death. These include the healing of a man born blind (John 9), Jesus's saying that he is one with the Father (John 10:30), the interaction with Nicodemus (John 3, oddly set in broad daylight), and the scene of the woman caught in adultery (John 8).[33] *Jesus of Nazareth* is just one example of how John has to be rearranged to accommodate a synoptic outline.

Son of God (2014)

Son of God (2014) was originally produced as episodes from History's miniseries *The Bible* (2013), with the portions dedicated to Jesus reedited, expanded, and then released in theaters. The film adopts a similar posture to that of *Jesus of Nazareth* (1977) by incorporating Johannine stories into the synoptic outline. Yet its harmonizing technique is much more complex because, although it follows a Lukan outline, it presents itself from beginning to end as being Johannine. It opens with a version of John's prologue and concludes with a vision of John the apostle on the island of Patmos, where John the Seer, who wrote Revelation (tradition identifies him as John the Apostle), received his apocalyptic visions. Additionally, early in the film, after a harmonized infancy narrative,[34] we see a retrospective with John the Apostle, several decades after the death of Christ, declaring that he is one of Christ's followers, further indicating to the viewer that the film is ostensibly based on the Gospel of John.

Nevertheless, following a series of miracles and teachings, the film's structure eventually reveals itself to be primarily Lukan. This is seen most clearly when Jesus reads from the scroll of Isaiah in the synagogue in Nazareth (Luke 4:16–21), which is thematically resonant for the Gospel of Luke and inaugurates Jesus's public ministry. In *Son of God*, however, this scene is the catalyst for Jesus's decision to start his journey to Jerusalem—a pivot that is prominent later in Luke (9:51). Only after arriving in Jerusalem does Jesus have the Johannine encounter with Nicodemus (John 3), as in *Jesus of Nazareth* (1977), once more revealing the Lukan structure of the film into which Johannine material has been inserted. This dynamic continues into the post-resurrection scenes, which contain many Johannine elements (e.g.,

33. As noted in chap. 1, the story of the woman caught in adultery is not original to John, which is why the episode does not appear in the Diatessaron (from the most plausible reconstruction of its sequence). We do see adjustments to John's sequence in the Diatessaron that are similar to those in *Jesus of Nazareth* (1977). For example, the story of the woman at the well in Samaria from John 4 (§21) appears before Jesus's encounter with Nicodemus in Jerusalem from John 3 (§32).

34. A transition from John's prologue to Jesus's infancy narratives also occurs in *The Greatest Story Ever Told* (1965). The Diatessaron likewise opens with John 1:1–5 and shifts to an infancy narrative, but Tatian chooses the story of John the Baptist's birth from Luke 1 (§1).

doubting Thomas), but shifts to Luke's conclusion and to the beginning of Acts (Luke's sequel volume), with Jesus appearing to his followers forty days after his resurrection (Acts 1:3) and promising to empower them with the (coming) Holy Spirit (Acts 1:8; cf. Luke 24:46–49).[35] Use of this Lukan ending is rare in Jesus films, and it likely happens in *Son of God* because the miniseries *The Bible* (2013) includes the storyline of Acts. This larger framework from which *Son of God* was edited also explains the Johannine ending and the elements from Revelation already noted.

The Chosen (2017–Present)

Unlike for *Jesus of Nazareth* (1977) and *Son of God* (2014), the Gospel of John clearly provides the framework for *The Chosen*—a crowdfunded multiseason streaming series about Jesus and his disciples. The primary storyline of season 1 covers John 1–4 and culminates with the story of Jesus's encounter with the Samaritan woman (John 4). Seasons 2–4 incorporate much more synoptic material, but the Johannine framework from season 1 continues to provide the narrative backbone through John 12. Yet even with the adoption of a Johannine outline, the show has Jesus making only one trip to Jerusalem during his ministry before the triumphal entry. In light of that fact, it does make some adjustments to the location of events. For example, Jesus's meeting with Nicodemus (season 1, episode 7, "Invitations," 2019) takes place in Capernaum rather than Jerusalem. The show also breaks from the Johannine order of events on a few occasions, as with the calling of Nathaniel in season 2 (cf. John 1) after Jesus's encounters with Nicodemus and the Samaritan woman, both of which take place in season 1 (cf. John 3–4). The most notable shuffling of the Johannine sequence in the first four seasons is the delay of the temple cleansing from John 2. Through four seasons, which end with the start of the triumphal entry and so just before any sort of temple-cleansing event (season 4, episode 8, "Humble," 2024), *The Chosen* has portrayed Jesus as tender, warm, and even humorous—so much so that within the show's own narrative arc it would not have made sense to portray him as responsible for something like the temple-cleansing incident in the first season.

Conclusion

As we have seen, harmonization is a consistent feature of retelling Jesus stories, even though the methods deployed are quite diverse. This is true from

35. With additional language harmonized from Matthew's final commission (Matt. 28:19–20).

the ancient world to the present. It seems that there are as many ways to harmonize as there are people interested in harmonizing. So, the Jesus film we direct in our heads when we read or recall the story of Jesus is likely as full of harmonization as the external films that we have analyzed in this chapter.

Yet even thoroughly harmonized stories about Jesus are still stories in their own right, with unique emphases and presentations of Jesus. As such, they should be interpreted as discrete stories. The uniqueness of a harmonized Jesus film is not necessarily found in the creation of new events for the life of Jesus (although plenty of Jesus films take such liberties). Rather, uniqueness lies in the selection and fresh ordering of events from the Gospels. A film's themes begin to emerge when attention is given to how its harmonizing impulses have been executed. In this way, harmonizing can help us analyze the goals and effects of a Jesus film. In the end, whatever our assessments of how a film has mined, reshaped, and woven together the canonical Gospels, we will inevitably bring that film into interaction with the distinctive ways we direct the films of our own imaginations.

3

A Need to Fill in the Gaps

Good stories stick with us. They captivate our imaginations and draw us into their worlds. Sometimes we find ourselves so present to the narrative world that we can't help but probe the parts of the story that haven't been told: a certain character's backstory that went unexplained or an unknown, even puzzling, motivation for a character's actions at a particular point in the plot. We may come to the end of a story—even if it wasn't a cliff-hanger—and immediately begin to wonder, What happens next for our beloved characters? Because every story is selective and limited in scope, there are always gaps. And because we, both ancients and moderns, are curious creatures, we are desperate to fill in those gaps.

This dynamic can be just as true with the Gospels as it is for a favorite novel or film. Many gaps in the Gospel narratives provoke readers to ask unanswerable questions. These are often fair and interesting questions, but for whatever reason the Gospel writers chose not to address them. When we turn to modern cinematic Gospels, we see that many of their makers share this same kind of curiosity, to know more than what the Gospels give us. The films that use one or more of the Gospels as sources routinely expand and supplement them, adding details or whole episodes that are not a part of the Gospels themselves. Some of us may be tempted to reject these moves as speculative or even inaccurate. In many cases this may be a fair conclusion, historically speaking. Yet usually what we are implying in this evaluation is that, *for our own part*, we wouldn't fill in the gaps in the same way. Nevertheless, there is something about this drive to fill in the gaps in the Jesus story that illuminates how that story has been retold from antiquity to the present day. If we consider how the Gospels were originally written, we can observe that the drive to fill in the gaps is already a tendency internal to the four Gospels themselves—a tendency that continues in extracanonical Gospels. Investigating some of the ways that gaps in the Jesus story are filled helps us realize how often we, too, might be making similar kinds of decisions, even if only in our imaginations. Much that we take for granted in Jesus's story might actually exist in the gaps within the Gospels.

How the Canonical Gospels Fill in Gaps

In the composition of the four canonical Gospels, there is already a tendency to add to the literary traditions about Jesus by incorporating new details and even new episodes to his story. If that weren't the case, there wouldn't be much point in having multiple versions of the same story! A significant majority of scholars agree that Mark was the first written Gospel and that Matthew and Luke utilized Mark as a literary source for their own compositions. Matthew and Luke, in turn, each contain unique material not found in the other. Most scholars also agree that John was written later, perhaps independently, but recent discussions have entertained the idea that John may have been familiar with the synoptic traditions and sought to supplement them with new material, or in some cases expand on their significance.[1] We may find it compelling to ask questions about the gaps in the Jesus story, but it is fascinating to consider first that Gospel productivity itself was motivated in part by this same interest.

The clearest place to explore how filling in the gaps occurs *within the canonical Gospels themselves* is Matthew's and Luke's use of Mark. Mark's Gospel begins with little preamble and ends quite suddenly, yet those features are not characteristic of Matthew and Luke. It appears, from their own compositions, that Matthew and Luke were not completely content with these features and other Markan "gaps." For the purpose of illustration, we will focus on three such gaps: (1) the lack of detail in the account of Jesus's temptation, (2) the way Mark ends without an explicit resurrection appearance, and (3) the absence of any account of Jesus's childhood (or any event before his baptism).

The Temptation of Jesus

We start by considering one of the noticeable gaps at the very beginning of Mark's Gospel. Mark's account of Jesus's temptation is brief and simple;

1. See, e.g., Barker, *Writing and Rewriting the Gospels*.

it covers a mere two verses (Mark 1:12–13). The narrator offers only four details of Jesus's temptation experience: (1) the Spirit leads Jesus into the wilderness, (2) Jesus is tempted by Satan for forty days, (3) Jesus is with the wild animals, and (4) angels minister to him. That is the extent of Mark's narration. We don't hear anything about the three specific temptations that often come to mind when Bible readers recall the story, nor do we find Jesus's three quotations from Scripture to combat the temptations (as Matthew and Luke provide). In other words, Mark's brief account has significant gaps—gaps that raise a variety of questions, such as *How exactly did Satan tempt Jesus? What were the nature of those temptations? How did Jesus respond?* Consider this: Forty days is a long time, and Mark does not even allow himself *forty words* for this account! (It is a mere thirty words in the Greek [NA[28] ed.]). When Matthew and Luke fill in these gaps, they provide some solid answers to questions that might occur to readers of Mark. But filling in gaps often creates new ones, so readers of Matthew and Luke will very likely continue to ask questions about this episode as the additional information in these two Gospels presses their imaginations in new directions.

When the Jesus story is retold outside of and beyond the canonical Gospels, the gaps related to the temptation narrative are often filled in highly creative ways. The medium of film virtually necessitates creative (and expansive) choices. How, for example, can a filmmaker represent Satan in Jesus's temptations? In some films Satan assumes the form of a man, like the creepy cave dweller in *The Greatest Story Ever Told* (1965), or he takes on the forms of a man and a woman at different times, as portrayed in *Kristo* (1996) and in *Jesus* (1999). In some films, Satan is manifested in several different forms (e.g., *Mesih* [*Jesus, the Spirit of God*, 2010]; *Forty Nights* [2016]; *40: The Temptation of Christ* [2020]). The most notable and varied characterization might be found in Martin Scorsese's *The Last Temptation of Christ* (1988), where Satan appears as a cobra, a lion, a blaze of fire, and then—unexpectedly, at Jesus's crucifixion—a little girl.

Although there are many more ways that Jesus films address the gaps in the temptation story, we provide one final example taken from *Last Days in the Desert* (2015), whose storyline is devoted to Jesus's forty days of temptation in the wilderness and his experiences immediately thereafter.[2] Here the gaps pertain to Jesus's return to civilization after his forty days come to an end. The film entertains various questions not addressed in any of the four canonical Gospels: When in the temptation process did Satan decide to leave Jesus alone? What did Jesus learn in the wilderness? How did Jesus reintegrate into

2. This film makes an intriguing choice for Satan's appearance, as the same actor playing Jesus (Ewan McGregor) also plays Satan.

Universal Pictures / Cineplex Odeon Films / Ufland Productions

Satan disguised as a little girl, claiming to be a guardian angel, in *The Last Temptation of Christ* (1988)

society after his temptation episode? While the film is highly imaginative and speculative, it follows the same impulse—exhibited within Scripture itself and shared by many readers—to probe more deeply into what this experience may have been like for Jesus. The film imagines that the devil continually tempts and harasses Jesus during his entire time in the desert, from beginning to end.

In the final shot of *Last Days in the Desert*, the film strikingly portrays the significance of what has happened to Jesus in the desert, along with the curiosity that the story has evoked. We see a modern couple in contemporary dress arriving by car at the same desert hills where Jesus has been tempted. They step out of the car to take some quick photos before returning to their vehicle and driving on. The scene evokes numerous emotions in light of the contemporary proclivity to reduce almost any experience to a quick photo opportunity. The movie has portrayed Jesus going out into the desert for a forty-day period of discernment and committing himself to fasting and prayer, overcoming tremendous struggles all along the way. In contrast, these tourists spend no more than a few seconds looking out into the vast desert landscape and then shrink its potential for transformation and reflection into a mere snapshot. This scene also speaks to the apparent reason the film was made—namely, curiosity and wonder about gaps in our knowledge of the past, a past from which we are separated by an immense temporal and cultural gulf. And human beings are rarely content to leave such gaps unfilled.[3]

3. The final scene also turns *Last Days in the Desert* into an intriguing example of a Jesus film that makes the "two horizons" of the story explicit, the ancient horizon and the modern one (cf. chap. 8).

The Ending of Mark

The second example for consideration involves the gaps that arise from the abrupt ending of Mark's Gospel. As we have previously discussed (chap. 2), the Longer Ending of Mark (16:9–20) exhibits several elements of harmonization with other Gospel resurrection accounts. In fact, its amalgamation is one of the signs that the entire passage is secondary and not originally part of Mark's Gospel. In light of the tendency to fill in Gospel gaps, the Longer Ending appears to have been added to fill in the gaps left by Mark's abrupt ending. The best and earliest manuscripts show Mark 16 ending with verse 8, after an angel-like figure tells the women at the tomb about Jesus's resurrection and instructs them to inform the disciples that the risen Jesus will meet them in Galilee (16:6–7). Mark's Gospel concludes with this line: "Trembling and bewildered, the women went out and fled from the tomb. They said nothing to anyone, because they were afraid" (16:8). Quite an abrupt ending! It's not difficult to see why later scribes sought to give Mark a more "fitting" conclusion (by adding vv. 9–20). Yet scholars are unsure whether Mark *intended* to end his Gospel with verse 8. Some wonder if Mark's original ending has been lost altogether,[4] or even if perhaps Mark was an unfinished Gospel still in production (i.e., the version we have is a draft).[5]

In our view, Mark likely did intend to end the Gospel at 16:8,[6] given how well this ending, however abrupt, aligns with the earlier action and themes of Mark. Mark's "abrupt" ending fits the mantra "Where you end a story depends entirely on the story that you're telling." The women running away in fear and saying nothing seems designed as an *inversion* of Mark's "messianic secret" motif. That is, Jesus routinely warns people not to say anything about the miracles that he has been doing (cf. Mark 1:43–44; 5:40, 43; 7:36; 8:30; 9:9); he also warns the demons he exorcises (1:25, 34; 3:11–12). This desire for secrecy seems to suggest that the Markan Jesus wants to control the message about who he is and what he is all about. And the message is this: Jesus cannot be understood apart from the cross (cf. 8:27–38)—a message that didn't exactly fit with messianic expectations of the time.[7] Despite Jesus's desire for secrecy, news of his fame spreads, attested by those who have experienced his miracles (cf. 1:28, 45; 7:36). In this light, the female

4. Perhaps through accidental mutilation of the text, since the front and back of a manuscript would have been most susceptible to deterioration; so, e.g., Witherington, *Gospel of Mark*, 48–49.

5. So, e.g., Stein, *Mark*, 737.

6. So, e.g., Wallace, "Mark 16:8 as the Conclusion."

7. For more on Mark's "messianic secret," see, e.g., Garland, *Theology of Mark's Gospel*, 368–87.

followers of Jesus at the narrative's end are allowed and even encouraged to share freely the great news of Jesus's resurrection, but they do not. Mark has inverted the secrecy motif at the climax of the story, drawing attention to not only the motif itself but also the motif's role within the narrative. It is entirely possible that Mark's abrupt ending was intended to galvanize early readers with this logic: Since the women did not say anything, we must go and tell of Jesus's resurrection! Yet no matter what modern readers make of it, the scribal record indicates that Mark's ending was clearly not satisfying to early Christians.

The added verses at the end of Mark effectively "fix" the story's ending.[8] In the process Mark becomes, in a real sense, a new Gospel. The meaning of Mark with the Longer Ending is quite different from the meaning of Mark without it; its presence alters the story being told. The original version of Mark's Gospel leaves a substantial gap regarding what happened after Jesus rose from the dead. We can also note that Matthew, Luke, and John chose to fill in this gap in their own retellings of the Jesus story, with each setting out to tell a distinctive story. And, as mentioned, filling in gaps exposes new gaps for readers' imaginations to fill in. There are plenty of retellings of the Jesus story that continue the trend of filling in gaps about the aftermath of Jesus's resurrection.[9]

Jesus's Childhood

The four canonical Gospels provide little information about Jesus's early years. Mark and John begin their stories about Jesus at his intersection with John the Baptist (i.e., when Jesus is already an adult). Only Matthew and Luke narrate any events of Jesus's birth or childhood, and they do so only briefly (Matt. 1:18–2:23; Luke 1:26–2:52). While such minimal attention to Jesus's early years may strike modern readers as odd or unsatisfying, it does fit the pattern of the genre of the Gospels. The Gospels participate in the genre of ancient biography (Greek: *bios*), which, unlike modern biography, gave fairly limited attention to a subject's birth and early years.[10] Instead, ancient biographies primarily focused on the public life of an individual and placed special attention on their death.[11] So, that

8. See de Bruin's discussion of "fix-it fic" within modern fan fiction as an analogue for reading the Longer Ending of Mark (*Fan Fiction and Early Christian Writings*, 29–57).

9. A cinematic example, set during the days after Jesus's resurrection, is the 2016 film *Risen*.

10. Adams (*Greek Genres and Jewish Authors*, 265) refers to Matthew's genealogy and birth narrative as "typical, although not requisite, features of individual biographies."

11. See, e.g., Burridge, *What Are the Gospels?*; Bond, *First Biography of Jesus*.

the Gospels are ancient biographies partly explains their gaps around the early years of Jesus.[12]

Mark, among the four Gospels, offers us absolutely nothing about Jesus's youth. The Gospel begins with the inauguration of Jesus's public ministry at his baptism (1:9, with 1:2–8 introducing John the Baptist's role). The reader might be left wondering, Who is this guy Jesus? As if to answer, a voice declares from heaven, "You are my Son" (Mark 1:11), yet that affirmation could raise even more questions than it answers.[13] Rather than answering the question of Jesus's identity directly, Mark's narrative moves with a frenetic energy that pulls the reader along, offering some answers to this identity question but doing so mostly implicitly and inductively. Mark drops us in medias res—in the middle of things.[14] The evangelist reveals who Jesus is within the storyline as it moves along.

While Matthew and Luke do not extensively treat Jesus's life before his public ministry, they do provide some amount of relevant backstory. Most notably, their infancy narratives fill in some gaps concerning Jesus's identity and origin.[15] But even this is not enough to satisfy the curiosity of many Gospels readers. *What was Jesus like as a child, a teenager, or a young adult?* Only Luke offers us something here—a brief account of twelve-year-old Jesus in the temple (Luke 2:41–50). There's still so much more that we would like to know! Since the gap of Jesus's childhood has arguably activated our collective imaginations more than any other gap in the Jesus story, we turn to explore how ancient noncanonical Gospels and modern cinematic retellings have filled in this fertile gap.

Jesus's Childhood in Noncanonical Gospels

A key question often asked about Jesus's childhood is whether anyone recognized early in his life that there was something different about him. Two

12. While we understand the Gospels to be examples of ancient Greco-Roman biographies, we would not want to limit their genre participation to this category alone. They also unsurprisingly fit (or participate in) the genre category of Jewish biography. See Adams (*Greek Genres and Jewish Authors*, 257–92), who highlights the four Gospels as *Jewish* biographies. We follow Judd's (*Modern Genre Theory*) notion of texts as "promiscuous"; i.e., being capable of drawing on multiple genres at once.

13. Mark's initial title in 1:1 has already affirmed Jesus as Messiah (and possibly as "the Son of God," a reading that is present in some manuscripts and not others).

14. Similar to the way readers experience Narnia alongside the Pevensie children in C. S. Lewis's *The Lion, the Witch and the Wardrobe* and the way that viewers come alongside Luke Skywalker in his experience of the wider galaxy beyond Tatooine in the first *Star Wars* film (1977).

15. John also provides insight into Jesus's origins (1:1–18) but moves quickly to the account of Jesus's public ministry (1:19) as the first events narrated in the Gospel.

notable noncanonical Gospels from the second century that portray Jesus's early years (among many so-called Infancy Gospels from early Christianity) include the Protevangelium of James—sometimes called the Infancy Gospel of James—and the Infancy Gospel of Thomas. The value of these Gospels for our purposes is not that they provide us with historical or biographical information about Jesus but rather that they illustrate how people have always been curious about the question of Jesus's earliest days and what some have supposed about it. Additionally, they help us recognize that we, too, might desire to fill in the gaps, even though we might be motivated by different assumptions or theological preferences.

Protevangelium of James (Infancy Gospel of James)

The Protevangelium of James is primarily a narrative about Mary, from her own miraculous birth (Prot. Jas. 1–5) to the birth of Jesus in a cave.[16] As this noncanonical Gospel pertains to filling in gaps about Jesus's childhood, it seems designed to address gaps around Jesus's virginal birth—specifically, the "real story" about Mary's pregnancy.[17] The Protevangelium of James fills in narrative gaps in two prominent ways. First, the Gospel includes a scene where Mary and Joseph are compelled to drink a kind of truth serum administered by a priest in the temple to determine whether their story about Mary's virginity is true (Prot. Jas. 16).[18] Second, a midwife is included in the scene of Jesus's birth, and she confirms Mary's status as a virgin—and then her associate, Salome, nearly loses her hand for doubting it (Prot. Jas. 19–20). This Gospel also serves to address another set of questions focused on Mary's virginity after Jesus's birth. The text communicates indirectly that Mary remains a virgin even after Jesus is born by establishing the tradition that Jesus's "brothers" (mentioned in the canonical traditions; e.g., Matt. 13:55; Mark 3:31–34; John 2:12; 7:3, 5, 10; cf. Gal. 1:19) come from a relationship that Joseph had before Mary.

One of those brothers is James, who is identified as the source of the traditions written down in the Protevangelium of James, since he would have been

16. Several Jesus films, dependent on the tradition that begins with this text, depict Jesus being born in a cave. See, e.g., *Ben-Hur: A Tale of the Christ* (1925); *Mary and Joseph: A Story of Faith* (1979); *Per Amore, Solo per Amore* (*For Love, Only for Love*, 1993); *Ben-Hur* (2003); *La Sacra Famiglia* (*The Holy Family*, 2006); *Io Sono Con Te* (*Let It Be*, 2010).

17. On the origins of this text, see, e.g., Foster, "Protevangelium of James." For an edition of the text itself, see, e.g., Hock, *Infancy Gospels of James and Thomas*.

18. If the "serum" causes them harm, their story is a lie, but if nothing comes of it, then they are telling the truth. They each drink it, enter the wilderness, and return unharmed, one at a time, thereby confirming their claims. The background for this story can be found in Num. 5:11–31.

older than Jesus in this scenario and thus able to witness Jesus's birth firsthand (Prot. Jas. 25). Some of the events that James purportedly recalls and that are then recorded in this Gospel involve a harmonization of Matthew and Luke. For example, the Matthean magi arrive (at the cave) to witness the Lukan birth of Jesus, with elements of Matthew 2:1–12 and Luke 2:1–20 woven together. But the Protevangelium of James is also prompted in this move to fill in gaps that emerge as the result of the harmonization, providing stories of what happens to Elizabeth, Zechariah, and the child John (from Luke's Gospel) during the slaughter of the innocents from Matthew (Prot. Jas. 22–24).

Infancy Gospel of Thomas

Although the Protevangelium of James fills in gaps from the infancy narratives of Matthew and Luke, it continues to leave the temporal gap between Jesus's birth and his adulthood unexplored. In contrast, Jesus's childhood is expressly addressed in the Infancy Gospel of Thomas, which offers a sustained focus on Jesus at ages five and six.[19] Throughout the narrative, the boy Jesus performs many miracles of various kinds, including healing (Inf. Gos. Thom. 16.1–2), controlling nature (2.1), miraculously fixing a broken object (11.1–2), increasing the size or quantity of objects (12–13), and rather famously, turning clay sparrows into real birds (2.2–5). The Infancy Gospel of Thomas clearly imagines that the boy Jesus had the same superordinary capacities as he did during his public ministry (as recorded in the canonical Gospels).

One of the shocking elements in the Infancy Gospel of Thomas is that Jesus inflicts harm on others out of frustration or spite, even to the point of killing other children (3–4). The villagers grow concerned that Jesus is causing their children to die, and Jesus reacts by blinding his accusers (5.1). When a child named Zeno falls from a house to his death and the townspeople blame Jesus for it, Jesus brings Zeno back to life simply so that Zeno can testify that Jesus didn't do it (9.1–3)! At various points, Jesus also displays extraordinary skill at reasoning and debate (cf. 6–8), yet he is also portrayed as taking revenge on a scribe who hits him over the head during a debate—by causing the scribe to fall over dead (14.1–2).

A charitable reading of the Infancy Gospel of Thomas recognizes that Jesus is portrayed as being just like any other child in one sense, even though he is unlike any other child in another sense. The text imagines Jesus making use

19. For an overview of the history and development of this text, see, e.g., Chartrand-Burke, "Infancy Gospel of Thomas." For critical editions of the various recensions of the text, see Burke, *Syriac Traditions*. For the purposes of this section, we are relying on recension "Sa" from Burke's volume (pp. 126–69).

of his unique abilities as one could expect any normal child to do—erratically and selfishly. Other characters are deeply puzzled over Jesus, with his teacher, Zacchaeus, even questioning whether Jesus might be an angel or a god (7.4). This confusion highlights how different Jesus is from the other children, and yet his outbursts simultaneously suggest that he is acting as we could expect any young boy to behave.

The Infancy Gospel of Thomas seems to be drawing from Luke's Gospel to fill in at least some of the temporal gaps in the Jesus story. The concluding scene of the Infancy Gospel of Thomas (19.1–5) shifts to Jesus at age twelve, drawing on the sole scene of Jesus's boyhood—Jesus in the temple from Luke 2. The final lines of the Infancy Gospel of Thomas borrow from Luke's narration about Jesus growing in wisdom, stature, and favor (Luke 2:52). One can see how the Infancy Gospel of Thomas—inspired by Luke's own attempts to fill in the gaps of knowledge about Jesus's childhood—goes further by filling in the additional gaps created when Luke fills in the gaps of Mark's Gospel.[20] The Infancy Gospel of Thomas seems to be addressing something akin to the question, What kind of "growing pains" did Jesus have as he grew in wisdom, stature, and favor?

For those used to reading about Jesus solely from the four canonical Gospels, a text like the Infancy Gospel of Thomas might evoke strong, even negative, reactions: *Jesus would never have acted like that!* To be frank, we find ourselves agreeing with this assessment. But there is an important lesson here that we should not miss—namely, that this kind of reaction is itself a result of filling in gaps. The truth of the matter is that we do not have much to go on for reconstructing Jesus's early years. Even if our own hunches or intuitions about that time frame in Jesus's life seem more plausible, they still reflect a method of filling in the gaps.[21] Our own internal "director" of the Jesus story is inevitably filling in gaps from the Gospels, and our reactions to other attempts at gap filling can tell us something about how we have already directed that story in our mind's eye. In short, even if we might do it differently, we, too, are implicitly filling in the same kinds of gaps. And noticing our reactions can cause us to reflect on our own theological starting points in conversation with what might have motivated the Infancy Gospel of Thomas to fill in the gaps as it does. At the very least, it seems that Luke's own statement about Jesus's maturation was one such influence on that Gospel. Additionally, we can see in the Infancy Gospel of Thomas a particular way of holding in tension the

20. Possibly also Matthew's Gospel, depending on the solution to the synoptic problem. See Goodacre, *Synoptic Problem*.

21. A method potentially based on comparing the four Gospels and reconstructing a fulsome composite from them (e.g., harmonization plus filling in gaps).

divinity and humanity of Jesus by envisioning Jesus with profound abilities even at a young age.

Jesus's Childhood in Film: *The Young Messiah* (2016) as a Case Study

In a similar move, several Jesus films imagine the boy Jesus as someone with special abilities wrestling with how to use them wisely, as well as discerning what his extraordinary abilities might mean.[22] *The Young Messiah* (2016), which is based on Anne Rice's novel *Christ the Lord: Out of Egypt* (2005), is a notable example. The film opens with a text caption that reads, "Inspired by Scripture and rooted in history, this story imagines a year in the boyhood of Jesus." As it visualizes the early years of Jesus's life, *The Young Messiah* displays some influences from the two apocryphal Gospels just discussed, the Infancy Gospel of Thomas and the Protevangelium of James. But *The Young Messiah* is not primarily derivative; instead, it offers its own way of filling in gaps about Jesus's earliest years.

The storyline of *The Young Messiah* begins with Jesus and his family in Alexandria, Egypt, where they have been hiding in the aftermath of Herod's murdering of the young boys in and around Bethlehem (Matt. 2:16). The opening scene imagines an incident that leads Jesus's family to leave Egypt and return to Nazareth. Another young boy, Eleazar, picks a fight with Jesus for "playing with girls." Eleazar appears as if he is going to knock a girl over when Jesus yells at him to stop and tells Eleazar not to touch her. The camera pans to an unidentified man dressed in all black and with long, curly blond hair who is standing nearby. After biting into an apple—a symbolic gesture that viewers are meant to interpret as satanic (cf. Gen. 3:1–7)—the man in black tosses the apple to the ground, causing Eleazar to trip, hit his head on a rock, and die. This mysterious man then turns to whisper to another boy standing close by, who then accuses Jesus of causing Eleazar's death. The accusation leads to an uproar within the nearby crowd. At this point, the viewer realizes that no one except Jesus (and the viewer) has seen the man or the apple.

Sometime after the opening incident, the young girl thanks Jesus for rescuing her; she tells him that he should help Eleazar like he helped "the little bird." The film cuts to a flashback of Jesus bringing a dead bird back to life.[23] From this flashback, the film shifts to a scene of Jesus sneaking into Eleazar's home

22. Cf., e.g., *Jesús, el Niño Dios* (*Jesus, the Child of God*, 1971); *Jesús, María y José* (*Jesus, Mary and Joseph*, 1972); *Un Bambino di Nome Gesù* (*A Child Called Jesus*, 1987); *La Sacra Famiglia* (*The Holy Family*, 2006); *Mesih* (*Jesus, the Spirit of God*, 2010).

23. In *Jesus* (1999), Mary recalls how the boy Jesus brought a dead bird back to life.

and miraculously reviving him. Jesus's actions in the film thus far share some clear points of resemblance with the Infancy Gospel of Thomas,[24] though in *The Young Messiah* Jesus is decidedly kindhearted and makes no attempt at any point to kill anyone. Additionally, the inclusion of the satanic figure seems designed to vindicate young Jesus's reputation from the kinds of motivations attributed to him in the Infancy Gospel of Thomas.

Pertaining to Jesus's self-understanding, throughout *The Young Messiah* Jesus does not fully grasp how he is able to do miracles. There's an emerging sense in the film that Mary and Joseph recognize they will need to explain everything to Jesus at some point, since they have privileged information given to them by angels about his true identity. Another character with more awareness of Jesus's identity than Jesus himself is his *cousin* James, who is neither his brother nor stepbrother in this film.[25] James is older than Jesus, and so he carries the memories of significant events in Jesus's early life, such as the visitation of the "noblemen" (i.e., magi), who hailed him as king, and the slaughter of the innocents. In *The Young Messiah*, as in the Protevangelium of James, James is an important holder of Jesus memories.[26] In *The Young Messiah*, it seems that the people closest to Jesus have a better grasp of Jesus's identity than Jesus himself does.

In the film, questions continue to build for the young Jesus. This uncertainty sends Jesus on a quest to discover his true identity, but an important plotline complicates that pursuit. The story imagines that Herod Antipas, who began ruling in Judea after the death of his father, Herod the Great, never forgot about his father's concern over a budding Messiah from Bethlehem. In some Jesus films, Herod the Great's concerns are so pronounced that they predate

24. Jesus films that portray a young Jesus bringing clay birds to life, in seemingly more direct dependence on the Infancy Gospel of Thomas, include *Jesús, María y José* (*Jesus, Mary and Joseph*, 1972); *Un Bambino di Nome Gesù* (*A Child Called Jesus*, 1987); *Mesih* (*Jesus, the Spirit of God*, 2010); *The Book of Clarence* (2023).

25. Usually James (the brother of Jesus) is not included in Jesus films. When he is, he is sometimes Joseph's son from a previous relationship, as in, e.g., *La Sacra Famiglia* (*The Holy Family*, 2006); *Io Sono Con Te* (*Let It Be*, 2010). For another Jesus film in which James is Joseph's nephew (as in *The Young Messiah*), see *Maria, Figlia del Suo Figlio* (*Mary, Daughter of Her Son*, 2000). In *Per Amore, Solo per Amore* (*For Love, Only for Love*, 1993), Joseph is fairly hedonistic before he settles down with Mary, which connects (in its own way) to the tradition that he had relationships before Mary.

26. James's memory of significant events in the early life of Jesus also raises questions about how Jesus's family (whether brothers or cousins) failed to believe in him during his lifetime. In some films, we see James fighting with Jesus (*La Espina de Dios* [*The Thorn of God*, 2015]) or doubting him (*Color of the Cross*, 2006), even into the early post-resurrection period (*Color of the Cross 2: The Resurrection*, 2008). *La Sacra Famiglia* (*The Holy Family*, 2006) imagines James to be the same age as Mary and wishing to be her husband, creating a strange love triangle that offers a unique explanation for James's reluctance to follow Jesus.

1492 Pictures / CJ Entertainment / Hyde Park International

Boy Jesus in *The Young Messiah* (2016)

the magi's arrival, with these films even depicting Herod as quite familiar with biblical prophecies (both plot elements contradict Matthew's portrait of Herod the Great).[27] In *The Young Messiah*, Herod the Great has long since died, but Antipas retains his father's anxiety about a messianic uprising.[28] Matthew includes no such characterization of Herod Antipas, but it is the sort of gap-filling invention that might suggest new gaps to be filled in (and on it goes!).[29] In a way that dramatizes Antipas's preoccupation with a messianic revolt, we are introduced to a Roman soldier named Severus (played by Sean

27. This characterization of Herod the Great can be seen in, e.g., *The Life of Christ* (*Mysteries of the Rosary* series, 1957); *The Greatest Story Ever Told* (1965); *The Nativity Story* (2006); *The Nativity* (2010); *Killing Jesus* (2015); *Mary* (2024). The Iranian film about Mary rooted in the Qur'an, *Maryam Moghadas* (*Saint Mary*, 2000), and the subsequent 2002 television series by the same name that was based on it, begins with Herod the Great's fear of a coming Messiah already at the time of Mary's birth.

28. Other films where Antipas has the same messianic concerns include, e.g., *Salome* (1953); *King of Kings* (1961); *Un Bambino di Nome Gesù* (*A Child Called Jesus*, 1987); *Secondo Ponzio Pilato* (*According to Pontius Pilate*, 1987); *Journey to Bethlehem* (2023).

29. Perhaps to explain why this was a gap in the canonical Gospels, *Journey to Bethlehem* (2023) has Antipas come up with the idea for the census from Luke 2 *for the purpose of* finding Jesus and murdering him (creatively harmonizing Matthew's slaughter of the innocents with Luke's census). But when Antipas goes to Bethlehem to hunt down Jesus on the night he is born, Antipas stops short of killing him. Instead, he warns Jesus's family to flee Judea because he cannot spare them from what his father is about to do (i.e., the actual slaughter of the innocents that would soon follow).

Bean) who participated in the slaughter of the innocents and continues to search for the young Messiah, while stories of a wunderkind from Alexandria have begun to spread. This soldier is on the hunt for Jesus, even as Jesus himself is on the hunt for answers about his own identity.

We see a similar storyline of a soldier continuing to hunt for Jesus in *King of Kings* (1961). In that film, the soldier Lucius is present for the slaughter of the innocents and is a part of the Jesus story until the very end. We also find the ongoing pursuit of Jesus in *Joseph and Mary* (2016), as well as in *Jesús, el Niño Dios* (*Jesus, the Child of God*, 1971), where the hunting soldier is Claudius, "the first convert," and in *Un Bambino di Nome Gesù* (*A Child Called Jesus*, 1987), where one of the assassins is actually a fourth wise man who has left the rest of the group.[30] But *The Young Messiah* is most indebted to *King of Kings* (1961) for this trope. When Lucius arrives in Nazareth twelve years after the slaughter of the innocents, he is concerned when he realizes that Jesus's birth was never registered. "I have no record of his birth," Lucius says. His suspicion only grows once he hears that Jesus was born twelve years earlier *in Bethlehem*. Lucius knows that there should be no one alive who was born in Bethlehem twelve years before. He continues his pursuit of Jesus all the way to Jesus's crucifixion. When he finally locates Jesus, the viewer then realizes that Lucius is the famous soldier who recognizes Jesus as the Son of God (cf. Matt. 27:54). Lucius is an example of a well-developed character in a Jesus film, a phenomenon we will explore in the next several chapters focused on characterization—itself a form of filling in the gaps.

Returning to *The Young Messiah*, Severus's quest for Jesus and Jesus's quest for the truth about himself converge in the temple during Passover, when the boy Jesus goes to Jerusalem on his own. (To be clear, this is not a rehearsal of the Lukan scene in which Jesus stays behind and interacts with the temple leaders.) While Jesus is at the temple, he finds an old rabbi who is blind and inquires subtly what the rabbi knows about the boy who was visited by magi from the East. As the rabbi tells Jesus about the slaughter of the innocents, Severus prepares to seize Jesus, moving closer and closer to him from across the temple precinct, being guided by the same figure dressed in black from the film's opening. But after Jesus heals the rabbi, a great commotion ensues

30. Other questions and gap-filling moves have been asked about the magi, who are also so closely linked to this story. Did they cease to be interested in the Messiah after he was born? What happened to the magi after they visited Jesus? Some imagine that at least one of the magi was present for Jesus's crucifixion, which provides a bookend to the appearance of the magi at his birth and the celestial signs that accompany both events (cf., e.g., Melchior in *Barabbas* [2019]; Balthazar in *Ben-Hur* [1959] and *Ben-Hur* [2003]). Similarly, *The Fourth Wise Man* (1985) has one of the magi, who was not present at Jesus's birth, eventually having the opportunity to see him, not only at his crucifixion but also in his resurrected state.

in a nearby area of the temple, and Severus loses track of Jesus. Suddenly, Jesus is standing in front of Severus, who is stunned and stares at him. Jesus declares that he knows Severus has "saved him once before." In this moment, Jesus is somehow fully aware that Severus had been there in Bethlehem during the slaughter of the innocents, had the opportunity to kill Jesus, and yet chose to spare him, which the viewer learns for the very first time just as Jesus comes to realize it. Jesus's words soften Severus's heart, and he allows Jesus to escape and return home.

Jesus's return sets up the climactic moments of the film, as Jesus reunites with his family and Mary discloses to him the full content of the angelic message she received before he was born. She explains that God is his father, and this is why he has power to do the miraculous. But she tells him to keep that power inside himself until God indicates to him the time for revealing it. This final scene in *The Young Messiah* functions to fill in the gaps about not only how Jesus came to have such a clear sense of self-understanding as portrayed in the canonical Gospels but also why people in Nazareth did not know who Jesus *really* was or what he was able to do before his public ministry.

The Young Messiah fills in gaps to answer important questions about Jesus's self-understanding—namely, when and how his self-understanding developed. Readers of the canonical Gospels often fill in their own answers to these questions. Readers might wonder, Did Jesus come to a clear self-understanding because of the nature of his relationship with God? By his engagement with Israel's Scriptures? By recognizing he had abilities that differed from other children? Through Mary and Joseph telling him about their own angelic visitations? Or some combination of these? However we answer these questions, we are filling in the gaps. If we reject *The Young Messiah*'s answer to this question in favor of another explanation, we have not rejected the exercise of filling in the gaps, just a particular way of doing so.

Conclusion

The Young Messiah (2016), as well as the Infancy Gospel of Thomas and the Protevangelium of James, each in its own way, probes the gaps of Jesus's origins and upbringing.[31] Each takes its cues from the canonical Gospels, and each speculates beyond those Gospels. Additionally, each story incorporates an assumed Christology (a portrait of Jesus) into its account of what the young Jesus was like or ought to have been like.

31. *Jesus* (1999) also alludes to Jesus's extraordinary adolescence; see Walsh and Staley, *Jesus, the Gospels, and Cinematic Imagination*, 244.

Filling in the gaps, as a phenomenon, goes well beyond the examples that we have explored in this chapter: the temptation narrative, the resurrection appearances, and Jesus's childhood. We have seen that filling in gaps is a feature internal to the four Gospels themselves, as well as a routine feature of subsequent retellings of the Jesus story in both ancient noncanonical Gospels and modern cinematic storytelling. Indeed, filling in gaps is an inevitable dynamic that affects anyone who wants to understand the story of Jesus. In addition to seeing how others fill in gaps in the Gospels, a significant value of Jesus films and other kinds of retellings is to highlight gaps we did not know existed. The invitation for people who value the story of Jesus is not to ignore the gaps in the Gospels or to resist the tug to fill them in but to grow in the recognition of this broader hermeneutical factor and to reflect on why one might be inclined to fill the gaps in ways that are different from how other people do so.

4

Characterization

Putting Flesh on the People of the Jesus Story

People are endlessly fascinating because people—in their motivations and commitments, their relationships and their actions—are rich and complex. When we come to read a story, the characters are often what we notice first. The "who" of the story captures our attention and keeps us engaged. In contemporary fiction and film, characters are often fully formed, complicated, and "works in progress." In other words, they are on a journey of self-discovery, with character development being an important part of most story arcs.

As readers shaped by these modern sensibilities, we often come to the canonical Gospels ready to see characters grow and change. We may find ourselves deeply interested in the motivations of biblical characters, ready to consider their "interior lives" and the forces that drive them to act as they do. From this angle, the Gospels may disappoint us. The Gospels, after all, give us very little information about how characters think (their interior lives). More often than not, the Gospels, like most ancient biographies, show who characters are by what they say and do—whether it is communicated directly or through long narrative expositions about a character—not by what they think. Attention to a character's thoughts is fairly unusual in the Gospels.[1]

1. Mark 5:28 is unusual in giving us a character's internal thoughts, in this case those of a woman coming to Jesus for healing: "If I just touch his clothes, I will be healed" (see the

Additionally, character development is often, though not always, less important in ancient narrative than in modern storytelling. In fact, characters in the Gospels can readily be used in service of the plot rather than the other way around. For these reasons, readers may intuit or try to imagine the motivations of certain characters in a given situation. Such inferences about motivation will then inform the meaning derived from the text, even if these motivations are not implied by the evangelist. Despite what may be a less-than-satisfying amount of detail about their internal lives, some Gospel characters have a more complex or rich existence that suggests we should avoid a one-size-fits-all approach to characterization.

In this chapter, we introduce the topic of characterization, and we will extend the examination through the next two chapters, where we will look more closely at the representation of Jesus (chap. 5) and his enemies (chap. 6) in retellings of the Jesus story. To explore the dynamics of how characterization works more broadly, in this chapter we will analyze some relatively minor characters who populate the canonical Gospels and yet go on to receive fuller backstories and more vivid portrayals in later Gospels and films. In particular, we will focus on Thomas and then give significant attention to how Mary Magdalene has been portrayed by ancient and modern storytellers. Our three chapters dedicated to characters emphasize how the inevitable gaps surrounding characters in the Gospels have provided tantalizing areas for expansion—for filling in the gaps of characterization.

Understanding Characterization in the Gospels

Scholars who study characterization in the Gospels often tap into contemporary characterization theory and use it in conversation with the ways that ancient biographies (*bioi*) and other narratives portray their characters.[2] This combination of resources for thinking about characterization has provided a number of productive insights.

Twentieth-century novelist E. M. Forster described characters using the categories of "flat" and "round," with a flat character functioning as a simple type and a round character having complexity and multiple traits.[3] Rather than employing these two categories as static containers, it is helpful to see character complexity on a continuum. Cornelis Bennema, in fact, suggests

parallel in Matt. 9:21). Luke, however, omits this "thought" from his narration of the story (see Luke 8:42–48).

2. E.g., Bennema, *Theory of Character*.

3. Forster, "Flat and Round Characters."

seeing at least two spectrums for analyzing characterization in the Gospels: a continuum addressing complexity and another addressing character development or change.[4]

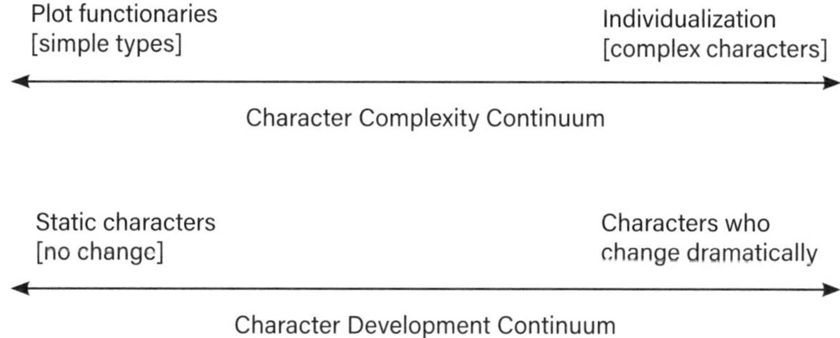

Character Complexity

The first continuum, which addresses character complexity, helps us see the range of ways the Gospel writers portray their various characters. Any number of Gospel characters function as simple types (the left side of the first continuum). For example, Luke introduces a man with a skin disease who is characterized by only a few details: "When he saw Jesus, he fell with his face to the ground and begged him, 'Lord, if you are willing, you can make me clean'" (Luke 5:12). Jesus heals the man, but we read of no response from the man himself. His portrayal consists solely of his desperate plea for healing (expressed physically and verbally). The man is not a complex character and instead functions to advance the plot around the theme of Jesus's healing power. James Resseguie identifies a few categories that fit on the left side of the continuum (flat characters), including stock characters, foils, and walk-ons. In the latter category we might put the soldiers in John's passion narrative, who appear and then disappear from that narrative and "simply do the bidding of either the Jewish leaders or Pilate."[5] On the other side of the spectrum of character complexity we can place characters who receive extensive treatment. Jesus, for example, is a complex character in each of the four Gospels, since a significant number of traits are woven together to represent who he is (for more on Jesus's characterization, see chap. 5).

Somewhere in the middle of the continuum are characters who are described by more than just one or two traits but lack significant complexity and often

4. Bennema, *Theory of Character*, 73–78.
5. Brown, *Gospels as Stories*, 69.

serve primarily to move the plot along. For example, Herod Antipas (tetrarch of Galilee) shows up a number of times in Luke's storyline and is uniformly portrayed negatively. According to Luke's characterization, Herod is an evil actor (Luke 3:19–20) who is initially confused by what he hears about Jesus (Is he John the Baptist come back to life?) and tries to see Jesus (9:7–9). According to some Pharisees, Herod wants to kill Jesus (13:31). Yet, after Jesus is arrested, Herod seems to consider Jesus someone who might entertain him (23:8–9), even as he ends up ridiculing and mocking Jesus before sending him back to Pilate (23:10–11). Herod Antipas is something more than a flat character, but we would not likely consider him "complex," given his uniformly negative portrayal in Luke. Additionally, Herod moves the plot along by playing a supporting role in Rome's condemnation of Jesus to crucifixion (cf. 23:12, 25).[6]

Character Development

The second continuum has to do with character development—a primary way that we frame characters in our contemporary Western context. To cite one example from contemporary fiction, consider the character of Amir in Khaled Hosseini's *The Kite Runner* (2003). Over the course of the story, Amir, who is the first-person narrator, moves from childhood to adulthood and from Afghanistan to Pakistan to California. This central character develops in significant ways, especially as he learns to grapple with his status and privilege in comparison to Hassan, the son of his family's servant. At a key point in the story, Amir witnesses Hassan being cruelly assaulted by another boy, yet out of fear Amir does nothing. Hassan's ongoing and unrelenting loyalty to Amir makes Amir's act of betrayal toward Hassan all the more poignant. That betrayal sets events in motion and changes Amir in ways that eventually lead to him adopting Hassan's son at the end of the novel. Amir changes in profound ways across the storyline, and the reader witnesses it through Amir's own first-person narration.

Ancient characterization, on the other hand, focuses less on character development than contemporary storytelling does.[7] Even when a character changes, a sustained development over time is typically lacking. Instead, what we might identify as character development in the Gospels most often consists of moments of transformation, about-faces that in Christian parlance are referred to as "conversions." When Jesus encounters people, the changes

6. Although Luke indicates that Pilate surrenders Jesus to the will of the Jewish leaders, only Rome has the power to enact the death penalty, and so Rome (with Pilate and Herod as its representatives in this case) holds primary culpability (cf. chap. 6).

7. Brown, *Gospels as Stories*, 68–69.

they experience are less about gradual, incremental development and more about decisive shifts from one path to another. Think of the Samaritan woman (John 4) or the man who had experienced blindness from birth (John 9). Or consider the dramatic change of vocation of the four fishermen who leave everything to follow Jesus (Matt. 4:18–22).[8] Nicodemus in John's Gospel provides an interesting character study, because it is not clear whether he changes in response to his initial conversation with Jesus (John 3). His portrait is ambiguous precisely because we have so little to work with; Nicodemus only reappears two times in the rest of the narrative (John 7:50–52; 19:38–42).

The dramatic shifts we see in certain characters are rightly understood under the rubric of character development, but they are distinct enough from character development as we know it in modern film and contemporary storytelling to put us on our guard. So, we will need to be cautious about importing modern notions of characterization into the Gospels (or other ancient biographies). Our tendency as readers may be to "psychologize" various characters (a modern interest), seeking to fill in details about their motivations and inner lives, which are given little attention by the evangelists.[9] In coloring in a character's interior life, we often follow the lead of our own cultural milieu rather than that of the evangelists.

Additionally, ancient characterization may at times play on the assumption, evident in some Greco-Roman narratives, that a person's nature is relatively fixed and what seems to be character development may very well be the "progressive revelation of . . . latent characteristics."[10] An example of static characterization in the Gospels comes in the character of Judas, who is introduced as a betrayer in Mark well before the betrayal occurs (Mark 3:19), though as the story is retold by the other Gospels, Judas does receive slightly more development after being similarly introduced as a betrayer (cf. Matt. 10:4; Luke 6:16; John 6:71; for more on Judas, see chap. 6). As a result, character complexity is more easily seen in the Gospels than development, which is somewhat more elusive.

Characterization Methods

Ancient characterization happens in indirect ways more than by direct description.[11] Characters are "fleshed out" or "filled in" by what they say

8. This about-face is followed by a fairly static portrait of the twelve disciples across Matthew. The twelve are consistently portrayed as exhibiting "little faith" (Matt. 8:26; 14:31; 16:8; 17:20; cf. 28:17), and they routinely misunderstand Jesus's messianic mission to serve his people (see Brown, *Gospels as Stories*, 85–104).

9. Brown, *Gospels as Stories*, 69.

10. Russell, "On Reading Plutarch's *Lives*," 146 (cf. n. 2).

11. Brown, *Gospels as Stories*, 71.

and do and by what other characters say and do in relation to them. Less frequently, a narrator might provide direct characterization about a character, whether about their attributes or motivations, or about their identity, status, vocation, or appearance.

As we consider how to analyze characterization, it can be helpful to pay close attention to relationships between characters or character groups. As we have already pointed out, the relationship between a character we are studying and others in the story significantly informs characterization.

Yet there are two other relationships that are crucial for characterization. The most important relationship is the one between a character and the *narrator*, since the narrator provides the POV from which to understand and evaluate any particular character. "By viewing the narrative and its characters from the perspective of the . . . narrator, we are able to hear a coherent perspective on the various words, actions, and (when they are apparent) motivations of the story's characters."[12]

The magi in Matthew 2 provide an interesting example. They are introduced by the narrator as (presumably) gentiles traveling to Jerusalem and inquiring about one "born king of the Jews" (Matt. 2:2). Their initial contact is with King Herod, who is troubled by the advent of a rival king and secretly arranges for the magi to report back to him when they find the child (Matt. 2:3, 7–8). Although we might be prone to think of the magi in a favorable light (e.g., via their initial expressed desire to worship or pay homage to the child; Matt. 2:2), this entanglement with Herod raises the possibility that they will betray the location of Jesus. The narrator, however, characterizes them as "overjoyed" when they follow the star and find Jesus, and they worship him and present him with expensive gifts (Matt. 2:10–11). The narrator signals an interior characterization ("overjoyed"), which provides the reader with the narrator's perspective on the magi. This positive portrait is confirmed when the narrator communicates that the magi readily respond to a divine warning in a dream and take another route home, thereby avoiding reporting anything back to Herod (Matt. 2:12).[13]

The other crucial relationship to consider is the one between characters and *readers*.[14] In their study on characters and characterization in the Gospels from the vantage point of cognitive psychology, Jan Rüggemeier and Elizabeth Shively

12. Brown, *Gospels as Stories*, 74.

13. Some films give sustained attention to the journey of the magi (e.g., *Cammina, Cammina* [*Keep Walking*, 1983]; *El Cant dels Ocells* [*Birdsong*, 2008]), and others add scenes in which the magi study together before embarking on their journey (e.g., *The Nativity* [2010]; *Chasing the Star* [2017]). These depictions provide more texture to their brief appearance in Matthew and so add clarification about their motivations and allegiances.

14. Brown, *Gospels as Stories*, 77–80.

stress how characterization is a result of what "actual readers" do when they read.[15] Characters are not merely developed by the author in the story but are also constructed by the reader or hearer on the basis of both prompts in the text and what they bring with them to the text,[16] including their own experiences and their previous exposure to the characters and story. When dealing with figures who appear in multiple stories, texts, and media, like biblical characters who appear in apocryphal texts, art, and even film, these experiences of characters from various contexts inform our mental models of them (i.e., "character migration"; see the introduction). The various relationships that characters have with other characters in the story, with the narrator, and with the reader highlight how characterization is both a "text-internal" and "text-external" phenomenon.[17]

Characterization Trajectories: From Gospels to Film

The characterization we see in the canonical Gospels is adapted and expanded in subsequent retellings of the Jesus story, and especially in modern films. We see this expansion in various ways—for example, making minor characters more prominent, as is done with Jairus's daughter in *The Miracle Maker* (2000).[18] Bringing Jesus to television and streaming, specifically, has provided a significant vehicle for taking Gospel characters on extended journeys, since an episodic show can provide a more sustained storyline, develop characters with more detail, and explore a greater number of themes. For example, we see such character expansions in TV miniseries like *Jesus of Nazareth* (1977), *The Nativity* (2010), *The Bible* (2013), *A.D.: The Bible Continues* (2015), as well as the lesser-known Iranian TV shows from a Muslim perspective: *Maryam Moghadas* (*Saint Mary*, 2002) and *Mesih* (*Jesus, the Spirit of God*, 2010).[19] Perhaps the most pronounced of all in regard to augmenting characters is the multiseason streaming show *The Chosen* (2017–present), which provides fertile ground for assessing characters. *The Chosen* makes a series of character-based expansions, including providing a backstory for Simon the Zealot to explain the historical oddity of his presence,[20] exploring the

15. Rüggemeier and Shively, "Introduction," 414.

16. Rüggemeier and Shively, "Introduction," 411.

17. Rüggemeier and Shively, "Introduction," 416.

18. The decision to develop Jairus's daughter (cf. Mark 5:22–23), who is called Tamar in the film, is partly rooted in this stop-motion cartoon's intended audience: children.

19. Each of these Iranian shows was also made into a feature-length film in a manner similar to the film *Son of God* (2014), which developed out of the series *The Bible* (2013).

20. In *The Chosen*, Simon the Zealot is the brother of the man in John 5 who has been unable to walk for nearly forty years, whom Jesus heals (season 2, episode 4, "The Perfect Opportunity," 2021). Although an imaginative choice, the decision serves as an explanation for why

interpersonal dynamics among the twelve disciples rooted in the diversity of their backgrounds,[21] and assigning characters specific personality traits, such as portraying Matthew on the autism spectrum.[22]

Already, though on a smaller scale, we see tendencies to expand character portraits among the four Gospels themselves. For example, John's characters are often more substantial than those we find in the Synoptics.[23] John portrays characters whom we also meet in the other Gospels—people like John the Baptist, Peter, Pilate, and Mary and Martha—but he typically offers fuller portraits of them. Further, we can consider the characters that only John introduces, like Nicodemus (John 3), the Samaritan woman (John 4), and the man born blind (John 9). Each of them is provided longer episode(s) than any individual character in the Synoptics. The trajectory of character expansion already begins in the Gospels themselves. And that trajectory continues into noncanonical Gospels and then into Jesus films on an even larger scale. To explore this phenomenon, we turn to consider first the development of Thomas and then that of Mary Magdalene.

The Character Development of Thomas

Thomas in the Canonical Gospels

In the Synoptic Gospels, Thomas is mentioned only in the list of the twelve apostles (Matt. 10:3; Mark 3:18; Luke 6:15). In John's Gospel, however, his portrait is expanded. Thomas is granted a few lines in the prepassion narrative (John 11:16; 14:5), but his most memorable scene comes after Jesus's resurrection (20:24–29; cf. also 21:2). After being absent from Jesus's first appearance to his disciples, Thomas expresses his doubts to the others: "Unless I see the nail marks in his hands and put my finger where the nails were, and put my hand into his side, I will not believe" (20:25). When Jesus reappears to his disciples,

---

a Zealot hell-bent on overthrowing Rome would follow Jesus and join a group of disciples that includes a tax collector, someone complicit with Roman rule. To highlight this oddity further, the show cleverly pairs Simon and Matthew together for dramatic tension when Jesus sends out the disciples in pairs (season 3, episode 2, "Two by Two," 2022). Cf. *La Espina de Dios* (*The Thorn of God*, 2015), where Simon the Zealot tries to kill Matthew at the beginning of the movie before they are each called to follow Jesus.

21. E.g., the relationship between Peter and Matthew is particularly fraught in *The Chosen* because Peter owed taxes to him. This is also part of their relational dynamic in *La Espina de Dios* (*The Thorn of God*, 2015). Cf. *Jesus of Nazareth* (1977), which portrays Matthew and Peter being reconciled during Jesus's telling of the parable of the prodigal son.

22. E.g., he is exceptionally good with numbers and details and interprets many jokes and figures of speech literally.

23. See, e.g., Skinner, *Characters and Characterization*; Hunt et al., *Character Studies in the Fourth Gospel*.

he shows Thomas his nail marks and corrects him: "Stop doubting and believe" (20:27). Only then does Thomas respond: "My Lord and my God!" (20:28). It is from John's portrait that we get the notion of a "doubting Thomas."

Thomas in the Noncanonical Gospels

This Johannine portrait of Thomas, already expanded from the synoptic depiction, is further developed in the Gospel of Thomas (written between 135 and 200 CE).[24] Even though Thomas functions as a character in only one location in the Gospel of Thomas, the way he is portrayed there, along with the attribution of the entire Gospel to him at its beginning and end, suggests an expansion and even a shift from Thomas's portrait in John 20. Thomas as a character appears in one scene (logion 13), where Jesus asks his disciples, "Compare me and tell me whom I resemble?"[25] After Peter and Matthew answer inadequately ("a righteous angel" and "a wise philosopher," respectively), Thomas answers, "Master, my mouth is completely unable to say whom you are like." Although not explicitly commended, this seems to be the "right" answer for the author of this Gospel, since Jesus then pulls Thomas aside and speaks three words, or sayings, to him alone.[26] When Thomas returns to the others and is asked what Jesus said to him, he warns, "If I told you one of the words which he spoke to me, you would pick up stones and throw them at me. But fire would come forth from the stones, and burn you." Thomas is thus portrayed in this Gospel as the bearer of esoteric secrets; he is, as J. P. Meier states, "exalted as the possessor of the secret knowledge of Jesus' nature."[27] This aligns with the Gospel of Thomas's prologue, which reads, "These are the secret sayings which the living Jesus spoke, and Didymus Judas Thomas wrote them down."[28] While the Johannine portrait of Thomas is of one who doubts and requires additional proof (and is admonished by Jesus for his doubts), his characterization in the Gospel of Thomas focuses on and commends him as the recipient of special knowledge that others are not able to understand.

Thomas On-Screen

In the cinematic stories that develop the portrait of Thomas, we see particular attention given to providing a rationale for his propensity to doubt.

24. Gathercole, *Gospel of Thomas*, 124.

25. All translations here are from Gathercole, *Gospel of Thomas*, 259.

26. Ehrman (*New Testament and Other Early Christian Writings*, 118) proposes the translation "things" rather than "words," which would allow that Jesus refers to sayings rather than three individual (and specific) words.

27. Meier, *Marginal Jew*, 3:256n17.

28. Gathercole, *Gospel of Thomas*, 189.

In *The Chosen* (2017–present), for example, Thomas is introduced as one of the suppliers of wine for the wedding at Cana (season 1, episode 5, "The Wedding Gift," 2019). This backstory provides a narrative explanation for his need *to see to believe* (John 20:24–29), since including him at Cana makes him a witness of Jesus's first sign—developing further the Johannine portrait. To this early signaling of Thomas's characterization, *The Chosen* adds moments when Thomas is overly analytical. For example, when asked his response to Jesus's Sermon on the Mount, he confirms he has some questions because he tends "to overthink things" (season 3, episode 1, "Homecoming," 2022). The primary way *The Chosen* develops Thomas into someone who would eventually doubt Jesus's resurrection is in its creation of a love story between Thomas and Ramah, a character who tragically dies when a Roman praetor (Quintus) stabs her accidentally during a riotous commotion (season 4, episode 3, "Moon to Blood," 2024). The difficulty of losing his beloved is exacerbated when Jesus chooses not to heal her, saying that it is "not her time," even as he resuscitates Lazarus a few episodes later (season 4, episode 7, "The Last Sign," 2024). The showrunners use this discrepancy to prepare viewers for Thomas's doubting, even as it raises more questions about their version of Jesus.

Other Jesus films also associate Thomas with early miracles of Jesus. *La Espina de Dios* (*The Thorn of God*, 2015) ties his belief to the fact that he directly witnesses the healing of Jairus's daughter. In *Jesús de Nazaret: El Hijo de Dios* (*Jesus of Nazareth*, 2019), by contrast, Thomas doesn't believe that a miracle has occurred when Jesus exits Jairus's house, and he remains suspicious when Jesus says the centurion's servant has been healed from a distance. In each case, Thomas can't see that the miracle has occurred, so he will not believe it has happened. Although *Jesús de Nazaret* develops Thomas as a doubting person, it surprisingly does not depict the Johannine moment when Thomas doubts Jesus's resurrection. Other films explain Thomas's doubts by imagining what he was doing elsewhere during the resurrected Jesus's first appearance to his disciples (cf. *Gli Amici di Gesú: Tommaso* [*The Friends of Jesus: Thomas, 2001*]). *The Book of Clarence* (2023) provides a twist on the doubting trope—it is not Thomas who doubts Jesus but rather his twin brother, Clarence, with the film exploiting the Aramaic meaning of "Thomas" as "twin."

Even though Thomas's portrait in the Gospel of Thomas stands out from these film versions, which develop in line with the Johannine representation,[29] all these characterizations of Thomas emphasize *his unique critical faculties*.

29. Although *The Book of Clarence* (2023) is clearly influenced by the Gospel of Thomas (with allusions to logia 5–6, 61).

Whether because he refuses to believe too quickly or because he has special insight into Jesus's teachings, these portrayals share that basic similarity. In contrast, the development of the character of Mary Magdalene is more complex and diverse and so warrants our attention for the remainder of the chapter.

The Character Development of Mary Magdalene

Mary Magdalene would be considered a minor character in each of the four canonical Gospels, but her prominence at the end of each Gospel as witness to Jesus's crucifixion and to his resurrection appearance suggests a level of significance that helps explain her prominence in later noncanonical Gospels and, most certainly, in Jesus films.

Mary Magdalene in the Canonical Gospels

In each Gospel except Luke, Mary Magdalene is not mentioned until late in the story, in the passion narrative. Luke, however, tells us more about Mary, going beyond his source Mark (and perhaps Matthew) by naming Mary as one of a larger group of women who, along with the twelve apostles, are with Jesus in his ministry and support the whole entourage from their means (8:1–3). In his description of Mary, Luke indicates she was "called Magdalene"[30] and that she had been healed of seven demons (8:2; cf. Mark 16:9, from the Longer Ending). That is all we know of Mary's background from the canonical Gospels, but later traditions fill in any number of details.

In the passion accounts, it is only in John that Mary is referenced *before* Jesus's death; she is stationed near his cross along with other women (John 19:25). In the Synoptics, she is included with the group of women who had followed Jesus from Galilee and were watching the crucified Jesus from a distance (Matt. 27:55–56; Mark 15:40; Luke 23:49; cf. 24:10 for specific reference to this Mary). All three Synoptics also place Mary Magdalene at Jesus's tomb (Matt. 27:61; Mark 15:47; Luke 23:55–56).

Mary Magdalene has the distinction of being the woman in all four Gospels who testifies that Jesus has been raised from the dead. She is the common thread across all four resurrection narratives (Matt. 28:1; Mark 16:1; Luke 24:1, 10; John 20:1; cf. Mark 16:9–11), even as each Gospel names and numbers the women who witness the empty tomb and resurrection announcement/appearance differently.[31] In John's account, Mary Magdalene's characterization

30. On the question of whether Magdalene is a place name or a nickname ("the Tower") given to Mary, see Schrader and Taylor, "Meaning of 'Magdalene.'"

31. Mark mentions two others, Matthew one, and Luke a larger group. John has only Mary Magdalene as the first witness to the empty tomb and to the resurrected Jesus.

expands, consistent with the Johannine pattern noted earlier, as the evangelist narrates an extended encounter between Mary and Jesus (20:11–18). Jesus comforts a distraught Mary, who believes Jesus's body has been moved (20:2, 13) and who at first thinks Jesus is the gardener (20:15).[32] Mary Magdalene recognizes Jesus when he speaks her name, and Jesus commissions her to tell of his resurrection and ascension to his disciples (20:17–18).

Mary Magdalene in the Noncanonical Gospels

As Mary Magdalene is taken up in later noncanonical Gospels, her portrait is expanded beyond the trajectory of the canonical Gospels. The Gospel of Mary (a second-century CE writing) builds on the few and fairly brief references to Mary Magdalene in the four Gospels to give her a more prominent role *after Jesus's ascension*.[33] Although the time after Jesus's ascension is not addressed much in the canonical Gospels (see Luke 24:50–52; cf. Acts 1), the Gospel of Mary is partially set within this time frame and highlights Mary's[34] role in encouraging the disciples in their task to preach the gospel by "turn[ing] their hearts to the Good" (Gos. Mary 9.21–22). In response, Peter notes that Mary was loved by the Savior more than any other of his female followers (10.2–3), and he asks her if there was anything Jesus had spoken to her to which the rest of the disciples had not been privy (10.4–6). Mary then describes a vision and teachings she received from Jesus. In this recounting, a few sayings resemble Jesus's teachings in the canonical Gospels, such as, "Where the mind is, there is the treasure" (10.15–16) and "Do not judge" (15.16). Nevertheless, much of the material in Mary's recounting is esoteric and Gnostic in flavor, such as a reference to "the All . . . being dissolved" (15.21), followed by a rehearsal of the soul's triumph over the four powers (15.21–16.4). When she concludes these descriptions, Andrew and Peter contest Mary's special knowledge (17.10–22), but both Mary and Levi defend what she has shared, with Levi's final commendation serving to validate both Mary and, by extension, the Gospel of Mary (18.1–15). This Gospel seems designed to fill in gaps inherent in the brief portrait of Mary from the canonical Gospels and to expand on what has already been provided. As Jennifer Pietz suggests, the

32. See Brown, "Creation's Renewal."

33. For translations and critical editions of the available manuscripts, see Tuckett, *Gospel of Mary*. All citations of the Gospel of Mary come from Tuckett's translation of Papyrus Berolinensis (*BG*) 8502 (cf. *Gospel of Mary*, 91–95).

34. There is some debate about whether the Mary of the Gospel of Mary is Mary Magdalene, Mary the mother of Jesus, or some conflation of the two or even of additional Marys. We think it most likely, for reasons connected to our discussion in this section, that the Mary here is Mary Magdalene. Cf. Tuckett, *Gospel of Mary*, 14–18.

Gospel of Mary was "perhaps inspired by the account of her one-on-one encounter with the resurrected Jesus in John 20:11–18."[35]

Mary Magdalene is similarly portrayed in the third-century CE text called the Gospel of Philip,[36] which stems from a branch of Gnosticism called Valentinianism. In this Gospel, Mary has unique access to, and unique understanding of, Jesus's teachings, and in this depiction, she seems to develop a romantic relationship with Jesus. In particular, Mary is identified not only as the most beloved of the disciples but also as Jesus's "companion" (cf. Gos. Phil. 59.6–11) and someone that he often kisses. The key passage is worth citing in full:

> As for the Wisdom who is called "the barren," she is the mother [of the] angels. And the companion of the [Savior is] Mary Magdalene. [But Christ loved] her more than [all] the disciples [and used to] kiss her [often] on her [mouth]. The rest of [the disciples were offended] by it [and expressed disapproval]. They said to him, "Why do you love her more than all of us?" The Savior answered and said to them, "Why do I not love you like her? When a blind man and one who sees are both together in darkness, they are no different from one another. When the light comes, then he who sees will see the light, and he who is blind will remain in darkness." (Gos. Phil. 63.25–64.9)[37]

Jesus's treatment of Mary and his enigmatic sayings about light and darkness and blindness and sight have prompted a variety of interpretations. Karen King has proposed that the Gospel of Philip imagines that Mary and Jesus had a romantic relationship (i.e., "companionship"), which functions as the paradigm for subsequent marriages in the community that this Gospel addresses.[38] Yet most scholars contend that, given the general asceticism of the text and the spiritualized language of "the bridal chamber," kissing here should be understood symbolically (cf. chap. 7).[39] Such a symbolic meaning is conveyed earlier in the Gospel of Philip when Jesus says this: "For it is by a kiss that the perfect conceive and give birth. For this reason we also kiss one another. We receive conception from the grace which is in each other" (59.2–6). However the kiss is interpreted, it is noteworthy that the Gospel of

35. Pietz, *Mary Magdalene*, 32. For Pietz's review of Mary's heightened role in other Gospels from the second century onward, see 31–35.

36. For an edition of the text, see Isenberg, "Gospel of Philip."

37. Isenberg, "Gospel of Philip," 138. In-text brackets indicate places in this fragmentary manuscript where words or letters are missing and have been surmised and reconstructed by Isenberg.

38. King, "Place of the *Gospel of Philip*."

39. Foster, "Gospel of Philip," 74–76.

Philip gives Mary a prominent status among the disciples, a portrayal that clearly surpasses how the canonical Gospels characterize her.

Mary Magdalene and Conflation with Other Marys

In what would become the traditional, orthodox strands of church tradition, Mary Magdalene did not attain the status of a prominent disciple as we see in the Gospel of Mary or the Gospel of Philip. On the contrary, she has often been conflated with other women and other Marys from the New Testament. As New Testament readers can attest, it can be difficult not to confuse characters, especially minor ones, and Mary Magdalene has been an unfortunate casualty in this regard. In some cases, she is conflated with Mary of Bethany (the sister of Martha and Lazarus; Luke 10:38–42; John 11–12),[40] who anoints Jesus's feet "for the day of [his] burial" (John 12:1–8). Other writers and artists have blended Mary Magdalene with other women who anoint Jesus in the Gospel stories: the woman identified as a "sinner," who anoints Jesus's feet (Luke 7:36–50),[41] or the unnamed woman who anoints Jesus's head for burial (Matt. 26:6–13; Mark 14:3–9). There has also been a pronounced tendency to conflate Mary Magdalene with the unnamed woman caught in adultery (John 8:1–11).[42] One problematic result of these conflations, especially with the women from Luke 7 and John 8, is that, since the time of the Middle Ages, Mary Magdalene has often been identified as a (reformed and penitent) sex worker.[43]

This conflation of Mary in Christian tradition with other women from the Gospels continues into cinematic Jesus stories. In many films, she is conflated with the women who anoint Jesus's head or feet,[44] and she is also identified

40. Potentially already in Hippolytus's *Commentary on the Song of Songs* (late second or early third century CE); see Pietz, *Mary Magdalene*, 37.

41. E.g., Gregory the Great in his Easter sermon on John 20; see discussion and references in Pietz, *Mary Magdalene*, 41, 80n71.

42. As noted in chap. 1, John 7:53–8:11 is text-critically suspect and unlikely to be original to John.

43. See discussion in Pietz, *Mary Magdalene*, 47–50.

44. E.g., *La Vie du Christ*, or *La Naissance, La Vie et La Mort du Christ* (*The Birth, the Life and the Death of Christ*, 1906); *La Vie et Passion de Notre Seigneur Jésus-Christ* (*The Life and Passion of Our Lord Jesus Christ*, 1902–5, 1907); *Christus* (1916); *I.N.R.I.* (*Crown of Thorns*, 1923); *Jesús de Nazareth* (*Jesus of Nazareth*, 1942); *María Magdalena, Pecadora de Magdala* (*Mary Magdalene, Sinner of Magdala*, 1946); *Day of Triumph* (1954); *The Prince of Peace* (1959); *El Proceso de Cristo* (*The Trial of Christ*, 1966); *Jesus* (1973); *Jesus Christ Superstar* (1973); *Jesus of Nazareth* (1977); *Karunamayudu* (*Ocean of Mercy*, 1978); *Jésus de Montréal* (*Jesus of Montreal*, 1989); *Kristo* (1996); *Maria Magdalena* (*Mary Magdalene*, 2000); *Santhi Sandesam* (*Message of Peace*, 2004); *Jezile* (*Son of Man*, 2006); *Judas* (2006); *Mesih* (*Jesus, the Spirit of God*, 2010).

as the sister of Martha and Lazarus.[45] The implication that Mary Magdalene was a financial supporter of Jesus's ministry (cf. Luke 8:1–3), combined with her conflation with the woman anointing Jesus with expensive ointment (e.g., Mark 14:3), has led to her portrayal in some films as an opulent courtesan who lives extravagantly.[46] As mentioned earlier, she is sometimes conflated with the woman caught in adultery (John 8:1–11).[47] Even in films where she is not that woman, Mary is at times portrayed as witnessing the John 8 scene, which functions as a catalyst for her to follow Jesus,[48] so even in these examples she is closely tied to the incident.

The Sexualization of Mary Magdalene

We have seen that Mary Magdalene is often portrayed as a reformed sex worker in Jesus films,[49] despite the fact that the New Testament at no point characterizes her (or even the women of Luke 7 and John 8) in this way. Even when Mary is not directly portrayed as a sex worker, she is often sexualized.[50]

45. E.g., *María Magdalena, Pecadora de Magdala* (*Mary Magdalene, Sinner of Magdala*, 1946); *El Mártir del Calvario* (*The Martyr of Calvary*, 1952); *The Sword and the Cross* (1958); *Mesih* (*Jesus, the Spirit of God*, 2010).

46. Cf. *Christus* (1916); *I.N.R.I.* (*Crown of Thorns*, 1923); *The King of Kings* (1927); *Jesús de Nazareth* (*Jesus of Nazareth*, 1942); *María Magdalena, Pecadora de Magdala* (*Mary Magdalene, Sinner of Magdala*, 1946); *El Mártir del Calvario* (*The Martyr of Calvary*, 1952); *The Sword and the Cross* (1958); *El Proceso de Cristo* (*The Trial of Christ*, 1966); *Jesus* (1973); *Mesih* (*Jesus, the Spirit of God*, 2010); *The Book of Clarence* (2023).

47. E.g., *The Sword and the Cross* (1958); *King of Kings* (1961); *The Greatest Story Ever Told* (1965); *The Thorn* (*The Greatest Story Overtold / The Divine Mr. J*, 1971); *The Last Temptation of Christ* (1988); *The Passion of the Christ* (2004); *Jezile* (*Son of Man*, 2006); *Jesus: The Desire of Ages* (2014); *Das Neue Evangelium* (*The New Gospel*, 2020). A connection is also implied in *Jesus Christ Superstar* (1973) when Jesus admonishes Judas to stop criticizing Mary for her "profession" unless he has a clean slate himself, even referring to Judas's verbal attacks as throwing stones (in the song "Strange Thing Mystifying").

48. Cf., e.g., *Karunamayudu* (*Ocean of Mercy*, 1978); *Jesus* (1999); *Mesih* (*Jesus, the Spirit of God*, 2010).

49. E.g., *The King of Kings* (1927); *The Sword and the Cross* (1958); *El Proceso de Cristo* (*The Trial of Christ*, 1966); *Jesus Christ Superstar* (1973); *Jesus of Nazareth* (1977); *The Last Temptation of Christ* (1988); *Marie de Nazareth* (*Mary of Nazareth*, 1995); *Jesus* (1999); *Maria, Figlia del Suo Figlio* (*Mary, Daughter of Her Son*, 2000); *Color of the Cross* (2006); *Color of the Cross 2: The Resurrection* (2008); *Maria di Nazaret* (*Mary of Nazareth*, 2012); *Risen* (2016); *Das Neue Evangelium* (*The New Gospel*, 2020); *The Book of Clarence* (2023). In *Das Neue Evangelium* (*The New Gospel*, 2020), the retelling of the story of Jesus is overlapped with a documentary about African migrant workers in Matera, Italy (cf. chap. 8), and the actor playing Mary Magdalene was formerly a sex worker.

50. E.g., *I.N.R.I.* (*Crown of Thorns*, 1923); *Jesús de Nazareth* (*Jesus of Nazareth*, 1942); *María Magdalena, Pecadora de Magdala* (*Mary Magdalene, Sinner of Magdala*, 1946); *El Mártir del Calvario* (*The Martyr of Calvary*, 1952); *Celui Qui Doit Mourir* (*He Who Must Die*, 1957); *Jesus* (1973); *The Gospel of John* (2003); *Mesih* (*Jesus, Spirit of God*, 2010); *Jesús de Nazaret: El Hijo de Dios* (*Jesus of Nazareth*, 2019).

In *The Gospel Road: A Story of Jesus* (1973), narrator Johnny Cash even asserts that Mary is more stained by controversy "than any woman I ever heard of." In one notable portrayal, the film *Maria di Nazaret* (*Mary of Nazareth*, 2012) contrasts Mary Magdalene explicitly with Mary the mother of Jesus, with the two having grown up together in this retelling.[51] After her mother is suspected of adultery and stoned to death, Mary Magdalene is captured for Herod Antipas's harem by Herodias, which provides a unique explanation for the origin of her opulence and association with sexuality, both of which were not her own choosing in this film.[52]

Several Jesus films develop their focus on Mary Magdalene's sexuality into a romantic relationship with Jesus. *The Last Temptation of Christ* (1988), for instance, implies that Mary resorts to sex work because Jesus has refused a romantic relationship with her out of his sense of duty to God's mission. This missed opportunity at love, and the devastation that it causes in both their lives, becomes the seed for the titular last temptation (cf. chap. 7). In *Jesus Christ Superstar* (1973), we also watch Mary Magdalene struggle with unrequited love and wrestle with whether to tell Jesus of her deeper feelings for him.[53] The high mark in our pop-cultural Zeitgeist about the nature of Jesus's relationship with Mary Magdalene comes in Dan Brown's 2003 novel, *The Da Vinci Code* (film, 2006), which suggests that Leonardo da Vinci's famous mural of the Last Supper portrays Mary Magdalene (rather than a beardless John) sitting beside Jesus as his secret romantic partner. In this portrayal, Mary herself is the famed "Holy Grail": Mary is the only one seated without a wine glass, with the void between Mary and Jesus creating a "V" shape resembling a chalice. Mary's womb, like a full wine glass, carries in it the child of Christ.

The Da Vinci Code also overtly appeals to Mary's role in the Gospel of Philip, specifically her portrait as a dearly beloved companion of Jesus whom he often kissed. As these examples demonstrate, there is a popular fascination with the notion of Mary having a romantic relationship with Jesus. This fascination has stretched from fanciful to even fraudulent in the case of a forgery called the Gospel of Jesus's Wife.[54] Although *The Da Vinci Code*

51. Other Jesus films also reimagine the relationship between these two Marys. *La Sacra Famiglia* (*The Holy Family*, 2006) imagines that Mary of Nazareth was the wet nurse of Mary Magdalene, implying that Mary Magdalene and Jesus grew up together (and the film even has Jesus raising her from the dead when they were young).

52. In *Maria Magdalena* (*Mary Magdalene*, 2000), Mary also becomes a slave of Herodias and thus becomes associated with wealth.

53. Cf. the sexual tension between the people playing Jesus and Mary Magdalene in passion plays, as in *Cristo 70* (1969) and *Celui Qui Doit Mourir* (*He Who Must Die*, 1957).

54. This account is devastatingly chronicled in Sabar's *Veritas*.

Promotional photo for *The Da Vinci Code* (2006) with Leonardo da Vinci's *The Last Supper* partially visible in the background

does not portray Mary Magdalene as a sex worker as often assumed, Mary's characterization is nevertheless still framed primarily by her sexuality.

One detail about Mary Magdalene from the canonical Gospels that also garners great interest in film is Luke's mention of Jesus exorcising her of seven demons (Luke 8:2). Interestingly, this Lukan detail often further contributes to Mary's sexualization in film. In Cecil B. DeMille's *The King of Kings* (1927), viewers witness a highly dramatic and visually intense exorcism, with demons departing from Mary one by one, each named after one of the seven deadly sins. In keeping with the film's portrayal of Mary as an opulent courtesan, Lust is the first demon to be expelled and Greed the second. Moreover, the presence of all seven deadly sins within Mary Magdalene clearly implies that she is one of the worst of sinners.

This portrayal of Mary in *The King of Kings*, and specifically of her exorcism, has been quite influential for subsequent films, including *María*

DeMille Pictures Corporation

The demon of Lust being exorcised from Mary Magdalene in *The King of Kings* (1927)

Magdalena, Pecadora de Magdala (*Mary Magdalene, Sinner of Magdala*, 1946) and *El Mártir del Calvario* (*The Martyr of Calvary*, 1952). The animated Jesus film *The Miracle Maker* (2000) introduces Mary Magdalene as an almost feral, animalistic woman known as "Mad Mary" before she is healed by Jesus, although in this film there is nothing sexual about her characterization before her transformation.[55]

In *The Chosen* (2017–present), the story of Mary Magdalene's demon possession and unsavory lifestyle in the Red Quarter is the subject of the very first episode (season 1, episode 1, "I Have Called You by Name," 2019). When we meet Mary, she goes by the name Lilith, a not-so-subtle reference to a demonic figure from Jewish tradition.[56] As the tradition develops, Lilith is a female demonic spirit married to Adam (before God created Eve). The decision in *The Chosen* to give Mary the name Lilith adds a layer of sexualization to Mary Magdalene's demon possession, a combination we also saw in *The King of Kings*. After Mary is healed by Jesus (because Nicodemus

55. Cf. also, e.g., *Magdalena: Released from Shame* (2007); *Jesus: A Deaf Missions Film* (2024).

56. E.g., Songs of the Maskil (4Q510–11); b. Shabb. 151b; b. Nid. 24b; Alphabet of Ben Sira 23a–b.

couldn't do it properly) and is called Mary for the first time in the episode,[57] she becomes one of Jesus's first disciples. Mary's character is fairly complex in *The Chosen*, as she becomes someone eager to learn the Scriptures and Jewish customs. Yet viewers are routinely reminded that Mary lived a sinful life. "You know my past," Mary says to Tamar when the two of them are discussing what they can learn from winemaking for their budding olive oil business. She adds, "You think I don't know the best vineyard in town?" (season 3, episode 6, "Intensity in Tent City," 2023).

By all accounts, *The Chosen* appears to perpetuate the reformed sex worker trope for Mary Magdalene,[58] but Dallas Jenkins, the director, producer, and cowriter of the series, has denied this on multiple occasions. Instead, he claims that Mary is portrayed as a victim of demonization and sexual assault.[59] Yet we could ask why Mary should be sexualized at all and why demonization ought to be represented as closely connected to sexuality. More importantly, even if Jenkins intended something different, the viewer is primed to interpret Mary in accordance with the well-established trope in Christian art, tradition, and film, so the mental model of Mary as a sex worker is easily activated. And a handful of suggestive moments reinforce the association. In a scene where Peter is suspicious about Jesus meeting with Nicodemus, Jesus suggests that Mary, who has vouched for Nicodemus, can be trusted since "she has known some of the worst kinds of men in this world" (season 1, episode 7, "Invitations," 2019). Mary's backstory is also raised when she recalls for John her first encounter with Jesus as John takes notes in preparation for his Gospel (in a flash-forward). She remembers how Jesus placed his hand on her hand when she was at a tavern. Then she stops abruptly, recognizing how damning her words could sound; she advises John to leave out that part lest people get "the wrong idea" (season 2, episode 1, "Thunder," 2021). Finally, there is an odd sequence in the second season in which Mary's character development is complicated by her reversion to drinking and gambling. While gambling in a bar, a man asks her how she has money to gamble, and she responds suggestively, "Wouldn't you like to know?" (season 2, episode 6, "Unlawful," 2021). At this point, we would propose she has become an archetype for a

57. Jesus calling her Mary foreshadows that her character arc will culminate in Jesus calling her by name in his resurrected state (cf. John 20:16).

58. See esp. Burnette-Bletsch's analysis of seasons 1–2 of *The Chosen* and the way Mary's storyline falls in line with established tropes for rescued sex workers in fiction and cinema ("'Tis Pity She's [Still] a Whore").

59. E.g., @TheChosenTv, which is the official handle for *The Chosen* on the social media platform X (then Twitter), tweeted the following on June 22, 2021: "Mary Magdalene is not portrayed as a prostitute; she is portrayed as a victim of past sexual assault and demon possession" (https://x.com/thechosentv/status/1407398832002981888).

"backslidden" Christian, a new development in the Magdalene tradition. These suggestive elements indicate that *The Chosen* has not provided sufficient prompts to help viewers revise their mental models of Mary Magdalene as a reformed sex worker. Yet such a revision can and has been offered in *The Miracle Maker* (2000), as we have seen, and in the film *Mary Magdalene* (2018), as we will see presently. These clear counterexamples highlight that *The Chosen* essentially reverts to the same broad archetype of the past for Mary Magdalene.

Mary Magdalene as "Apostle" of Jesus

Mary Magdalene (2018) provides a portrait of Mary that is radically different from its predecessors. When the viewer is introduced to Mary, she is most definitely not a sex worker. Her family does suspect that she is demon possessed because she defies cultural expectations for a woman: She refuses to get married and prays by herself as men do, actions that her family deems shameful. Her first encounter with Jesus comes after Mary's parents ask him to exorcise her demons. When Jesus sees her, he declares, "There are no demons here,"[60] an overt discrepancy with Luke 8:2 (or perhaps a unique take on the exorcism itself). As the film progresses, Mary joins Jesus's followers and takes on a central role in Jesus's inner circle. She is directly baptized by Jesus and then ministers to and baptizes the women who are drawn to Jesus's ministry. Mary is even present at the Last Supper and sits next to Jesus, which may be intended as a deromanticization of *The Da Vinci Code*, or perhaps a signal that she is the unnamed "beloved disciple" of John's Gospel (John 13:23).[61] In either case, the film draws our attention to Mary's position of honor during the meal by showing Jesus and Mary circling the group and then taking their seats side by side as the last to join the table.

In *Mary Magdalene*, Mary is also depicted as having a better grasp on Jesus's teachings than his male disciples do. She alone understands the deeper meaning regarding his message of the kingdom, interpreting his message of the kingdom as focused on the internal life of believers and brought about through love and care rather than violence. Her recognition of the spiritual nature of the kingdom contrasts with the revolutionary expectations of the

60. Other characters also mistakenly think Mary is possessed a few times in *Maria Magdalena* (*Mary Magdalene*, 2000), such as when her husband suspects her of being oppressed by demons when she fails to bear him a child. In *Mesih* (*Jesus, the Spirit of God*, 2010), Mary Magdalene spurns the advances of men, which leads them to think she's possessed.

61. Although the film *Mary Magdalene* does not suggest romantic associations, it is perhaps worth noting that the actors Rooney Mara (Mary) and Joaquin Phoenix (Jesus) were romantically involved and had children together after filming.

male disciples (especially Peter). The ending of the film, with its vindication of Mary's interpretation of the teachings of Jesus, is similar in several respects to the ending of the noncanonical Gospel of Mary.[62]

When *Mary Magdalene* cuts to black immediately before the final credits, three captions appear. The first mentions that, according to the canonical Gospels, Mary was a principal witness to the resurrection. The second says that Pope Gregory the Great in the sixth century CE invented the idea that Mary was a prostitute. The final caption adds that the Catholic Church reclaimed her as an "Apostle of the Apostles" in 2016.[63] From the canonical Gospels, to noncanonical portraits and church tradition, to contemporary film, Mary Magdalene has captured the collective imagination to produce one of the most diverse sets of portraits of any character from the Jesus story.

Conclusion

In this chapter, we introduced characterization theory and method and noted how ancient characterization differs from that of contemporary storytelling. In the process, we have looked at some characters from the canonical Gospels, especially Thomas and Mary Magdalene, who have been reframed, developed, and "filled out" in retellings of the Jesus story, starting within the four canonical Gospels themselves and then in later apocryphal Gospels and on into modern films. As readers of the Bible who are influenced by the broader portrayals of these and other characters, we all inevitably bring fuller and richer presentations of them with us when we return to the text, whether explicitly or implicitly. These fuller portraits can significantly influence our understandings, as has been the case with both Thomas and Mary Magdalene. As has been suggested throughout the book, each of us already has in our minds a portrait of Gospel characters, almost inevitably filled in beyond their portrayals in the Gospels. And we will intuitively compare other portraits of these characters—whether offered in films, in noncanonical Gospels, or even in Matthew, Mark, Luke, and John—with our own versions. The director in our heads will weigh in on other portrayals accordingly.

Over the next two chapters, we will continue our exploration of characters and characterization in the ancient Gospels and on-screen, always aware that the characters who populate the story of Jesus have captivated people for two

62. *Mary* (2005), a film about the making of a Jesus film based on the apocryphal Gospels, similarly portrays Mary coming into conflict with her male counterparts regarding the private information she has received from Jesus.

63. Cf., e.g., Esteves, "Pope Francis Raises Memorial."

thousand years and that the traditions about them are not easily disentangled in readers' minds when they engage the Gospels. We turn first to the central character of the Gospels, Jesus himself (chap. 5), and then to those who have been cast as the "villains" of the Jesus story, particularly Judas, the Roman Pilate, and the Jewish leaders (chap. 6).

5

The Centerpiece

Portraying Jesus

At the center of the Jesus story, from the early Gospels to modern film, is Jesus himself. Yet translating Jesus to film is a tricky task on several fronts. The biblical material is meant in part to elicit worship and reverence for Jesus, leaving many Christian viewers hoping that film versions will do the same. How a Jesus film is received largely depends on its portrayal of Jesus. If audiences don't appreciate how Jesus looks, acts, or is otherwise portrayed on-screen, they are unlikely to regard the film favorably. Highly individualized metrics for what makes "a good Jesus" complicate the matter further. Each of us has preconceived notions about Jesus's demeanor and appearance, conditioned by the Gospels themselves as well as by art, culture, tradition, and film. None of us function from a clean slate regarding Jesus's characterization. So, when we cast the part of Jesus for the films playing in our minds, we are making a calculus like filmmakers do, except that we have the luxury of our internal "Jesus reel" escaping scrutiny.

We consider in this chapter various aspects of displaying Jesus on-screen, specifically the challenges involved in portraying his characterization, giving him a physical depiction and a "filled-in" personality. As we do so, a crucial issue will emerge, sometimes addressed explicitly and other times implicitly—namely, the tension involved in depicting Jesus as both human and divine. Which physical and personality traits cohere more with one or the other? And how does a film strike a balance (if that's the aim)? To prepare for a closer look at the Jesus of cinema, we start by applying the two spectrums of character complexity and character development from chapter 4 to the characterization of Jesus we find in the four canonical Gospels.

The Characterization of Jesus in the Gospels

We can affirm generally that the Jesus of each of the canonical Gospels receives a *fairly complex* portrayal, since he has many attributes, sayings, and kinds of actions ascribed to him. For example, in Matthew 4:17–9:35, which narrates Jesus's early Galilean ministry, Jesus is portrayed as (1) an authoritative teacher who announces God's kingdom, (2) a compassionate and powerful healer who takes away people's diseases and casts out demons, (3) a rabbi who has high expectations for those who would be his disciples, and (4) someone who celebrates at meals with "tax collectors and sinners" (Matt. 9:10). On occasion we can also discern some of Jesus's motivations, such as when he indicates his intention to preach the good news widely rather than staying in one location or focusing on any one group of people (Mark 1:38; cf. Luke 4:43), or when Jesus refrains from going to Bethany despite Mary and Martha's plea for their sick brother, Lazarus (John 11:3–6), intending his absence to spark his disciples' belief (John 11:14–15). All four evangelists provide Jesus with a wide variety of traits and characteristics, even as their individual portraits of Jesus are also somewhat distinctive.

At the same time, the portraits of Jesus in the four Gospels remain *quite static*, showing few clear signs of character development apart from Luke's explicit mentioning of Jesus's growth into maturity and adulthood: "Jesus grew in wisdom and in stature and in favor with God and all the people" (Luke 2:52 NLT; cf. 2:40).[1] This summary occurs at the conclusion of the Lukan birth narrative, just before the evangelist turns to narrate Jesus's public ministry, indicating that this growth happens during Jesus's time in Nazareth between the age of twelve (2:42) and his baptism by John when he was about thirty years old (3:21–23). By the time Luke narrates the baptism scene, we hear the divine voice affirming Jesus: "You are my Son, whom I love; with you I am well pleased" (3:22). In this affirmation, Luke (indirectly) characterizes Jesus as having fully matured into God's favor.

Some scholars have also suggested something of a trajectory of development in Jesus's characterization related to moments when he seems to change his

1. The ending of the Infancy Gospel of Thomas (19.1–5), which occurs at the same temporal point as Luke 2:51–52, highlights how this Lukan passage was likely understood in terms of Jesus developing self-control over his divine abilities.

mind. One such moment comes in Matthew 15, when a gentile mother comes to Jesus, imploring his help with her daughter, who is possessed by a demon (15:22). Despite being initially ignored by Jesus and then told by him that he has been "sent only to the lost sheep of Israel" (15:24), this woman persists in pleading for her daughter (15:25). Jesus's response and her reply only ramp up the rhetoric: "He replied, 'It is not right to take the children's bread and toss it to the dogs.' 'Yes it is, Lord,' she said. 'Even the dogs eat the crumbs that fall from their master's table'" (15:26–27). As Jesus hears her rejoinder, he marvels at her faith and grants her request to heal her daughter (15:28). Does Matthew portray Jesus, in this change of mind, as developing or growing in his understanding of God's mission for him, as some have argued? Elaine Wainwright, for example, argues that this woman points Jesus back to his earlier, more inclusive vision of the kingdom.[2] Yet Matthew does provide something of a stable view of Jesus in his mission, especially if we read Jesus's response to a centurion (the only other clear interaction with an individual gentile requesting help) as a question and not a statement: "Shall I come and heal him?" (8:7; cf. CSB). In both cases, Jesus is portrayed as hesitating to expand beyond his (God-given) mission to Israel (15:24; see also 10:5–6).

The (mostly) static portrait of Jesus in the canonical Gospels continues in other early Gospel narrations. This isn't surprising, given the tendency in ancient biographies toward more static portraits of their characters (see chap. 4). Film portrayals of Jesus, especially more recent ones, more readily allow for a complex and developing portrait of Jesus, although this has not always been the case.

The Challenges of Portraying Jesus in Film

The task of portraying on film a protagonist like Jesus from the Gospels, who is fairly complex yet lacks development, is less than straightforward. Ostensibly, filmmakers want their Jesus to be a compelling figure, but this is not often accomplished on-screen. Richard Walsh articulates the problem: "We want interesting, identifiable heroes in film. Jesus is not that. We know him too well for him to interest us, but he is also too different from us to interest us."[3] At the heart of this tension are the interrelated questions of (1) whether Jesus can be portrayed on camera as both human and divine (with character development suggesting a more human Jesus) and (2) whether Jesus can develop and change as a character (i.e., going beyond the Gospels' portraits) without alienating viewers.

2. Wainright, *Shall We Look for Another?*, 88.
3. Walsh, *Reading the Gospels in the Dark*, 25.

Traditionally, Gospels scholarship has identified the synoptic portrait of Jesus as focused more on his humanity and the Johannine portrait as concentrated on his divinity. This continues to be a default assessment despite its oversimplification. Across all four Gospels, Jesus's claims about himself (e.g., Matt. 21:41–46; John 8:58), the significant authority with which he speaks (e.g., Luke 4:32), his powerful miracles (e.g., Mark 3:1–6) and exorcisms (e.g., Mark 1:34), and his claim to forgive sins (e.g., Mark 2:1–12) suggest Jesus shares in the divine identity or, at minimum, that he is no ordinary human. Alternatively, signs of Jesus's true humanity include his acknowledging that there are things he doesn't know (e.g., Matt. 24:36; cf. Mark 13:32), being surprised and amazed (e.g., Matt. 8:10; Mark 5:30; 6:6; Luke 7:9), expressing (certain) emotions (e.g., Mark 1:41; John 11:35), being hungry (Mark 2:16; Luke 4:2), being tired (Matt. 8:24; Mark 4:38), and ultimately suffering physically and dying (John 19:1–2, 30, 34).

Given all this, translating Jesus from text to screen has undoubtedly been the most fraught task of the Jesus film industry, not least because the physical appearance and personality of Jesus are inevitably scrutinized in detail, making it difficult for both actors and casting directors. Whatever decisions are made, viewers are likely going to be dissatisfied with some part of Jesus's portrait in any particular Jesus film. Yet the implicit director in our mind's eye rarely receives such scrutiny and critique.

One way to avoid such potential dissatisfaction, or even offense, is to simply avoid representing Jesus at all. The makers of the show *VeggieTales* determined early on that they would never depict Jesus, not because they were opposed to the idea in principle but because they thought it would be strange to portray him as a vegetable.[4] Yet even human actors can elicit controversy. For example, in *The Jesus Film* (2001), an expanded version of *Jesus* (1979), the narrator maintains that, with respect to playing Jesus, "no actor is worthy of such a role" but adds that an actor (Brian Deacon) will nevertheless perform the role so that viewers can understand and benefit from Jesus's story. In other words, depicting Jesus is a concession rather than an ideal.

In some Christian traditions, especially in some conservative Reformed circles, depicting Jesus is considered blasphemous and a violation of the second commandment, the prohibition against making physical representations of God (Exod. 20:4–6).[5] This tension can be seen in the history of Christian art, which has an ancient pedigree (dating to the late second and early third

4. Cf. Huckabee, "Never Forget That 'VeggieTales' Weren't Allowed to Show Jesus."

5. This is at least one way of understanding question 109 from the Westminster Larger Catechism.

century)[6] and became more prominent after the Edict of Milan declared that Christianity was no longer an illegal sect (313 CE).[7] Yet Christian concerns about the use of images and icons in worship became controversial during the Byzantine period. The "iconoclastic controversy" was addressed at the Second Council of Nicaea in 787 CE (also called the Seventh Ecumenical Council). The council's determination, stated simply, was that prohibition of images of Jesus would be at cross-purposes with the truth of the incarnation that the invisible God became visible (see 2 Cor. 4:4; Col. 1:13–15). Yet some Christians remain reticent about visual depictions of Jesus, even though the inescapably visual nature of reading virtually necessitates evoking some image of Jesus in the reader's mind.

A few decades into the silent film era, a desire to *avoid* portraying Jesus or to limit how Jesus was represented began to preoccupy the growing industry. Producers of Jesus films were met with new policies concerning the handling of sensitive religious figures and subjects, policies developed in Hollywood's Hays Code of 1927. In 1934 another restrictive force came on the scene: the Legion of Decency. This Catholic organization would blacklist films, boycott theaters, and lobby against certain developments in the broader business. The evolution of the medium from silent films to "talkies" played a role in this suppression. As Richard Ascough explains, "The use of sound added a unique problem to cinematic depictions of Jesus. While audiences were familiar with what Jesus 'looked like' through the ubiquity of Western Christian art and iconography, it was not clear what Jesus would have sounded like, and directors and producers seemed reluctant to hazard a guess and risk offending audiences."[8] These developments and strictures significantly affected the Jesus film industry for the next several decades, until Hollywood revoked the Hays Code in 1968 and the Legion of Decency disbanded in 1980.

For the first three decades of this period of film history (1930–60), Jesus films tended to play it safe. Many production companies thought Cecil B. DeMille's *The King of Kings* (1927) couldn't be topped—financially, artistically, and even reverentially—so they were reticent to make full-scale Jesus films under these restrictions.[9] Non-US productions continued mostly unaffected (although international distribution was certainly impacted). The first Jesus film made with sound, *Golgotha: Ecce Homo* (*Behold the Man*, 1935),

6. Jensen, *Understanding Early Christian Art*, 9.

7. Jensen, *Understanding Early Christian Art*, 16. Why there wasn't more Christian art before the edict could be due to concerns about idolatry, but it could also be an accident of history (i.e., the artwork is not extant or yet discovered). More likely, the political and social climates affected the means and safety of making Christian art.

8. Ascough, "Jesus," 180.

9. Reinhartz, *Jesus of Hollywood*, 14–15.

Metro-Goldwyn-Mayer (MGM)

Jesus offers Judah Ben-Hur water from off-screen in *Ben-Hur* (1959).

allowed audiences to both see and *hear* an actor playing Jesus.[10] Although American outliers were produced,[11] filmmakers during this period often chose to tell stories adjacent to, and at times intersecting with, the story of Jesus. Doing so gave them enough distance to draw in audiences while avoiding any scandal. When Jesus is incorporated as a character in these films he remains off camera, is viewed from afar, has his face obstructed, or is only visible from behind or by one of his extremities.[12] The most famous example undoubtedly comes from the water cup scenes in the 1959 film adaptation (starring Charlton Heston) of Lew Wallace's 1880 novel *Ben-Hur: A Tale of the Christ*.[13] And *The Life of Christ* (*Mysteries of the Rosary* series, 1957) is perhaps the most

10. Other non-US Jesus films from this period unhindered by the Hays Code include *Jesús de Nazareth* (*Jesus of Nazareth*, 1942); *María Magdalena, Pecadora de Magdala* (*Mary Magdalene, Sinner of Magdala*, 1946); *Reina de Reinas: La Virgen María* (*Queen of Queens: The Virgin Mary*, 1948); *El Mártir del Calvario* (*The Martyr of Calvary*, 1952).

11. See, e.g., *The Pilgrimage Play* (1949); *I Beheld His Glory* (1953); *Day of Triumph* (1954); *The Prince of Peace* (1959).

12. E.g., *Quo Vadis* (1951); *Salome* (1953); *The Robe* (1953); *The Big Fisherman* (1959); *Barabbas* (1961). The film *The Prodigal* (1955) provides an example of Jesus's absence; it tells an (expansive) version of the parable of the prodigal son without ever showing Jesus or even acknowledging him as narrator. The Indian film *Snapaka Yohannan* (*John the Baptist*, 1963) follows a similar degree of modesty. *The Power of the Resurrection* (1958) may represent something of a transitional example near the end of this period, with viewers at times gaining a partial glimpse of Jesus's face.

13. The first adaptation from 1907 is so short that it does not contain any of the scenes with Jesus, and the 1925 silent version similarly conceals Jesus's appearance (before the Hays Code was implemented). Remakes of *Ben-Hur* after the 1959 version showcase Jesus on a few more

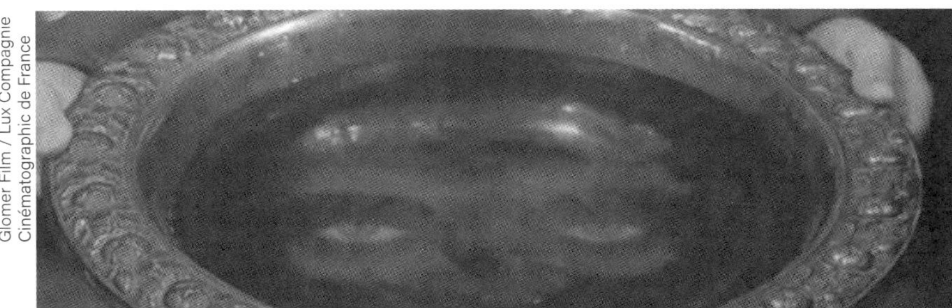

Glomer Film / Lux Compagnie Cinématographic de France

Jesus's eyes appear in the water basin before Pilate washes his hands and it becomes filled with blood in *Ponzio Pilato* (*Pontius Pilate*, 1962).

unappealing example of this broader trend: Jesus is consistently the center of attention but always has his back to the camera because the filmmakers refuse to show his face.

A couple of films during this era reveal Jesus's face a single time. In *El Beso de Judas* (*Judas' Kiss*, 1954), Jesus's face is seen only indirectly from the imprint left on Veronica's bloody towel. *The Sword and the Cross* (1958) reveals Jesus's face for only a moment on the cross in a quick flash of lightning after he has died. And in *Ponzio Pilato* (*Pontius Pilate*, 1962), only Jesus's eyes are visible. When Caiaphas is interrogating Jesus, we see an intense close-up of Jesus's eyes. Their piercing quality is foreshadowed earlier in the film, when Judas tells Caiaphas that those same eyes have been haunting him. Jesus's eyes appear a final time in the basin of water just before Pilate washes his hands and declares himself innocent of Jesus's blood. As he does so, the basin fills with blood (cf. chap. 6).

This era of reticence is lampooned in the Coen Brothers' film *Hail, Caesar!* (2016), which provides a fictional account of Hollywood in the late 1950s. In the film, Capitol Pictures is producing a Jesus film in the style of the biblical epics. This fictional film within the film revolves around Antoninus, a Roman tribune (played by George Clooney), and is meant to evoke *Ben-Hur* (1959). This evocation is clear from a parody of the water cup scene and from the full title of their film, which shares the same original subtitle: *Hail, Caesar! A Tale of the Christ*. In a scene designed to ridicule the influence of the Hays Code and the Legion of Decency, an executive from Capitol Pictures, Eddie Manix (played by Josh Brolin), has a meeting with four clergy members—a Protestant pastor, Catholic and Orthodox priests, and a rabbi—to review the script. Manix assures them that the actor playing Jesus "is seen only fleetingly

occasions, give him a few more lines, and make no attempt to conceal his appearance (see the 2003 and 2016 versions).

and with extreme taste." The humor around the implementation of this *extremely tasteful* representation is that it is not limited to the film within the film. Viewers never see the actor playing Jesus apart from his feet, and his voice is heard only from off-screen when a producer asks the actor—still hanging on the cross on a break between takes—whether he's an "extra" or a "principal" and whether he remembered to choose the box lunch for the day. The voice we hear in response, hesitatingly affirming that he is a "principal," is the voice of comedian Michael Cera, who is uncredited for the role.

Concealing Jesus's appearance may stem from a desire to avoid offense, but it also has theological consequences for the viewer. Steven Greydanus describes the choice to hide Jesus in film as a kind of "cinematic apophaticism,"[14] referring to a mode of theological discourse characterized by denials rather than affirmations. Indeed, it is hard to escape the implication that these films inadvertently deny Jesus's humanity. Consider how, in the "grammar" of films, those who remain just off camera or who receive only oblique visibility are usually otherworldly creatures or monsters.[15] Viewers during this era saw little to confirm that Jesus was genuinely human, with a rich and complex interior life. Portraits from the heyday of the Hays Code and the endurance of similar sensitivities in subsequent films tend toward docetism, with Jesus only appearing to be human. Avoiding or minimizing the portrayal of Jesus in film communicates something to audiences, whatever the motivation. Alternatively, much is communicated through the physical portrayal of Jesus and the kind of personality he is granted. Both of these features have implications for how Jesus is perceived in terms of his humanity and divinity as well as for his character development.

Portraying the Physicality of Jesus

Gospels, canonical or otherwise, exhibit virtually no interest in the physical appearance of Jesus. Given the genre similarities between the canonical Gospels and Greco-Roman biographies (*bioi*), this may seem somewhat surprising. Ancient *bioi* tended to include descriptions of their subject's physical appearance because physical descriptors were held to convey insight into someone's *characteristics*.[16] In other words, if you knew what someone *looked like*, you

14. Greydanus, "Through Other Eyes," 78.

15. Noted by Walsh on *The Two Cities* podcast (John Anthony Dunne, Stephanie Kate Judd, and Daniel Parham, hosts, episode 131, "Depicting Jesus in Jesus Films with Dr. Richard Walsh," July 27, 2022, https://www.thetwocities.com/biblical-studies/depicting-jesus-in-jesus-films-with-dr-richard-walsh-podcast/). See also Walsh's reference to such Jesus depictions as "sheer externality," never getting to the heart of who he is (*Reading the Gospels in the Dark*, 26).

16. Taylor, *What Did Jesus Look Like?*, 5–6, 10.

could infer what they *were like*. This correlation is known as physiognomy, a pseudoscientific means of determining character through appearance.[17] To be clear, this is by no means a relic of the past. Hollywood was built on this misguided idea. Assumptions about the alignment of character and appearance explain why certain actors tend to consistently be typecast as villains because they may have a "menacing look," while others are typecast as heroes. Such assumptions also explain why some actors and not others are cast in the part of Jesus.

Joan Taylor suggests that the dearth of information in the Gospels about what Jesus looked like may stem from Jesus being "average in every way."[18] She goes on to give the following plausible description of Jesus as a first-century Jew living in Roman Palestine based on historical and archaeological data. He was probably about five feet five inches in height (or 1.67 meters), had "olive-brown skin, brown-black hair and brown eyes," with shorter hair and a beard, though not necessarily well groomed (since philosophers were known to care more about their ideas than their appearance).[19]

Short hair is perhaps the most incongruous part of Taylor's proposed description compared with many representations of Jesus. Countless paintings, sculptures, and films portray a Jesus with long hair. This feature is reinforced by alleged artifacts like the Shroud of Turin—burial cloths that some claim feature an impression of Jesus's body, including his face. A long-haired Jesus is even depicted in one of the oldest known portraits of him (a mural painting) from the fourth century CE (from the Catacomb of Commodilla).[20] Yet there is good reason to doubt that Jesus had long hair. First, as Taylor points out, short hair for men was common practice in the first-century world, including, it seems, in Judaism of the time.[21] Second, Paul's negative attitude toward long hair for men would likely have been shared by Jesus (1 Cor. 11:14).[22]

17. Consider how Dorothy, when she meets Glinda in *The Wizard of Oz* (1939), responds in shock at the thought of a good and beautiful witch, with Glinda assuring her that "only bad witches are ugly." This sentiment reveals a deep prejudice about what it means to be "ugly" or different, which the musical *Wicked* (2003) turns on its head. Alternatively, people responded with surprise at the thought of Ted Bundy being a serial killer—he was *too handsome* to be capable of such evil! Cf. the Netflix docuseries *Conversations with a Killer: The Ted Bundy Tapes* (2019).

18. Taylor, *What Did Jesus Look Like?*, 194.

19. Taylor, *What Did Jesus Look Like?*, 194; cf. 129.

20. Cf. Jensen, *Understanding Early Christian Art*, 103.

21. Taylor, *What Did Jesus Look Like?*, 194. An exception to this would pertain to men undertaking the Nazarite vow for an extended period, as perhaps with John the Baptist. See McGrath, *Christmaker*, 17.

22. Turner, "Representation of New Testament Figures," 85. If Paul knew Jesus (as Porter argues) and Jesus had long hair, Paul would not likely have argued as he does in 1 Cor. 11:14. See Porter, *When Paul Met Jesus*.

Another physical characteristic of Jesus is his circumcision. Luke records that Jesus was circumcised when eight days old in keeping with Torah requirements (Luke 2:21; cf. Lev. 12:3). Yet few films portray this event (exceptions include *The New Media Bible: The Gospel According to Luke* [1979]; *La Sacra Famiglia* [*The Holy Family*, 2006]; *The Savior* [2014]).[23] As part of its feminist critique of religion's violence and paternalism, *Io Sono Con Te* (*Let It Be*, 2010) subverts the circumcision story through Mary's refusal to allow the procedure. Yet from a historical perspective, it is likely that mothers oversaw and even performed the circumcisions of their sons before the ritual became institutionalized (cf. Exod. 4:24–26; 1 Macc. 1:60–61; 2 Macc. 6:10; 4 Macc. 4:25).[24] Luke makes no mention of an agent performing Jesus's circumcision ("when he was circumcised," Luke 2:21 ESV), and it is only *after* Jesus is circumcised that his parents bring him to Jerusalem to present him in the temple (Luke 2:22). His circumcision isn't portrayed as a priestly action, and so Mary could have performed the rite. While Jesus's circumcision would have been a hidden physical feature, it would have been publicly displayed when he was crucified unclothed, something that film directors have understandably avoided (at least through camera work).[25] Jesus is usually afforded more honor in film and other visualizations of the crucifixion than he probably would have historically. However sensitive a subject, Jesus's circumcision serves to reinforce his humanity and his Jewishness.[26]

Another aspect of Jesus's physicality may be hinted at in Luke 19:3, where the report of shortness of stature is applied by Luke either to Zacchaeus or to Jesus: "Because he [antecedent unclear] was small in stature" (ESV). This phrase comes at the end of the Greek sentence and so could apply to either Zacchaeus (the subject of the previous lines) or Jesus (the direct object in the opening line). Traditionally, the description has been attributed to Zacchaeus, but the logic of the narrative could go either way. Zacchaeus could have climbed a tree to see Jesus among the crowds because he (Zacchaeus) was short and unable to see over the crowd or because Jesus was short, with taller people surrounding him.[27] Returning to Taylor's description of Jesus's height, though, five feet five inches (or 1.67 meters) would have been the average height for first-century Jews in Roman Palestine. The reticence to portray

23. The film *The Gospel of Luke* (2015) gives voice-over narration, coupled with vague editing decisions, to convey that Jesus's circumcision took place even as he lay in the manger; cf. also *Jesus* (1979).

24. Blanton, "Did Jewish Women Circumcise Male Infants?"

25. Although see Jesus in *The Last Temptation of Christ* (1988) and Daniel (playing Jesus in the passion play) from *Jésus de Montréal* (*Jesus of Montreal*, 1989); both are portrayed as being crucified naked, with their legs twisted to the side to avoid nudity.

26. Notably, one of the few films to portray the rite is a Palestinian film (*The Savior* [2014]).

27. See Soon, "Little Messiah."

Jesus as short in art and film probably has nothing to do with historicity but rather with *physiognomic associations* with height.

Within the Christian tradition, that Jesus was unattractive has been a common assumption based on Isaiah's description of the Lord's Servant as "disfigured," "marred," and lacking in beauty (Isa. 52:14; 53:2). We find this application of Isaiah 52–53 as early as Irenaeus in the late second century CE (*Haer.* 3.19.2; 4.33.12), and it has continued to inform many people's thinking ever since.[28] Yet the description of the Servant should be understood in its context as poetry, with attention to its metaphorical qualities. More importantly for our purposes, the connection fostered by the Gospel writers (and other New Testament authors) between Jesus and the Isaianic Servant isn't a direct one but rather rests on a representational view of the Servant (an individual from Israel standing in for Israel), which is then applied to Jesus as the utterly faithful representative of his people (e.g., Matt. 8:17; 12:18–21; 20:28; 26:28).[29] Simply put, it is unlikely that any of the New Testament authors understood Isaiah to be describing the physical appearance of Jesus.

Despite this traditional theological association with unattractiveness, Jesus is almost never portrayed that way in film, perhaps because doing so might offend some moviegoers. One notable exception comes from the Sardinian film *Su Re* (*The King*, 2012), which portrays Jesus with close-cropped hair and a short beard, accentuating his bulging eyes and cleft lip. This actor is also slightly heavier in frame, with ample dark body hair. To put it bluntly, he would not be most people's first choice to play Jesus, and his appearance certainly clashes with preferences for a handsome Jesus.

As these examples demonstrate, the paucity of information about Jesus's appearance in the Gospels provides a gap to fill. The casting decision of who will play Jesus comes down to imaginative possibilities that fill in gaps about his height, size, skin color, shape (and even count) of teeth, length and shade of hair and facial hair, hygiene and grooming, and more. And since each of us functions as the casting director for the Jesus film in our own mind, it can be illuminating to ask who we would choose to play Jesus as we read the Gospels. Consider the way that film adaptations have affected our experience of reading novels. If we read (or reread) a book after seeing a film adaptation, especially a successful one, it can be difficult to get the actors' faces out of our head. When reading *Harry Potter*, for example, who doesn't imagine Daniel Radcliffe as "the Boy Who Lived" after being introduced to the movies?[30] The

28. Taylor, *What Did Jesus Look Like?*, 141–42.

29. See Brown, "Jesus Messiah as Isaiah's Servant."

30. Once the new *Harry Potter* series arrives on HBO Max, the new actor playing the role of Harry (Dominic McLaughlin) will similarly affect how readers engage the novels.

ITC Films / RAI Radiotelevisione Italiana

Image of Robert Powell from *Jesus of Nazareth* (1977)

same phenomenon occurs with the proliferation of Jesus images that have been impressed on us. It's not clear whether humans can visualize in their minds wholly new faces they've never seen before, so it is an open question whether it's even possible to imagine a new face for Jesus. Chances are many of us conjure up images from art or from the more famous actors who have portrayed Jesus: Jim Caviezel (*The Passion of the Christ* [2004]), Brian Deacon (*Jesus* [1979]), Jonathan Roumie (*The Chosen* [2017–present]), or Robert Powell (*Jesus of Nazareth* [1977]), for example. Powell's appearance was specifically influenced by Warner Sallman's classic painting of Jesus, *Head of Christ* (1941), so Powell closely resembled the modern era's most popular artistic rendering of Jesus.[31]

Many other prominent actors have played Jesus over the years, including Max von Sydow (*The Greatest Story Ever Told* [1965]), Willem Dafoe (*The Last Temptation of Christ* [1988]), Christian Bale (*Mary, Mother of Jesus* [1999]), Ewan McGregor (*Last Days in the Desert* [2015]), and Joaquin

31. Reinhartz, *Jesus of Hollywood*, 49.

Phoenix (*Mary Magdalene* [2018]).[32] Yet we would venture to guess these are *not* actors many of us would cast as Jesus in our "internal films," perhaps because we have seen them in too many other films for them to play *Jesus* in our minds.

In the history of film, Jesus has typically been depicted according to popular conventions and associations.[33] Viewers are bound to have a sense of prototypical expectations of what Jesus "ought to look like" based on extensive visual reinforcement through art, film, and other representations.[34] Yet from the time that images of Christ were first produced, these have hardly been uniform. Early Christian art evinces a diversity of images for Jesus; sometimes he is older and bearded with long hair, and other times he is youthful and beardless.[35]

Outliers from the standard depictions of Jesus in film do exist (cf. *Su Re* [*The King*, 2012], noted above), and the range of portraits can help viewers recognize their standing assumptions about Jesus's appearance. For example, virtually every Jesus film presents him as able-bodied. An exception comes in *Jesus: A Deaf Missions Film* (2024), in which Jesus is deaf and communicates through ASL. Such a presentation invites viewers to reflect on ableist assumptions they may be bringing to their internal portrayals of Jesus. Jesus is also typically presented as being on the younger end of middle age, with only a handful of counterexamples. An older Jesus is found in *The King of Kings* (1927); the actor playing Jesus, H. B. Warner, was in his fifties. The oldest actor to play Jesus was Krishna Ghattamaneni in the Indian film *Santhi Sandesam* (*Message of Peace*, 2004); he was in his sixties during filming.[36] Yet Warner from *The King of Kings* retains the status of the *oldest-looking* Jesus, and with the strong emphasis on children in the film, his Jesus resembles a loving grandfather. Warner's depiction also taps into popular paternalistic conceptions of God as "an old guy with a beard." This connection is fostered by the film's lighting effect that causes Jesus to glow as if he is constantly experiencing transfiguration,[37] contributing to a sense of divinity in his physical depiction.

The dominant physical representation of Jesus is as white with European features—with the whitest and blondest Jesus being Robert Elfstrom from Johnny Cash's *The Gospel Road: A Story of Jesus* (1973). Contributing to

32. Although he did not appear as Jesus, Ralph Fiennes provides Jesus's voice in *The Miracle Maker* (2000).

33. This can be seen especially in caricatured depictions of Jesus in, e.g., *Dogma* (1999); *Le Tout Nouveau Testament* (*The Brand New Testament*, 2015).

34. On the notion of prototypicality, see Stockwell, *Cognitive Poetics*, 15–31.

35. Jensen, *Understanding Early Christian Art*, 113.

36. Bakker, *Challenge of the Silver Screen*, 223.

37. Cf. Walsh, "Reading the Gospel(s) in the Dark," 111.

DeMille Pictures Corporation (left); Padmalaya Studios (right)

Image of H. B. Warner (left) in *The King of Kings* (1927) and Krishna Ghattamaneni (right) from *Santhi Sandesam* (*Message of Peace*, 2004), the oldest actors playing Jesus

the perpetuation of a white Jesus in film is Hollywood's long-standing appropriation of Jesus as a uniquely *American* figure. This is clear already in D. W. Griffith's *The Birth of a Nation* (1915), a racist film about the merits of the Ku Klux Klan for American society. In the film, Jesus is superimposed over the final scene to authorize the film's messages. An American Jesus is simply taken for granted, and the legacy of this unreflective association continues into modern cinema.[38] The "Americanization" of Jesus is on full display in *The Greatest Story Ever Told* (1965) through the choice of film locations in Utah and Arizona, where the story of Jesus is performed by a predominantly white cast and set amid a quintessentially American landscape of mountains, cacti, and desert terrain. Walsh comments on the effect of this setting: "The West's iconography naturalizes Jesus as the American—or Western—hero."[39]

Despite the ubiquity of the white American Jesus, plenty of non-white and non-American Jesus portrayals can be found. A number of films offer Hispanic[40] and Indian[41] Jesus portraits, and others provide Filipino (*Kristo* [1996]), Palestinian (*The Savior* [2014]), and Iranian perspectives (*Mesih*

38. Walsh, "*Birth of a Nation*." As Walsh describes it, Jesus functions as a "talisman" in *The Birth of a Nation*, something that also occurs in *Civilization* (1916), in which Count Ferdinand is indwelled by the Spirit of Christ and then conveys messages of peace during a time of war.

39. Walsh, *Reading the Gospels in the Dark*, 157.

40. E.g., *Jesús, Nuestro Señor* (*Jesus, Our Lord*, 1971); *Reina de Reinas*: *La Virgen María* (*Queen of Queens: The Virgin Mary*, 1948); *El Mártir del Calvario* (*The Martyr of Calvary*, 1952); *María Magdalena, Pecadora de Magdala* (*Mary Magdalene, Sinner of Magdala*, 1946); *El Proceso de Cristo* (*The Trial of Christ*, 1966); *Cristo 70* (1969); *La Espina de Dios* (*The Thorn of God*, 2015); *Jesús de Nazaret*: *El Hijo de Dios* (*Jesus of Nazareth*, 2019).

41. E.g., *Jesus* (1973); *Thomasleeha* (*Saint Thomas*, 1975); *Snapaka Yohannan* (*John the Baptist*, 1963); *Karunamayudu* (*Ocean of Mercy*, 1978); *Santhi Sandesam* (*Message of Peace*, 2004); *Mulla Kireetam* (*Crown of Thorns*, 2006).

George Stevens Productions

John the Baptist amid the Southwestern terrain of the United States in *The Greatest Story Ever Told* (1965)

[*Jesus, the Spirit of God*, 2010]).[42] There are a few African Jesus films,[43] along with other movies that portray Jesus as Black.[44] Cultural features are clearly present throughout these films, which may appear striking for viewers accustomed to the "Jesus of Hollywood" (as Adele Reinhartz calls him). In Indian films, for example, Jesus often poses in a way that resembles Hindu deities, especially in the ascension scenes.[45] In the South African film *Jezile* (*Son of Man*, 2006), Jesus undergoes the coming-of-age Xhosa ceremony, *ulwaluko*.[46]

Yet even when films originate far beyond the confines of Hollywood, pressure to cohere with normed depictions of Jesus is still felt. It is striking that

42. One prominent American film recently cast an Israeli actor (Avraham Aviv Alush) in the role of Jesus (*The Shack* [2017]), and *Martin Scorsese Presents: The Saints* (season 1, episode 2, "John the Baptist," 2024) cast a Moroccan actor (Hatim Abdelghafour).

43. E.g., *Jezile* (*Son of Man*, 2006); *Lamentations of Judas* (2022).

44. E.g., *Color of the Cross* (2006); *Color of the Cross 2: The Resurrection* (2008); *Das Neue Evangelium* (*The New Gospel*, 2020); *The Book of Clarence* (2023). In *The Chosen* (2017–present), Jesus's father, Joseph, is Black, but this is ostensibly intended to highlight the virgin birth and how much Jesus does not look like Joseph (cf., e.g., season 1, episode 5, "The Wedding Gift," 2019).

45. E.g., *Jesus* (1973); *Thomasleeha* (*Saint Thomas*, 1975); *Karunamayudu* (*Ocean of Mercy*, 1978); *Santhi Sandesam* (*Message of Peace*, 2004); cf. Page, *100 Bible Films*, 123.

46. Cf. Erlank, "'Brought into Manhood.'"

Nu-Lite Entertainment

Jesus in *Color of the Cross* (2006)

in *Mesih* (*Jesus, the Spirit of God*, 2010) the Iranian actor who plays Jesus (Ahmad Soleimani Nia) has bleached his hair and beard blond even though the rest of the cast has dark hair. This is undoubtedly intended to conform to what has become a "visual standard" for the representation of Jesus. In an interview, the director (Nader Talebzadeh) does not mention the hair dye but does acknowledge that Nia was chosen in part because of his resemblance to Western depictions of Jesus.[47]

The Book of Clarence (2023), which depicts a Black Jesus, offers a critique of the physiognomic assumptions at work in depicting Jesus's ethnicity. After a poor, disheveled man named Benjamin (played by Benedict Cumberbatch) is healed by Jesus, he is granted the miraculous ability to multiply gold coins. This allows him to get cleaned up and attract large crowds of his own, even to the point of "looking the part" of a white Jesus, although he is a messianic pretender with an out-of-control gift. Nevertheless, people say he is "pure and white, so trustworthy"—an obvious parody of cinematic representations of Jesus intended to critique physiognomic associations of whiteness.

The Black Jesus of *Color of the Cross* (2006) and *Color of the Cross 2: The Resurrection* (2008) is overtly a transgressive choice. Unlike most films with a non-white Jesus, in these films Jesus is racially dissimilar to the majority of the cast, and the notion of a Black Jesus is addressed within the story world of the films.[48] In fact, Jesus's ethnicity is part of the controversy surrounding

47. Appendix 4 in Malone, *Screen Jesus*, 295.

48. *Lamentations of Judas* (2022) also explores race and ethnicity, but it specifically uses the story of Judas to frame societal perception of Black Angolan soldiers fighting alongside white South Africans (see chap. 8).

his messianic movement (he is called the Black Nazarene and the Black Jew), and the Jewish leaders overtly debate whether it is possible for the Messiah to be Black. The handling of this controversy in these two films has a meta quality to it, since many (white) filmgoers may balk at the idea of a Black Jesus. Despite the historical implausibility of a white Jesus, films like these raise the issue of our own implicit casting choices for Jesus around skin color and ethnicity. Strong responses to a Black Jesus likely illuminate something about these already-made choices.

Portraying the Personality of Jesus

Not only have cinematic Jesuses been largely lacking in melanin; they've also been largely lacking in personality—our final topic of discussion in this chapter. Portraits of Jesus in film, especially in the first half-century of film history, were short on personality, potentially because filmmakers wanted to avoid taking liberties with the biblical text. As a result, Jesus is often fairly stoic and emotionally stilted, as in *The Greatest Story Ever Told* (1965), *The Passover Plot* (1976), and *Jesus* (1979). The net effect of Jesus's rather flat affect in film conveys that Jesus wasn't fully human, lacking in the full range of human emotions. The portrait was decidedly docetic across this period. Nevertheless, as the Hays Code was being phased out, humanizing portrayals of Jesus began to appear. The first film to attempt a thoroughgoing portrayal of a human Jesus was Dennis Potter's *Son of Man* (1969), but the most prominent example is *The Last Temptation of Christ* (1988). Both films humanize Jesus through their portrayals of a man struggling through his own confusion and anxiety about the nature of his divine calling (see chap. 7).

When it comes to our earliest sources, the question of how to read Jesus's personality is both difficult and hermeneutical. Ask two different people to describe the Jesus they read from the pages of the Gospels, and you will likely get two different sets of personality traits. Since we each direct our own version of the Jesus story as we read the Gospels, it may be that certain emotions or personality traits simply do not fit our internal Jesus reel. Which characteristics might we downplay or augment without realizing it?[49]

Adding to the complexity, the portraits we glean from the four Gospels feel rather different from one another. In Mark, Jesus seems to be a man

49. When teaching a Gospels course at our seminary, some students in Jeannine's class were struck on a second reading of Mark that Jesus seemed angrier than on their first reading (e.g., Mark 1:41; 3:5; 10:14). The director in their heads may have been muting this particular characteristic of the Markan Jesus during their first reading.

of few(er) words, whereas in John, Jesus is a man of many (more) words. There are also clear differences among the Gospels (and especially between the Synoptics and John) in *how* Jesus speaks. Does Jesus sound more like a prophet, announcing judgment and salvation? Or does he speak like a sage—a wise teacher, wielding at times pithy sayings that guide and at other times riddles that confuse? These various determinations will contribute to the fairly impressionistic question of Jesus's "personality" in terms of his approachability (Is he distant, or is he aloof?) and his emotional state (Is he calm and composed, or is he passionate and fiery?). Whatever impressions we glean from a Gospel on these kinds of spectrums, writers and directors of Jesus films have no choice but to make decisions about these questions as they create their portraits of Jesus.

At key points in the Gospels, Jesus refuses to respond to a question or answers a question by asking one of his own (cf., e.g., Matt. 15:23; 21:23–27; Mark 15:2; John 19:9), and these moments could give the impression that Jesus was often evasive. But this isn't the only way to understand Jesus's nonresponses. While in the silent film era, Jesus was rendered silent by the medium itself;[50] in *Last Days in the Desert* (2015), Jesus chooses to remain silent to avoid saying something unwise or less than ideal. Instead, he decides to let his actions "speak" for him. This film potentially challenges ways of understanding Jesus's "evasive" portrait. It can cause us to wonder if there is more than one way to interpret a facet of Jesus's behavior.

At the heart of the problem is the difficulty of determining emotion through text. Unless we read an explicit statement of someone being sad or happy or angry, we might misunderstand the attendant emotion, or read the tone differently than intended, or ascribe a different emotion than other people do. Given contemporary habits with text messaging, we should acknowledge that we are not always correct in our ways of reading emotions from texts. It is not always clear from a text when someone is being sarcastic, snippy, dryly humorous, or straightforward.[51]

Yet humans seem wired to identify emotions and intentions. Cognitive psychologist Keith Oatley (with Nicola Yuill) reconducted a famous experiment (originally conducted in 1944 by Fritz Heider and Mary-Ann Simmel) in which viewers watched a short cartoon of shapes (triangles, a circle, and a box) moving around the screen.[52] The cartoon had no plot or storyline, just

50. Shepherd, "Introduction," 1.

51. See the comedic "Text Message Confusion" skit by Keegan-Michael Key and Jordan Peele from Comedy Central's *Key and Peele* (season 4, episode 3, "Old Ladies and Satan," directed by Peter Atencio, aired October 8, 2014).

52. Oatley, *Such Stuff as Dreams*, 130–32.

movement. At the end of the cartoon, viewers somehow ascribed emotions and intentions to the shapes without any direct evidence of either of those things. This experiment illustrates how readily we anticipate, and at times import, emotions into scenarios without explicit direction and even when there is little evidence to go on.

To illustrate the wide-ranging ways people read the Gospels and assume Jesus's emotional state from them, we can compare films that offer visual translations of the same Gospel (see chap. 1). Both Pasolini's *Il Vangelo Secondo Matteo* (*The Gospel According to St. Matthew*, 1964) and van den Bergh's *The Gospel According to Matthew* (1993) rely on the text of Matthew for Jesus's lines of dialogue, and yet Jesus reads his lines quite differently in each film. In Pasolini's film Jesus gives the lines of Matthew's text with intense passion and anger,[53] whereas in van den Bergh's version the same words are whimsical, delivered with a smile, and even play for laughs. The same Matthean text has inspired radically different conceptions of Jesus's tone and thus his overall personality.

The addition of humor to Jesus's personality in *The Gospel According to Matthew* (1993) has been unique among visual translation films. While *Godspell* (1973) was the first film to veer toward lightheartedness in retelling the Jesus story, *The Gospel According to Matthew* does more than simply sprinkle in humor; it systematically applies humor throughout. This becomes quite jarring when a jovial Jesus is saying something painful, calling out the Pharisees, cleansing the temple, or announcing his imminent death. In a latter scene (Matt. 26:2), Jesus abruptly informs his disciples of his coming death while they are bathing together, and he somehow manages to conclude his horrific news with a smile. Bruce Marchiano, the actor playing Jesus in *The Gospel According to Matthew*, also played Jesus in the films *Apostle Peter and the Last Supper* (2012) and *My Son, My Savior* (2015), but in those films his use of humor is toned down significantly. Although Walsh and Staley suggest that Jeremy Sisto from *Jesus* (1999) is "the happiest Jesus" of them all,[54] we propose that no one can top Marchiano's original portrayal (also on display, briefly, in *The Visual Bible: Acts* [1994]).

Laughter in Jesus films serves as a way of making Jesus more relatable and personable—indeed, more human—moving his portrait away from the more stoic, docetic side of the spectrum. Jesus's laughter in films can also prompt us to reflect on the Gospels to consider their use (or lack) of humor.

53. The actor who plays Jesus in Pasolini's film (Enrique Irazoqui) makes an appearance in the documentary *Das Neue Evangelium* (*The New Gospel*, 2020), which has a delightful moment when, behind the scenes, Irazoqui coaches the new actor playing Jesus (Yvan Sagnet) to smile more.

54. Walsh and Staley, *Jesus, the Gospels, and Cinematic Imagination*, 244.

Visual Bible / Visual International

Jesus in *The Gospel According to Matthew* (1993)

Nowhere in the canonical Gospels does Jesus himself laugh. Yet the Gospels do provide examples of Jesus teaching with images and figures that may have originally evoked laughter.[55] Did it strike early audiences (within the story or in early reception of Matthew) as funny when Jesus told them not to focus on the speck in someone's eye but rather to focus on the log in their own (Matt. 7:3–5)? This saying is understood as funny in *The Gospel According to Matthew* (1993), though not in *The Chosen* (season 3, episode 1, "Homecoming," 2022). Is a response of laughter intended when Jesus declares that it is easier for a camel to pass through the eye of a needle than for a rich person to enter the kingdom (Matt. 19:24)? *The Passion* (2008) certainly thinks so, but (surprisingly) *The Gospel According to Matthew* (1993) does not. If someone chuckles at the parable of the unjust steward (Luke 16:1–13), they may be perceiving it as dark humor, as does *La Voie Lactée* (*The Milky Way*, 1969). And if Jesus's command to Peter to pay taxes with a coin he'll soon find inside a fish (Matt. 17:25–27) sounds to you like a humorous scenario, you'd be in agreement with *The King of Kings* (1927). Our point is that finding humor in what we read is itself an act of projection—it is hermeneutical and is not independent from our mental and emotional states as we read.

55. People do laugh at Jesus when he claims the young woman they are mourning "is not dead but asleep" (Mark 5:39–40). This is a mocking kind of laugh rather than humorous laughter. Additionally, Jesus teaches that in the great reversal to come, those who laugh now will weep, while those who weep now will laugh (Luke 6:21, 25).

Although Jesus never actually laughs in the canonical Gospels, he does do so in some noncanonical Gospels. If laughter in Jesus films serves to humanize Jesus, it has the opposite function in the noncanonical Gospels. Jesus laughs out of derision, with the effect of creating even greater distance between himself and the other characters in the story and highlighting his otherness and incomprehensibility. In the Gospel of Judas (second century CE), Jesus laughs at his disciples when they ask questions or express mistaken assumptions, even as they try to understand his difficult and esoteric teachings (Gos. Jud. 34.1–9; 36.22–23; 44.18–22; 55.14–22).[56] The child Jesus laughs in the Infancy Gospel of Thomas "as one far superior to those he laughs at" and thereby humiliates his elders (cf. Inf. Gos. Thom. 8.1).[57] When Jesus emerges from the baptismal waters, according to the Gospel of Philip, he comes up laughing out of contempt for the world (Gos. Phil. 74.25–75.2).[58] The same scene in the film *The Gospel According to Matthew* (1993) shows Jesus full of joy as he exits the water, but the connotation is utterly different from the Gospel of Philip. In Jesus films, unlike noncanonical Gospels, laughter consistently serves to humanize Jesus.

The portrait of Jesus in *The Chosen* (2017–present) incorporates humor in a humanizing way and does so with balance by including the full range of human emotion. Jonathan Roumie's portrayal of Jesus throughout this serial show is playful, kind, empathetic, and gracious, and yet he also gets into heated exchanges with Pharisees. This Jesus plays games during Rosh Hashanah, although he is not very good at them (season 3, episode 3, "Physician, Heal Yourself," 2022). He laughs, winks, smiles, and shares inside jokes with his disciples (such as the recurring gag about the elastic meaning of the word "soon"). When Jesus teaches in parables, he does so in a more Socratic fashion, asking questions and then dynamically incorporating the disciples' responses into his teaching.[59] The Jesus from *The Chosen* is perhaps the most well-rounded depiction of Jesus yet captured on film.

As we've been discerning, we have no clear indication of Jesus's personality from the canonical Gospels. Do the accounts indicating that he would withdraw privately to pray and sometimes avoid large crowds (e.g., Mark 1:35–39, 45; Luke 5:16) suggest that he was an introvert? Or does his regular

56. For a detailed analysis, see Nel, "He Who Laughs Last," 5.

57. Nel, "He Who Laughs Last," 5.

58. Isenberg, "Gospel of Philip," 145.

59. An interactive and playful teaching style is also present in *La Espina de Dios* (*The Thorn of God*, 2015), where Jesus jokes with his disciples about misunderstanding his parables, and they push back jokingly about how he adds unnecessary details that don't have any particular significance.

eating and drinking with people suggest extroversion (cf., e.g., Mark 2:15–17)? (Maybe he was an ENFP on the Myers-Briggs, or an 8 wing 7 on the Enneagram.) While we can only speculate on these questions, key storyline features of Jesus's life probably tell us something worthwhile about his demeanor—namely, that some people wanted to party with him and others wanted to kill him. Yet the stoic and docetic Jesuses we see throughout film history hardly cohere with either point. The anxious Jesuses of *Son of Man* (1969) and *The Last Temptation of Christ* (1988) are hardly "party worthy." And although a happy and funny Jesus (e.g., *Godspell* [1973]; *The Gospel According to Matthew* [1993]; *Jesus* [1999]) could be a great party guest, it is hard to imagine someone wanting to kill him. In our estimation, no celluloid Jesus has truly pulled off both aspects convincingly. While a truly authentic portrayal of the personality of Jesus proves to be an ever-elusive goal, for us, any depiction of Jesus that makes it believable that no party would be complete without him *and* that he was executed as a state criminal would be truer to the stories we find in the Gospels.

Conclusion

Even though Jesus is so difficult to depict on film, Jesus films continue to be produced at an ever-increasing pace. Anyone who has seen even a handful of them will be able to identify one or more preferred performances. Yet what we tend to dislike in a portrayal speaks less to an actor's ability and more to the reality that we regularly cast a different Jesus in our minds and direct him to act in ways at odds with what we are seeing on-screen. In other words, we bring much to a Jesus film that remains unstated and assumed. Our tendency is to make Jesus "in our own image" within our minds, and so we inevitably protest when he looks and acts differently in text or film *from that image*. Once again, the director in our heads is alive and well as we read or view retellings of the Jesus story. And, maybe when it comes to Jesus, our sensitivities and sensibilities are especially activated because many of us have so much invested in the question of who he really was.

6

Casting the Villains

Portraits of Judas, Pilate, and the Jewish Leaders and Crowds

Good stories need good villains. The Gospels are no exception. Readers, if they at all identify positively with Jesus as they read the Gospels (as their authors intend), will put the blame for the climactic moment when Jesus is crucified squarely on one or more of the story's antagonists. This would likely be all fine and good if the Gospels were just fictional accounts that had no bearing on real people and their lives. Yet the ways that Jesus's antagonists are portrayed in the Gospels have sometimes directly—and devastatingly—affected people across the last two millennia. Especially in our post-Holocaust era, there are ethical dimensions to thoughtfully considering how Jewish characters and character groups from the Jesus story have been villainized.

As we think about Jesus's antagonists in the Gospels—and their "afterlives" in subsequent noncanonical Gospels and modern film—we can notice a rather wide mix of characters who oppose Jesus and his mission, in either brief or sustained ways. Even in the shortest of the canonical Gospels, Mark, we can notice the following antagonists:

- Demonic entities (Satan, demons, impure spirits; 1:13, 23, 34)
- Teachers of the law (or scribes; 2:6; 3:22; 12:12; 14:53)

- Pharisees (2:16, 24; 3:6)
- Herodians (3:6)
- Jesus's family (3:21)
- Mourners at Jairus's home (5:38–40)
- Residents of Jesus's hometown (6:1–6)
- Herod Antipas (toward John the Baptist; 6:27; cf. 8:15)
- The elders (8:31; 11:27; 12:12; 14:53)
- The chief priests (8:31; 11:18; 12:12; 14:53)
- Peter (8:31–33; 14:71)
- Gentiles (i.e., Rome; 10:33–34)
- Sadducees (12:18–23)
- Judas (14:10, 21, 43–46)
- A crowd sent by chief priests, scribes, and the elders (14:43)
- The high priest (14:53)
- The Sanhedrin (15:1)
- Pilate (15:1–15)
- The crowd at Jesus's trial before Pilate (15:11–14)
- Roman soldiers (15:16–20)
- Passersby at the cross (15:29)
- Rebels crucified alongside Jesus (15:32)

From this list, we can restrict our focus to the people or groups who are the central antagonists in bringing about Jesus's death: Judas, the Roman governor Pilate, and the Jewish leaders (coming from a number of sects or groups), as well as the crowds. We'll explore these antagonists in this chapter, from their portrayals in the canonical Gospels, to the ways they are characterized in later Gospels, and finally to their roles in films. We will see that the way we imagine their villainy might vary considerably from how it is actually portrayed. At each stage we will also consider how the representations of Judas, Pilate, and the Jewish leaders relate to the commonplace tendency to portray the Jewish people themselves—as a whole group—as "villains" in the Jesus story.

The Portrait of Judas

Judas in the Canonical Gospels

Judas is perhaps the quintessential villain of the Jesus story because he is infamously remembered as Jesus's betrayer, although not much else is communicated about him in the four canonical Gospels. When he is first introduced in Mark, he is already identified as the one "who betrayed" Jesus (Mark 3:19), foreshadowing his future action but also potentially identifying a key trait about his nature. When Judas eventually turns Jesus over to the Jewish leaders, the reader has been prepared for his actions (14:10, 43–46). The other Gospels also straightforwardly introduce Judas as the one who betrayed Jesus (Matt. 10:4; Luke 6:16; John 6:71). Clearly a "villain," Judas is nevertheless a quite flat character in the Gospels. Both Luke and John explain that Satan entered Judas as Jesus shared the Passover meal with his disciples (Luke 22:3; John 13:2, 27).[1] Inversely related to conversionist character development (see chap. 4), this development of Judas's character might be understood as a "deconversion."[2] Providing a different trajectory, Matthew portrays Judas as changing his mind, or at least feeling remorse, after Jesus is delivered to Pilate by describing his returning the money and ending his life (Matt. 27:3–5), with Luke in Acts also recording his suicide (albeit differently; Acts 1:18).

Yet readers do not discover Judas's full motivation for betraying Jesus. The demonic influence in Luke and John could explain Judas's motives as coerced, but a human motivation is implied in the Johannine comment that Judas was the keeper of the money bag and routinely stole from it (John 12:4–6; cf. 13:29). This note has contributed to the idea that Judas was motivated to betray Jesus for money (cf. Mark 14:11; Luke 22:5). Yet, perhaps surprisingly then, John does not mention that Judas *received* any money for betraying Jesus (cf. John 13:26–30; 18:2–3). It is Matthew alone who portrays Judas asking for payment and receiving thirty pieces of silver (Matt. 26:14–16; 27:3, 9). Some have found potential motivation for Judas's actions in his surname, "Iscariot," interpreting the name as connected to the daggers (*sicarii*) used by Zealots (with Judas betraying Jesus for not being revolutionary enough)[3] or, more likely, as a transliteration of the Aramaic *ish kerioth* ("a man from Kerioth"), thus designating Judas's family origin (with Judas potentially an outsider from the south and so thought to be more likely to betray Jesus).[4] In the end, "Iscariot" is unlikely to illuminate Judas's motivations, although Jesus films have not hesitated to draw conclusions from the surname.

1. For a sketch of John's development of Judas, see Bennema, *Theory of Character*, 76.

2. Green, *Conversion in Luke-Acts*, 148–50.

3. The Epistle of the Apostles from the second century CE refers to "Judas the Zealot" in a list of named disciples (Ep. Apos. 2). Due to several oddities in the list, not to mention that the list concerns the disciples after Jesus's resurrection, it is most likely that "Judas the Zealot" is a reference to Simon the Zealot.

4. There are actually two possibilities: the Moabite town of Kerioth (cf. Jer. 48:24; Amos 2:2) and, more likely, the town south of Jerusalem called Kerioth Hezron (Josh. 15:25).

Judas in the Gospel of Judas

The noncanonical Gospel of Judas (second century CE) provides two early developments around the character of Judas. The first adds his motivation for betraying Jesus. In this Gospel, Judas is given access to secret information from Jesus and uniquely displays insight into those teachings (Gos. Jud. 35.14–24); it is this knowledge that propels Judas to betray Jesus.[5] Specifically, Judas betrays Jesus because he sees it as a necessity that is rooted in Jesus's overall mission. While the specifics remain opaque, Jesus's secret teaching to Judas explains his motivation. As Brakke says, "That [Judas] hands Jesus over suggests that he has learned what Jesus wanted him to know" (cf. Gos. Jud. 56.6–7, 20–21).[6]

The second development involves a certain kind of rehabilitation for Judas, whose act of betrayal was "wicked but necessary."[7] And importantly, Judas's suicide is not the end for him in this Gospel. Instead, the Gospel promises that Judas will have a role in the greater cosmos as an intermediary being, the "thirteenth demon" (Gos. Jud. 44.21);[8] that is, he is given future jurisdiction over the thirteenth aeon (Gos. Jud. 46.18–23; 55.12–13).[9] A partial rehabilitation of Judas is affirmed in the description of Judas "groaning" for the kingdom of God instead of being a part of it (Gos. Jud. 35.23–25; 46.11–13).[10] This is a more sympathetic portrayal of Judas than we can glean from the canonical Gospels, where the lack of development leaves room for readers' imaginations to fill in the gaps. Such imaginative explorations of Judas only develop further on-screen.

Judas in Jesus Films

Judas's reception in Jesus films is perhaps the most interesting of any character from the Gospels, given the varied ways filmmakers have attempted to make sense of him. Likely because he is named last in the list of apostles in the Gospels (e.g., Mark 3:19), and perhaps because he may not have been a Galilean, Judas is often the last disciple to join the group of Jesus's disciples in films.[11] Few

5. Brakke, *Gospel of Judas*, 58, 60, 82.
6. Brakke, *Gospel of Judas*, 61.
7. Brakke, *Gospel of Judas*, 61.
8. Brakke, *Gospel of Judas*, 84.
9. Brakke, *Gospel of Judas*, 61.
10. Brakke, *Gospel of Judas*, 82, 84.
11. Cf. *El Beso de Judas* (*Judas' Kiss*, 1954); *Son of Man* (1969); *Jesús, Nuestro Señor* (*Jesus, Our Lord*, 1971); *The Passover Plot* (1976); *Judas* (2004); *Santhi Sandesam* (*Message of Peace*, 2004); *Mesih* (*Jesus, the Spirit of God*, 2010); *Killing Jesus* (2015); *The Chosen* (season 2, episode 8, "Beyond Mountains," 2021). As a counterpoint, Judas is Jesus's first disciple in *The Greatest*

films portray Judas as negatively as the canonical Gospels do, opting instead to make his actions appear more compelling to audiences.[12]

The earliest depictions of Judas are quite simplistic ("flat"), adding little nuance to his biblical characterization. Cecil B. DeMille's Judas in *The King of Kings* (1927) is particularly one-sided, with the added trait that Judas is highly ambitious. In this film, Judas resembles the villain of a melodrama, being even cartoonlike in his nefarious pursuit of power, fame, and money.[13] Notably, Judas wishes that Jesus would neglect the poor and instead heal rich people, hoping the latter will propel him to a high position of honor. Fittingly, Judas ultimately chooses to betray Jesus because he is *bitter* that he does not get to experience the earthly kingdom and the personal advancement that it would offer. Judas is so villainized that he alone is admonished by Jesus for being unable to cast out a demon (which Jesus attributes to Judas's rather than the disciples' unbelief; cf. Matt. 17:14–20) and for trying to dismiss little children when they come to Jesus (cf. Mark 10:13–16). After betraying Jesus, Judas does show some remorse and decides to end his own life. Here the film harmonizes the accounts from Matthew and Acts: Judas hangs himself and then falls into a yawning chasm during the earthquake accompanying Jesus's death.[14]

A trope about Judas that stems from the emphasis on his relationship to money involves a romantic interest in Mary Magdalene. Once Mary Magdalene's characterization in art and film transforms her into a wealthy and extravagant person (cf. chap. 4), her appeal to a greedy Judas is an obvious connection for filmmakers.[15] Judas's romantic inclination for Mary Magdalene in several Jesus films also provides an intriguing contrast because their

Story Ever Told (1965), and in *The Last Temptation of Christ* (1988) Judas is a long-standing friend before Jesus starts his ministry (cf. also *Histoire de Judas* [*Story of Judas*, 2015]).

12. Although, see *Christus* (1916); *Blade af Satans Bog* (*Leaves from Satan's Book*, 1920); *The Passion of the Christ* (2004); *Apostle Peter and the Last Supper* (2012); *The Savior* (2014).

13. A very similar portrait appears in *El Mártir del Calvario* (*The Martyr of Calvary*, 1952). In some films, Judas is so deeply connected with money that he becomes "the rich young ruler," as in *Son of Man* (1969).

14. Similar harmonizations appear in *El Mártir del Calvario* (*The Martyr of Calvary*, 1952) and *The Day Christ Died* (1980). In *The Passion* (2008), Judas hangs himself by jumping into a well, which leaves open the potential for harmonization. In *King of Kings* (1961), Judas's body falls as the tree branch snaps, but just a few feet. Most Jesus films, however, opt for Matthew's account alone. *The Greatest Story Ever Told* (1965) is distinctive in portraying Judas throwing himself on the flames of the temple's altar. As Hebron argues, this screen version of Judas's death probably alludes to the Holocaust and reinforces "an emerging sympathy for the Jews and the growing abhorrence of anti-Semitism" (*Judas Iscariot*, 142).

15. Already in *The King of Kings* (1927); see also, e.g., *María Magdalena, Pecadora de Magdala* (*Mary Magdalene, Sinner of Magdala*, 1946); *El Mártir del Calvario* (*The Martyr of Calvary*, 1952); *Celui Qui Doit Mourir* (*He Who Must Die*, 1957); *Color of the Cross* (2006).

character arcs are inverted.[16] Mary is typically introduced as a sinner who becomes a devoted follower of Jesus, whereas Judas goes from disciple to traitor. This pairing of Mary Magdalene and Judas also leads to their conflation into a composite character in *Monty Python's Life of Brian* (1979); Judith is both Brian's love interest and his betrayer.[17]

One way that Jesus films complexify Judas as a character is by adjusting his canonical relationship to money. In *Jesus Christ Superstar* (1973), for example, Judas is completely uninterested in ambition, fame, or money; he declares that he has no concern for his "own reward" and initially rejects the "blood money" the Jewish leaders offer him (in the song "Damned for All Time / Blood Money"). In fact, it is precisely aversion to ambition that causes Judas to show *disdain* for Jesus, who embraces public adoration and seems to Judas to have lost sight of his original mission.[18] In *The Chosen* (2017–present), Judas's relationship to money is central to his characterization, but he undergoes significant development in this area. Initially, he is an honest businessman (season 2, episode 8, "Beyond Mountains," 2021) concerned with the unjust practices of his business partner during a land acquisition deal for the purpose of cutting tombs in the rocks (intended to foreshadow how his "blood money" is later used to purchase a burial field; cf. Matt. 27:7; Acts 1:19). Because of his expertise, Judas becomes the keeper of funds and lends his business acumen to help support Jesus's ministry (cf. season 3, episode 1, "Homecoming," 2022). This background explains why Judas, not Matthew, is in charge of the common purse even though Matthew's vocation in the canonical Gospels involves handling money as a tax collector (cf. season 3, episode 2, "Two by Two," 2022). Yet Judas becomes disillusioned with Jesus and the other disciples for not following through with his ideas (season 4, episode 6, "Dedication," 2024) and so begins to take some money for himself, signaling his belief that he deserves to be paid for his consultant work.

The most common way filmmakers have chosen to make Judas's character more complex, especially since World War II, is to associate him with the Zealot movement (as with one interpretation of "Iscariot," noted above).[19] This connection first appeared in 1951 in *The Living Christ Series*; was developed at length in two films from 1954, *Day of Triumph* and *El Beso de Judas* (*Judas' Kiss*); and can be found in many later films in varying degrees—from

16. Reinhartz, *Jesus of Hollywood*, 177.

17. See Telford, "*Monty Python's Life of Brian*," 7, 16.

18. For more on how this influences the film's "second horizon," see chap. 8.

19. *Gli Amici di Gesú: Giuda* (*The Friends of Jesus: Judas*, 2001), *Judas* (2004), and also likely *The Living Christ Series* (1951) combine both possible meanings of "Iscariot" by making Judas revolutionary minded and from a family based south of Jerusalem.

Judas having revolutionary sympathies to being in direct partnership with Zealots like Barabbas.[20] In some films the temple cleansing is a sign to Judas that Jesus is capable of extreme action befitting a revolutionary,[21] though in other films this event dashes Judas's hopes for an uprising.[22] Yet, in these films, Zealot and revolutionary ideology usually provide the source for his growing tension with Jesus. In some iterations, Judas intends his betrayal to (finally) incite a revolt against Rome: Either the people will revolt in response to Jesus's arrest (*Day of Triumph* [1954]) or Jesus himself will be forced to act (*King of Kings* [1961]).[23] The most sympathetic version of the latter option occurs in *Mary Magdalene* (2018). In that film, Judas's motives are less political than relational. He longs for the resurrection of the dead that accompanies the kingdom's arrival, because then he will be reunited with his wife and daughter, whom the Romans killed. Judas's dashed hopes compel him to turn Jesus in—to force his hand. Once Judas recognizes there is no revolt ahead, he hangs himself to be reunited with his family.

Some films go further in their attempts to make Judas a sympathetic character by absolving him of Jesus's betrayal. A few films imagine that Judas's sister (called Judith) is ultimately responsible, due to her influence either on Judas (*The Shadow of Nazareth* [1913]) or on Caiaphas (*Barabbas* [2019]). Other films portray Jesus himself pressuring Judas, whether because the betrayal is part of God's plan (*The Last Temptation of Christ* [1988]) or to put in motion a rather convoluted plan to trick people into thinking that Jesus has come back from the dead (*The Passover Plot* [1976]). In *Jesus Christ Superstar* (1973) Judas's perspective receives vindication when he returns from the dead, before Jesus's crucifixion, to sing "Superstar" while dressed in white with an angelic backup ensemble (see chap. 8).[24]

20. E.g., *Barabbas* (1961); *King of Kings* (1961); *The Passover Plot* (1976); *Jesus of Nazareth* (1977); *Karunamayudu* (*Ocean of Mercy*, 1978); *The Day Christ Died* (1980); *The Last Temptation of Christ* (1988); *Jesus* (1999); *The Miracle Maker* (2000); *Gli Amici di Gesú: Giuda* (*The Friends of Jesus: Judas*, 2001); *Judas* (2004); *Color of the Cross* (2006); *Mesih* (*Jesus, the Spirit of God*, 2010); *Barabbas* (2012); *La Espina de Dios* (*The Thorn of God*, 2015); *Mary Magdalene* (2018); *The Book of Clarence* (2023).

21. *Jesús, Nuestro Señor* (*Jesus, Our Lord*, 1971); *Judas* (2004); *Killing Jesus* (2015). In *Jesús de Nazaret: El Hijo de Dios* (*Jesus of Nazareth*, 2019), it is Barabbas who approves of the temple cleansing.

22. E.g., *Gli Amici di Gesú: Giuda* (*The Friends of Jesus: Judas*, 2001); *Mary Magdalene* (2018).

23. In *The Power of the Resurrection* (1958), a similar "hopeful betrayal" is posed to Judas by Annas, who leverages Judas's zealotry and desire for revolution.

24. Another film that arguably vindicates Judas is *La Última Cena* (*The Last Supper*, 1976), since the slave who fulfills the role of Judas in the reenactment of the Last Supper survives and escapes at the end; cf. the discussion on this film in chap. 8.

Universal Pictures

Judas and his angelic entourage singing triumphantly while Jesus is on trial in *Jesus Christ Superstar* (1973)

Histoire de Judas (*Story of Judas*, 2015) aims to exonerate Judas altogether, upending several cinematic tropes. This film portrays Judas as a close friend to Jesus; he collaborates with Jesus as he cleanses the temple, leading the charge and declaring that nothing belongs in cages—not even chickens, pigeons, or doves. Judas's desire to press against Roman occupation is in view, but with no sense of any tension with Jesus in this regard.[25] Notably, none of the *negative* actions associated with Judas in the canonical Gospels ever transpire in *Histoire de Judas* (*Story of Judas*). When a woman pours expensive perfume on Jesus's head, viewers hear nothing from Judas (cf. Matt. 26:8–9; John 12:4–6). And, quite strikingly, Judas never betrays Jesus. Instead, while Jesus is washing the disciples' feet (cf. John 13), Judas informs Jesus that there are some people from Qumran copying down Jesus's teachings and distributing them.[26] Hearing this, Jesus sends Judas to Qumran, borrowing from John 13:27 ("What you are about to do, do quickly"). Judas breaks the jars, rips up the scrolls, and burns everything in sight; he then is attacked by someone from Qumran on his return. When Judas recovers, he finds out that Jesus has

25. Earlier in *Histoire de Judas* (*Story of Judas*) there is a private meeting between Judas and a small band of armed men (Sicarii, a.k.a. Zealots), who ask Judas about Jesus's attitude toward Rome. The group is obviously violent and wants Jesus to act violently as well, but Judas is not interested in violence.

26. With Qumran, where the Dead Sea Scrolls were discovered, being the site of great scribal activity.

already been crucified. After mourning at the foot of his cross, Judas lays down in an empty tomb and dies. The film seems to suggest that Judas's role as a villain in the narrative was contrived by those controlling the narrative about Jesus—in this story, those from Qumran.

These distinctive perspectives on Judas are designed to make Judas more compelling and complex than the relatively flat characterization of the Gospels. Yet there is likely more at work than the aesthetic preferences of contemporary storytelling. As Carol Hebron has argued, the timing of these major cinematic alterations to Judas's characterization coincides with the aftermath of the Holocaust; Judas is given a more sympathetic interpretation to counterbalance his frequent association in Christian polemics with the Jewish people more broadly.[27] The rehabilitation of Judas in film, then, seems partly to be an effort to redress the antisemitism that led to the Holocaust. The effect that more sensitive Jewish-Christian relations has had on Jesus films is not, however, limited to Judas. It also affects the depictions of Pilate and the Jewish leaders. Although such sensitivity is not a consistent feature, as we will see.

The Portrait of Pontius Pilate

Pontius Pilate in the Canonical Gospels

The Roman governor (or "prefect") Pontius Pilate is the most prominent Roman figure in the four Gospels, ahead of Herod the Great and Herod Antipas, both client rulers established by Rome. Yet Pilate's characterization in the Gospels has been hotly debated, especially as it relates to his role and culpability in Jesus's death, in part because Pilate's portrayal is not identical among the four Gospels.

On the whole, Luke seems to get closest to exonerating Pilate. Three times in fairly short succession (Luke 23:4, 14–16, 22), Luke's Pilate disavows any basis to the charges levied against Jesus: subverting the Jewish nation, opposing paying the imperial tax, and claiming to be king (23:2). Pilate states his preference to punish Jesus (presumably by scourging) before releasing him (23:16, 20, 22). This willingness and even desire to release Jesus, most emphasized in Luke, finds its way into many later portrayals of Pilate. That Pilate is the one who sends Jesus to his death by crucifixion (23:24–25) is less important in these later portraits than his initial desire to free Jesus. Pilate may be ineffective, but his heart is in the right place (so the thinking goes).

27. Hebron, *Judas Iscariot.*

Yet Warren Carter, in his thorough and careful study of Pilate's characterization, suggests that Luke portrays a Pilate who is *arrogant*, not weak: "He is arrogant in his facile dismissal of the 'nobody' Jesus as posing no threat to Rome, and arrogant in his unwillingness to listen to the complaints of his allies, the Jerusalem elite, against Jesus. . . . Pilate finally consents because Jesus is not worth a rift with his allies. His action has little to do with whether he thinks Jesus is innocent."[28]

Matthew's Pilate, who attempts to claim innocence by washing his hands of the matter (Matt. 27:24), should also be read in the context of Roman power, and especially in light of the first-century reality that only Rome could enact the death sentence. Since Pilate does not abdicate his authority, he cannot remove the responsibility that he holds for the outcome of the trial.[29] Matthew's unique note about a warning sent from Pilate's wife to Pilate (27:19) only serves to emphasize further Pilate's culpability when he ignores her plaintive admonition.[30]

If we read the Gospels in light of their setting within Roman imperial domination and military might, we will be less likely to see Pilate as a sympathetic figure. While the evangelists answer with some amount of complexity the question of who is responsible for Jesus's death, Pilate is not acquitted. As Helen Bond concludes in her extensive study on the canonical representation of Pilate, "There is no evidence of a linear progression throughout the gospels in which Pilate becomes progressively friendlier towards Christianity."[31] Pilate represents Roman power and control, and Jesus dies on a cross after all—a uniquely Roman form of execution. Pilate, as Rome's representative, remains a key antagonist in the canonical Gospels. Yet many ancient and modern storytellers have been inclined to present Pilate more sympathetically.

Pontius Pilate in the Gospel of Peter

Later Christian writings exhibit increased tendencies to exonerate Pilate, and the Gospel of Peter illuminates this tendency at an early stage. The Gospel of Peter itself is fragmentary, with the beginning of the text missing. The first few extant lines were likely preceded by something akin to Matthew 27:24, where Pilate washes his hands, declares his innocence, and tries to pass off responsibility.[32] The first lines we have read, "But of the Jews [*tōn Ioudaiōn*]

28. Carter, *Pontius Pilate*, 104–5.
29. Brown and Roberts, *Matthew*, 519.
30. Brown, "Interpreting Gentile Women in Matthew."
31. Bond, *Pontius Pilate*, 206.
32. Foster (*Gospel of Peter*) approximates, in light of the relative length of Matthew's passion narrative and the scope of material covered in the fragment, that what we have is possibly only a quarter of the full text of this Gospel.

no-one washed the hands, nor did Herod, nor one of his judges. And when they were not willing to wash, Pilate rose up. And then Herod the king commanding the Lord to be brought, saying to them, 'Whatever I commanded you to do to him, do'" (Gos. Pet. 1.1–2).[33] As Foster suggests with due caution, "It does appear highly plausible that a report of Pilate's hand-washing was present, and that the author of the Gospel of Peter created the scene in Gos. Pet. 1.1–2 to juxtapose the innocence of Pilate with the guilt of those who refuse to wash their hands [i.e., the Jewish figures mentioned]."[34] Foster goes on to suggest that Pilate's authority in the Gospel of Peter "is made subservient to that of Herod Antipas and [Pilate] becomes a figure of protest against the injustice of the trial, albeit without power to right the wrongs he observes."[35]

Later, the Gospel of Peter reframes and magnifies Pilate's assertion to the crowd in Matthew 27:24 that he is innocent of Jesus's blood by including a similar but heightened sentiment expressed by Pilate after Jesus's body has been buried.[36] When the news of the empty tomb is reported, Pilate replies, "I am clean from the blood of the son of God, and this is recognized by us" (Gos. Pet. 11.46).[37] In the Gospel of Peter, "this man" from Pilate's words in Matthew has become "the son of God"—a confessional title for Jesus across the Gospels. In both places (Gos. Pet. 1.1–2; 11.46), the author seems interested in absolving Pilate of responsibility for Jesus's death by capitalizing on Matthew 27:24 and heightening its potential for Pilate's exoneration. In subsequent texts and traditions, Pilate even sometimes emerges as an explicitly Christian figure, as in the writings of Tertullian (*Apol.* 21.24)[38] and in the Gospel of Nicodemus.[39] In the latter Pilate is identified as "uncircumcised in the flesh, but circumcised in heart" (cf. Deut. 30:6; Rom. 2:25–29), establishing Pilate as a Christian convert (Gos. Nic. 12.1).[40]

Pontius Pilate in Jesus Films

Although in the canonical Gospels Pilate appears only at the end of the story, many Jesus films introduce him earlier, often with the aim of highlighting the pervasiveness of Roman rule in first-century Palestine. It can be easy to

33. Foster, *Gospel of Peter*, 199.
34. Foster, "Passion Traditions," 52–53.
35. Foster, "Passion Traditions," 53.
36. Foster raises the possibility that the author of the Gospel of Peter has portrayed Pilate washing his hands twice (just before the first extant lines and at 46) as "an *inclusio* in the text" (*Gospel of Peter*, 446–47).
37. Foster, *Gospel of Peter*, 203.
38. Cited in Carter, *Pontius Pilate*, 6–7.
39. Carter sketches five broad views of Pilate across the centuries, ranging from tyrant to saint (*Pontius Pilate*, 3–11).
40. Elliott, *Apocryphal New Testament*, 178.

underestimate the role that Rome plays in the Gospels, since Roman presence often sits in the background of these narratives. Yet Jesus films helpfully address Roman realities through their visual medium. By doing so, these films reinforce that Jesus was indeed executed by Rome as a Roman criminal. Yet the degree to which Pilate, as the most powerful Roman character in the story, remains culpable for Jesus's death varies across films along a wide spectrum.

Particularly after the Holocaust, some films make it clear that Pilate was responsible for Jesus's crucifixion. *King of Kings* (1961) is probably the best example and is notably self-conscious of its post-Holocaust context in several respects. The film's characterization of Pilate disallows any antisemitic assumption that the Jewish people were responsible for Jesus's death. Instead, Pilate emphatically declares to Jesus, "I, and I alone, have the authority to sentence you to crucifixion." Another example is the conniving Pilate of the film *Jesus* (1999), whose Machiavellian promotion of order in Judea—a refrain across the film—makes clear his culpability for Jesus's death. "Watch this," Pilate tells Caesar's historian Livio, "I've thought of the final blow," referring to the culmination of all his machinations: declaring his innocence to the crowd, washing his hands, and then calling for Jesus to be crucified. This Pilate is not at all sympathetic; even his question to Jesus about truth is asked sarcastically. Another film also firmly places full responsibility on Pilate, but it does so less explicitly. A rather simple villainizing approach is offered in BBC's *The Passion* (2008), where Pilate is brash and "othered" through his noticeable Irish accent and is characterized in sharp contrast to a highly sympathetic Caiaphas (see below).

Yet the most typical quality that Pilate possesses in film is *indecision*. This trait usually engenders sympathy, though not in the case of *Monty Python's Life of Brian* (1979). In that film, Pilate is lampooned as weak and silly, qualities conveyed in an ableist fashion through the character's lisping speech impediment. This exaggerated portrayal does not, however, erase the fact that Pilate wields immense power; he casually crucifies large groups of people—an act suggesting he will be just as cruel to Jesus. Additionally, there are no Jewish leaders in these scenes lobbying Pilate and sharing culpability.[41]

Pilate's indecision tends to create sympathy for him. He is frequently portrayed as performing small acts of kindness toward Jesus and struggling emotionally with what is taking place. In *The Passion of the Christ* (2004), Pilate appears fairly subdued throughout the trial and mildly disgusted by the violence of his soldiers. (He requests that it be "severe," though, with the hope that it will be enough to prevent crucifixion.) He is

41. Tatum, *Jesus at the Movies*, 153.

Pilate and Jesus in *The Passion of the Christ* (2004)

even modestly generous toward Jesus by offering him something to drink when they first meet. And in a private conversation with his wife, Pilate appears troubled by Jesus's comment about "truth" and the "catch-22" of an uprising (led by either Caiaphas or Jesus's followers) regardless of which decision he makes.

In *Jesus Christ Superstar* (1973), Pilate is given pretrial scenes that work to create a sympathetic portrait. When first introduced, Pilate sings of a dream he has had about Jesus in which a large crowd is maligning his own name (in the song "Pilate's Dream"). Although in the film Pilate oversees Jesus's flogging, counting out the thirty-nine lashes, he also holds and consoles the bloodied Jesus, even as the crowds insist Pilate could be "demoted" or "deported" if he doesn't crucify Jesus (in the song "Trial Before Pilate"). After the crucifixion, as the musical ends and the acting troupe is getting back on the bus, the actor who plays Pilate looks back at the cross (as do Mary and Judas separately). This action not only engenders sympathy for Pilate's apparent remorse but further suggests he was an unwilling participant in Jesus's execution.

A sympathetic account of Pilate's alleged catch-22 in Jesus's trial leaves open the possibility that he could experience redemption. The cowardice of Pilate is crucial to Mikhail Bulgakov's satirical novel *The Master and*

Margarita (1940/1967),[42] which has been adapted into several films.[43] In this story, a writer ("the master") has written an unfinished and unpublished novel about Pontius Pilate, depicting him as indecisive and distressed by the execution of "Yeshua Ha-Nozri." His regret continues to haunt him in the afterlife because he recalls Ha-Nozri's teachings about the vice of cowardice. When this story within the story is completed, Pilate is able to walk with Ha-Nozri, and Pilate begs him to ease his own conscience and say the execution never happened. Ha-Nozri agrees, thereby absolving Pilate of his feelings of guilt, and they continue to walk together into the hereafter. This unusual scene depicts the redemption of Pilate based solely on his own remorse.

Taking the redemptive trajectory further, a few films imagine that Pilate's guilt leads him to repentance and conversion. *Ponzio Pilato* (*Pontius Pilate*, 1962) makes it clear that Pilate is guilty for Jesus's death. Jesus's piercing eyes are superimposed in the water basin to signify Pilate's guilt (see chap. 5), and when he washes his hands to declare his innocence, the water basin fills with blood to indicate that Pilate has "blood on his hands."[44] Despite this explicit indictment of Pilate, he is later "shaken" into faith by the earthquake at Christ's crucifixion. His wife, Claudia, is fatally wounded by the upheaval, but with her dying words she implores Pilate to pursue "the truth." The final few seconds of the film show Pilate's subsequent trial scene before Caesar; Pilate quotes part of the Lord's Prayer and expresses that he has come to faith in Christ and that he himself will be executed as Jesus was. The film *Secondo Ponzio Pilato* (*According to Pontius Pilate*, 1987) develops these last moments further by portraying Pilate as one of the five hundred witnesses of Jesus's resurrection (cf. 1 Cor. 15:6), a recipient of angelic visitation, a miracle worker, and ultimately, a martyr. These two films offer the most sympathetic portraits of Pilate in film and are in keeping with some ecclesial traditions that regard him as a saint.

As we have seen, Pilate often becomes a rather sympathetic character in film, even when films stop short of portraying him as a Christian convert. Pilate's portrait falls along a similar trajectory to Judas's characterization,

42. The novel was completed in 1940 but remained suppressed during Bulgakov's life. Yet, proving that "manuscripts don't burn," it was published posthumously in 1967.

43. Cf. *The Master and Margaret* (1972); *The Master and Margarita* (1994); and the TV show *Master i Margarita* (*The Master and Margarita*, 2005). Films that have adapted the first-century storyline embedded within the larger narrative are *Pilatus und Andere: Ein Film für Karfreitag* (*Pilate and Others*, 1972); *Incident in Judaea* (1991). Influences from the original novel can also be found in, e.g., *Histoire de Judas* (*Story of Judas*, 2015).

44. *The Gospel of Matthew* (2016) has a similar effect signifying Pilate's guilt. In *Jesus Christ Superstar* (1973), Pilate washes off Jesus's blood in the basin, but to different effect since it is Jesus's actual blood from Pilate holding Jesus after his flogging.

but with a quite different effect. Whereas Judas's increasingly sympathetic portrayal can be understood as a reaction to the evils of the Holocaust and of anti-Jewish sentiment, Pilate's character development works in the opposite direction. The more sympathy that is given to Pilate, the more culpability is placed squarely on the Jewish people. If Pilate is off the hook, who else is to blame?

The Portraits of Jewish Leadership and Crowds

Jewish Leadership and Crowds in the Canonical Gospels

In the four canonical Gospels neither the Jewish leaders nor the Jewish crowds are homogeneous groups, especially when we pay close attention to their portrayals across each individual Gospel. Yet these crowds and leaders are frequently treated as monolithic; even more, they are often problematically conflated, with blame falling on the entire Jewish people for Jesus's death, bringing horrific consequences. Close study of the Gospels, however, does not support the types of conflations we so often see in subsequent retellings of the Jesus story.

Jewish Leadership

Jewish leadership, consisting of several distinct sects or groups, is a prominent character group across Jesus's ministry and his passion. In the Synoptics (Matthew especially), scribes and Pharisees are Jesus's primary interlocutors during his Galilean ministry because of their shared assumptions about the law,[45] and a variety of additional Jewish groups populate the landscape of Jerusalem, including priests, elders, Sadducees, and Herodians. According to Matthew, when Jesus arrives in Jerusalem, various Jewish leadership groups come together to catch him in a trap (21:23–22:46). Once the passion account begins (26:1–5), Matthew focuses primarily on "the chief priests and elders of the people" as the key antagonists working to have Jesus executed by Rome (e.g., 26:3, 47; 27:1, 12, 20).[46] Even the large crowd that appears during Jesus's arrest has been "sent from the chief priests and the elders of the people" (26:47). If we were to read only Matthew's Gospel, we'd be unaware of exceptions to the characterization of the Jewish leaders as Jesus's antagonists.

45. Brown, "Reconstructing the Historical Pharisees," 174.

46. Additionally, Matthew includes scribes at the cross (27:41) and Pharisees at the request for Jesus's body (27:62).

Yet there are positive portrayals of Jewish leaders from the other Gospels. Mark identifies Joseph of Arimathea, who buries Jesus's body, as "a prominent member of the Council" (i.e., the Sanhedrin). Joseph is portrayed positively as one "who was himself waiting for the kingdom of God" and who "boldly" asks Pilate for Jesus's body (Mark 15:43; see also Luke 23:50).[47] Luke offers a more varied portrait of the Pharisees by narrating the presence of Pharisees who take an opportunity to warn Jesus about Herod's nefarious intentions (Luke 13:31; cf. Acts 15:5). John introduces Nicodemus, a Pharisee and member of the ruling council (John 3:1), whose portrayal moves from one who questions Jesus to one who is sympathetic to Jesus and prepares his body for burial (7:50–51; 19:38–40).[48] The Gospels, while generally highlighting the Jewish leaders as key antagonists of Jesus, also provide relief to this portrait by characterizing some leaders as aligned with Jesus's interests.

Caiaphas deserves specific attention, given his central role in Jesus's trial before the Sanhedrin. Caiaphas was high priest during the time of Jesus's execution by Rome (with his tenure spanning about 18–36 CE).[49] He interrogates Jesus on behalf of the Jewish council before sending him to Pilate (Matt. 26:57–68; cf. Mark 14:53–65).[50] In Matthew, Caiaphas questions Jesus about the testimony against him and, when Jesus doesn't answer, places him under an oath to reveal if he is the Messiah (26:59–63). Jesus responds cryptically and alludes to Daniel 7:13 to identify himself with the vindicated Son of Man (26:64).[51] Caiaphas accuses Jesus of blasphemy, and the council confirms he should die (26:65–66) and delivers him to Pilate for judgment (27:1–2). In each presentation of Caiaphas, he is a crucial Jewish authority propelling Jesus's execution.

Jewish Crowds

Reading through Mark's passion narrative, another Jewish group that emerges during Jesus's Roman trial is the crowd that "the chief priests stirred up" (15:11), who calls out twice for Pilate to crucify Jesus. Shortly before that, we hear of "a crowd armed with swords and clubs, sent from the chief priests,

47. Matthew makes no mention of Joseph of Arimathea being a leader within Judaism, offering no positive portraits of Jewish leadership.

48. Culpepper, "Nicodemus."

49. For a detailed analysis of the historical and literary figure, see Bond, *Caiaphas*.

50. John includes an additional hearing before Annas (also called "high priest"; cf. John 18:19, 24), who is Caiaphas's father-in-law. See Luke's indication (3:2) that John the Baptist's ministry began "during the high-priesthood of Annas and Caiaphas" (with the word for "priest" [*archiereus*] used in the singular here). Annas was high priest from 6 to 15 CE (see Josephus, *Ant*. 18.2.2 [18.35]) and may have continued his influence thereafter.

51. For the import of his answer, see Brown and Roberts, *Matthew*, 244–45.

the teachers of the law, and the elders" (14:43) that joins Judas for Jesus's arrest. If this specific crowd or mob is identified with "the crowds" as they are portrayed more generally across Mark, it can be easy enough to assign central blame for Jesus's death to the Jewish people.[52] Yet already in Mark's Gospel, the culpability of the Jewish crowds is mitigated by the significant influence of the Jewish leaders on them. They act as these leaders want them to act. It is also crucial to check the tendency to read the crowds uniformly across the narrative. We should not assume that Mark wants his audience to identify the crowds in Galilee, who are often portrayed as positively responding to Jesus's ministry (e.g., 1:45; 2:12; 6:33–34; 7:37), with the Jerusalem crowd sent by the Jewish leadership (14:43) and later "stirred up" to call for Jesus's crucifixion (15:11) in the passion narrative.

In Matthew's Gospel, there is a clear distinction drawn between the Galilean crowds and a Jerusalem "mob" organized by Jewish leaders to ensure that their plans against Jesus succeed. For Matthew, the Galilean crowds respond positively to Jesus's ministry even as they do not always understand everything he is about (e.g., 9:33; 12:23; 15:31). Those who have faith in Jesus and experience his healing power are almost always Jewish individuals who come from the Jewish crowds following Jesus around Galilee (e.g., 9:2, 22, 29). When Jesus and his disciples travel to Jerusalem for Passover, crowds from Galilee also making that Passover journey hail him as prophet and king ("Son of David") as they all enter Jerusalem (21:9, 11). In this episode, Matthew distinguishes this Galilean crowd from people in Jerusalem wondering who Jesus is (21:10). As R. T. France comments, "The people of the city have every reason to see trouble ahead as the unruly Galilean crowd bring 'their' prophet into Jerusalem in a royal procession."[53]

In Matthew's passion narrative, the crowd sent by Jewish leaders for Jesus's arrest, a crowd that is then present for Jesus's Roman trial (26:47; 27:17, 20), is not likely to be identified simply with the Galilean crowds, given the earlier distinction in Matthew 21. Instead, it functions narratively as a "mob put together by the Jerusalem leadership."[54] This careful differentiation provides context for interpreting Matthew's inclusion of the cry of the Jewish people (*laos*) at Jesus's trial: "And all the people [who were present] answered, 'Might his blood be upon us and on our children!'" (27:25, our translation). This line

52. Since we can affirm that most of the characters across Mark's Gospel (and in each of the four Gospels) are Jewish, including Jesus and his followers, we can conclude that the Jewish crowds that each Gospel highlights cannot be read—as they too often have been read—as representative of all Jewish people in Jesus's day.

53. France, *Gospel of Matthew*, 782.

54. Brown and Roberts, *Matthew*, 242.

has reverberated across history in harmful ways, but it is not to be imputed to all Jewish people in all times. It is not even applicable to all Jewish people in the first-century world, or even all Jewish people in Matthew's narrative. Additionally, Matthew's final word on the "people" (*laos*; 27:64) describes their susceptibility to the "deception" that Jesus has been resurrected.[55] They continue to be open to the report that Jesus has been raised.[56]

In John's Gospel, the routine use of *hoi Ioudaioi* (traditionally, "the Jews") for Jesus's opponents contributes to the tendency to assign blame for Jesus's death to the Jewish people across history. While *hoi Ioudaioi* has traditionally been rendered "the Jews" in English translations, a careful look at each usage shows that its referents shift between at least two Johannine character groups: Jewish crowds and Jewish leadership. The Jewish crowds show a mixed reception of Jesus, with some seeing him in a favorable light and others questioning his identity and actions. The Jewish leaders as a character group are uniformly portrayed as Jesus's antagonists.[57] The clearest example of John making a distinction between these groups comes in John 7, where *hoi Ioudaioi* are watching out for Jesus at the Festival of Tabernacles (7:11). John then notes a disagreement among the crowds—*en tois ochlois*—about Jesus, with some affirming that he is good and others claiming he "deceives the crowds [*ton ochlon*]" (7:12, our translation). This scenario concludes, "No one [from the Jewish crowds] was saying anything about him openly because they feared *tōn Ioudaiōn*" (7:13, our translation). In this scene, the disagreement among the Jewish crowds about Jesus helps us recognize that *hoi Ioudaioi* here cannot refer to all Jews in John's storyline. Instead, it is used in this case to refer to a smaller group, likely the Jewish leaders, that is pressing the crowds to take a negative view of Jesus (cf. 7:31–32).[58]

Thus, there are layers of complexity in the canonical Gospels that disallow monolithic and uniformly negative views of the Jewish people. Instead, the Jewish people (apart from their leaders) are usually portrayed either positively or at least neutrally in relationship to Jesus. We should add here a historical note about the Gospels' literary portrayal. First, we cannot ignore the way that Roman power provoked the conflict and made it worse. Second, few, if

55. Carter, *Matthew and the Margins*, 528.

56. Brown and Roberts, *Matthew*, 251.

57. Even as a few specifically identified leaders are positively portrayed; e.g., Joseph of Arimathea (John 19:38) and Nicodemus (7:50; 19:39).

58. To represent this distinction between two referents for *hoi Ioudaioi*, the NIV translates *hoi Ioudaioi* as "Jewish leaders" in 1:19; 5:10, 15, 16; 7:1, 11, 13; 9:22; 18:14, 28, 36; 19:7, 12, 31, 38; 20:19, including a footnote at 1:19 that reads, "The Greek term traditionally translated *the Jews* (*hoi Ioudaioi*) refers here and elsewhere in John's Gospel to those Jewish leaders who opposed Jesus."

any, in the Gospels' original audiences would have viewed the Jewish people portrayed in them as representative of all Jewish people in the first century. They would have been acutely aware that the first generation of Jesus followers was overwhelmingly made up of Jewish people (e.g., Acts 1–7). It is only as the church gained greater numbers of gentiles that the Gospels could even begin to be read as an indictment of the whole of the Jewish people.

Jewish Leadership and Crowds in Later Gospels

Fueled in part by anti-Jewish polemic, subsequent Gospels exhibit a growing trend of both laying the blame for Jesus's crucifixion on the Jewish people as a whole and portraying Jewish leaders as particularly obstinate. In contrast to the canonical Gospels, the Gospel of Peter (which follows a tendency to exonerate Pilate; see above) narrates Jesus being delivered over to the Jewish people (Gos. Pet. 2.5), who proceed to mock, beat, and crucify him (3.6–5.16).[59] The writer then summarizes, "And they [the Jewish people] fulfilled all things and they accumulated the sins on their head" (5.17).[60] The Gospel of Peter thus adjusts and emphasizes the earlier canonical stories of Jesus to "incriminate Jews for the death of Jesus."[61]

In the Gospel of Nicodemus (fourth–fifth century CE),[62] the Jewish leaders are singularly inflexible, trying to mislead the people to keep them from discovering the truth about Jesus. In the first part of the Gospel of Nicodemus (i.e., the Acts of Pilate), set during Jesus's trial before Pilate, the Jewish leaders, including Annas and Caiaphas and other named figures, attempt to persuade Pilate to crucify Jesus. They claim that Jesus blasphemes, breaks the Sabbath, and has illegitimate parentage (cf. Gos. Nic. 1.1; 2.3–4). Yet eyewitnesses refute these claims, and Pilate does not go along with the Jewish leaders (Gos. Nic. 2–9). Later, Caiaphas and Annas aim to discredit witnesses of Jesus's resurrection and ascension (Gos. Nic. 13–16) and even those who were raised to life at the time of Jesus's death (Gos. Nic. 17.1; cf. Matt. 27:52). These characterization choices make the Jewish leaders appear foolishly immovable in the face of clear evidence. In a Latin recension of the Gospel of Nicodemus that includes the Epistle of Pilate to Claudius, Pilate goes so far as to write to Caesar about all that the Jewish leaders have done to cover up Jesus's resurrection and so keep the news from spreading among the people.[63]

59. Henderson, *Gospel of Peter*, 59.

60. Foster, *Gospel of Peter*, 199.

61. Ehrman, *New Testament and Other Early Christian Writings*, 124.

62. Composed of the Acts of Pilate, Christ's Descent into Hell, and, in one Latin recension, the Epistle of Pilate to Claudius.

63. Elliott, *Apocryphal New Testament*, 206.

In their respective ways, the Gospel of Peter and the Gospel of Nicodemus illustrate how the Jewish crowds and leaders are increasingly villainized in subsequent retellings of the Jesus story, even as more sympathetic approaches to Pilate are offered—a trajectory that continues into film.

Jewish Leadership and Crowds in Jesus Films

The Jewish leaders and crowds are routinely depicted as evil in Jesus films, one of the enduring problematic features in visualizations of the Jesus story. This tendency precedes the invention of film; it was already evident in the medieval passion play tradition, such as the well-known play in Oberammergau, Germany, that continues to the present. From its origins, this famous passion play, in Jeremy Cohen's words, "demonized Jesus' Jewish enemies on stage."[64]

A common choice for villainizing Jewish figures is costuming them in black or dark attire—the most common visual trope for villains in theater and film. Yet wearing black was uncommon in antiquity outside of particular settings—for example, times of mourning[65]—so something other than historical considerations perpetuates this costuming choice. *Jesus Christ Superstar* (1973) stands out for its black costuming of all Jewish leaders (including a tall Caiaphas with a bass voice), collapsing the differing Jewish sects "into a single amorphous but markedly Jewish opposition" to Jesus.[66] As Jesus enters Jerusalem, the Jewish leaders are strewn about on scaffolding overlooking the city, singing, "He is dangerous" (in the song "This Jesus Must Die"). In their black attire, they resemble vultures, ready to swoop in and feast on his dead flesh.[67]

The Jewish leaders and crowds are also often portrayed as unkempt relative to their Roman counterparts, creating a sharp physiognomic contrast between these ethnic groups. This disparity is notable in the silent German film *Der Galiläer* (*The Galilean*, 1921), where the Jewish characters have bulging eyes and untidy beards—never mind their visible horns. This presentation persists even in more recent Jesus films. In *The Passion of the Christ* (2004), Jewish characters have longer beards and are missing teeth, while the Romans are clean-cut. Historically, it is unlikely that Caiaphas, Annas, and other priests would have had long beards, given scriptural requirements for priests to keep their hair trimmed (Ezek. 44:20).[68] Yet in Jesus films, Jewish leaders are often depicted with long hair and beards, in unkempt fashion.

64. Cohen, *Christ Killers*, 214–15.
65. Turner, "Representation of New Testament Figures," 236.
66. Mills, "Politics of Jesus' Death."
67. Cf. Walsh and Staley, *Jesus, the Gospels, and Cinematic Imagination*, 134.
68. Turner, "Representation of New Testament Figures," 97.

Jewish leaders in *Jesus Christ Superstar* (1973) portrayed as vultures

While Jewish characters are demonized with horns in *Der Galiläer* (*The Galilean*, 1921), the Danish film *Blade af Satans Bog* (*Leaves from Satan's Book*, 1920) is more creative but just as horrendous with its demonization. At one point, Satan takes the form of a Pharisee to manipulate Judas and Caiaphas to proceed with the plan to execute Jesus. This choice to portray the devil in the guise of a Pharisee not only villainizes but demonizes the Jewish leadership. Moreover, the lurking presence of Satan in *The Passion of the Christ* (2004) does not merely convey satanic interest in the death of the Son of God; it also suggests his malevolent influence among those whom the film portrays as most unwavering in their determination to crucify Jesus—chief among them being Caiaphas.

Although not precisely a demonization, *Godspell* (1973) displays a monstrous version of the Pharisees. A giant mechanical head aggressively confronts Jesus, inquiring about the source of his authority. Jesus responds with a litany of woes for "lawyers and Pharisees" drawn from Matthew 23:13–32 and Luke 11:37–52. Some scholars interpret this Pharisaic monster to be a representation of technology, a transposition of Jesus's canonical critique of Pharisees and legal experts to a modern set of concerns.[69] Adele Reinhartz also contends that this characterization "circumvents the problem of anti-Judaism,"[70] although the degree to which it does so depends on how readily the viewer can make the same association between the Pharisaic monster and technology. Lloyd Baugh, conversely, calls it a "disturbing episode."[71] At the very least, the villainization of the Pharisees will be reinforced for many viewers through this monstrous representation.

69. Walsh, *Reading the Gospels in the Dark*, 87.
70. Reinhartz, *Jesus of Hollywood*, 202.
71. Baugh, *Imaging the Divine*, 44.

Another negative Jewish stereotype reinforced in Jesus films involves associations with greed. In DeMille's *The King of Kings* (1927), the character of Caiaphas is flattened into a greedy miser motivated only by money, even though there is no such indication in the canonical Gospels. A similar trope is perpetuated in the series *Mesih* (*Jesus, the Spirit of God*, 2010), where Pilate confronts the Jewish leadership about vaults of gold hidden underneath the temple's holy of holies and declares to Caiaphas later on, "Your god is money!" In *The King of Kings*, Caiaphas's greed propels him to plot behind the scenes to trap Jesus at several points in his ministry. For example, the question to Jesus about whether taxes should be paid to Caesar originates with Caiaphas (cf. Matt. 22:15–22).[72]

There are a few exceptions to these thoroughly negative representations of Caiaphas. For example, *Jesus of Nazareth* (1977) offers a more sympathetic version of Caiaphas while creating a new (Jewish) character, Zerah, to be the mastermind behind Jesus's execution. This substitution diverts blame from Caiaphas, who shows empathy for "our brother" Jesus, although it doesn't eradicate concerns about cinematic representations of Jewish leadership. Though fictional, Zerah is still a Jewish leader who is seen pulling the strings to bring about Jesus's death. The most positive and expansive portrayal of Caiaphas comes in BBC's *The Passion* (2008). In that series, Caiaphas is portrayed as empathetic and personable, someone who cares deeply for the people in his community. He's a family man, and he and his wife share many tender moments throughout the series. His personability sharply contrasts with the arrogance of Pilate. While Caiaphas is depicted as keen to stop Jesus, he intends to turn him over to the Romans only "if he doesn't repent." After the crucifixion, Caiaphas needs to be consoled by his wife about all that has transpired.

Caiaphas's portrayal in Jesus films vis-à-vis the characterization of Pilate often raises concerns about antisemitism. A sympathetic or even neutral Pilate paired with a malevolent Caiaphas is a particularly problematic combination. The main culprits in this regard are films like *Jesus Christ Superstar* (1973) and *The Passion of the Christ* (2004).

Concern about anti-Judaism in Jesus films, however, most often centers on the inclusion of the "blood cry" from Matthew 27:25 (i.e., "His blood is on us and on our children"). In response to worries about possible antisemitism, *The Passion of the Christ* (2004) retained these words in Aramaic but with subtitles removed.[73] Perhaps due to its inflammatory quality, the "blood cry"

72. Caiaphas also sentences the woman caught in adultery (cf. John 7:53–8:11) in *The King of Kings*. Caiaphas has long-term antagonism toward Jesus in *Jesús, María y José* (*Jesus, Mary and Joseph*, 1972), where he is cast as young Jesus's overbearing schoolteacher.

73. Malone, *Screen Jesus*, 160–61, 167. Additionally, the words are rather indistinct.

BBC / Deep Indigo Productions / HBO Films

Caiaphas and his wife, Abigail, in *The Passion* (2008)

is absent from many Jesus films. The only films "required" to include it are the films committed to representing the whole of Matthew's text—for example, *Il Vangelo Secondo Matteo* (*The Gospel According to St. Matthew*, 1964), *The Gospel According to Matthew* (1993), and *The Gospel of Matthew* (2016). For these films ("visual translations"; cf. chap. 1), the "blood cry" presents a difficulty. Since a film cannot easily convey Matthew's nuanced distinction between different crowds (see above), the challenge is how to forestall the problematic implication that Jewish culpability lasts into perpetuity. Yet the visual medium does afford filmmakers a unique opportunity to invite viewers to think about the passage differently. In *The Gospel of Matthew* (2016), for example, the camera fixes on Pilate's water basin in an overhead shot as the cloth that Pilate uses to wash his hands now spreads blood throughout the basin. The camera does not shift to the crowd with the words of Matthew 27:25 but continues to linger on the basin. This choice suggests that Pilate is the one who is ultimately responsible for Jesus's death despite what is said by the people.

Conclusion

With this chapter, we conclude our examination of characterization in the Jesus story (chaps. 4–6). The antagonists of the Jesus story have been easy to villainize, especially as their literary characterizations in the Gospels are not particularly well developed and so provide many gaps to fill in. As ancient and modern storytellers have pondered these cursory portraits to understand the motivations and actions of Jesus's antagonists, they have either intensified negative traits through stereotyping ("vilifying") or found ways to make these characters more compelling and thus (usually) more sympathetic. As we have seen, there have been trends toward making Judas and Pilate more sympathetic, and the Jewish leaders (specifically Caiaphas) less so. Significantly, increased sympathy for Judas has quite different implications than sympathy for Pilate. If both characters are portrayed sympathetically in a film, then the Jewish leaders are typically collateral damage (e.g., *Jesus Christ Superstar* [1973]). A sympathetic portrayal of Pilate paired with an unsympathetic portrayal of Judas or Jewish leaders can (sometimes inadvertently) communicate an anti-Jewish message (e.g., *The Passion of the Christ* [2004]).[74] Either way, Jewish characters are easily villainized and vilified, with potentially negative stereotyping of actual Jewish people—as history has shown. These stark realities invite those of us who are committed to reading and retelling the Jesus story thoughtfully and accurately to interrogate the Jesus film that we already are directing in our own minds for themes of antisemitism and for any tendency to vilify a particular people group as we fill in characterization gaps.

74. We'd do well to remember the historical realities that Pilate executed Jesus's sentence and that Jesus died as a criminal of Rome—something Christians confess in the Apostles' Creed: "He suffered under Pontius Pilate."

Themes Woven into the Jesus Story

When stories are retold, especially those about Jesus, storytellers tend to expand on earlier iterations through harmonizing, filling in gaps, and developing characters in new directions (as we have seen). In the process, certain themes also often take on greater prominence—themes that stress different parts of a story's message than previous iterations. Such themes may arise from patterns that readers recognize within the story, or they may be imported into the story wholesale. The emergence of fresh themes with each retelling of the Jesus story is already detectable within the four canonical Gospels themselves, and new themes emerge in the cinematic retellings of the Jesus story. While we could provide almost as many examples as there are Jesus films, we will focus our attention on a few particularly interesting examples, touching on other films along the way. After analyzing some distinctive themes in the Jesus story that appear in our earliest literary sources, we will closely examine *The Last Temptation of Christ* (1988), *Jesus* (1999), *Mesih* (*Jesus, the Spirit of God*, 2010), and *The Chosen* (2017–present).

Themes in Ancient Retellings

Each of the four canonical Gospels develops themes, many of them distinctive, and incorporates them into its storyline. In Matthew's Gospel, Jesus recapitulates (or relives) key moments in Israel's history (e.g., the exodus and exile; Matt. 2:15) and fulfills "the Law and the Prophets" (a recurring phrase). In addition to the theme of *fulfillment*, Matthew emphasizes Jesus as the divine presence among his people (Matt. 1:23; 28:20; cf. 18:20) and the Davidic Messiah, who nonetheless gives up his kingly rights to serve others and "give his life as a ransom for many" (Matt. 20:28). In Mark's Gospel, Jesus is the enigmatic Messiah who cannot be understood apart from the cross. While even his own followers struggle to understand his identity, his power over sickness and evil is palpable. Despite this Gospel's "cliff-hanger" ending (Mark 16:8)—with his female followers leaving the tomb in fear—the promise that the resurrected Jesus will rejoin his disciples rings out from its final lines.

In Luke's Gospel, Jesus is the Messiah who brings good news to the poor and the marginalized, a motif that is signaled in his preaching in Nazareth at the beginning of his Galilean ministry (Luke 4:14–20). Other groups that receive particular attention in Luke include women, Samaritans, "sinners," and tax collectors. In this Gospel, the wide inclusiveness of Jesus's ministry is emphasized, even as Luke introduces motifs like salvation, repentance, and gentile inclusion, which will be prominent in his second work, the book of Acts. In John's Gospel, Jesus is portrayed as the Messiah of life in line with the theme of creation's renewal in that Gospel.[1] Consistent with John's penchant for metaphor, Jesus is also characterized as the Passover lamb, the bread of life, the light of the world, and more. These christological themes are mobilized to engender belief and trust so that John's readers might have life in Jesus's name (John 20:30–31). These are just some of the distinctive emphases and themes that we find in each of the four Gospels.

Given the ways the Jesus story has inspired so many, it is perhaps unsurprising that its retellings have generated a great variety of themes. Early examples include the concise retellings embedded in the New Testament outside of the Gospels. For example, in the poetic material of Philippians 2:5–11, Colossians 1:15–20, and 1 Peter 3:18–22, we find clear, albeit brief, story-shaped summaries of the Jesus story—sequences of events that include preexistence, incarnation, death, and exaltation (cf. also Acts 2:22–36; Rev. 12:1–6). In these retellings of the Jesus story in miniature, themes that are only minimally addressed in the Gospels are incorporated or highlighted (e.g., the metaphor of Jesus as a "slave" [*doulos*] in Phil. 2:7; the notion of Jesus being the "image" [*eikōn*] of God in Col. 1:15).

The noncanonical Gospel of Philip emphasizes a theme that is nowhere present in the canonical Gospels—the soteriological theme in Valentinian

1. Brown, *Gospels as Stories*, 135–43.

Gnosticism pertaining to the ritual of the "bridal chamber," which some see as serving to develop Mary Magdalene's "companionship" with Jesus (see chap. 4; cf. Gos. Phil. 63.25–64.9). In the Gospel of Philip, Jesus says, "The Lord [did] everything in a mystery, a baptism and a chrism and a eucharist and a redemption and a bridal chamber" (67.27–30),[2] with the bridal chamber possibly being either a distinct ritual or a reality that is true of those who are baptized.[3] It becomes apparent elsewhere in the Gospel of Philip that this bridal chamber does not establish a marital union between a man and a woman, although it may be that earthly marriage prefigures it.[4] Instead, the "bridal chamber" ritual reunites a person with their masculine or feminine spiritual counterpart (65.7–12). In this text, the human plight is the division of Adam and Eve from the singular person who originally inhabited the primeval garden, with that division leading to death (68.22–26; cf. Gen. 2:18–25). The good news, according to the Gospel of Philip, is that Christ has come to overcome this division, restoring humanity to its original wholeness with no more death (Gos. Phil. 70.9–22). The theme of the "bridal chamber" is woven into the implied storyline of Jesus's mission and purpose, and in the process, changes the story substantially.

Themes in Jesus Films

Our earlier discussions of gaps, harmonization, and characterization have already surfaced any number of themes in Jesus films. We explored the theme of Jesus discovering his true identity in *The Young Messiah* (chap. 3) and the effect of the motif of race on Jesus's messianic legitimacy in *Color of the Cross* (2006) and *Color of the Cross 2: The Resurrection* (2008) (chap. 5). In one of the earliest Jesus films, *La Vie du Christ* (or *La Naissance, La Vie et La Mort du Christ* [*The Birth, the Life and the Death of Christ*, 1906]), we observed how telling the Jesus story through Jesus's interactions with female characters emphasizes the theme of good news for women (chap. 2), already a motif in Luke's Gospel. In recent decades, feminist themes have been developed more robustly in Jesus films like *Mary Magdalene* (2018) and *Io Sono Con Te* (*Let It Be*, 2010). This focus is perhaps most pronounced in the latter film, as it presents Mary struggling against the violence of religious ritual and patriarchy (noted in chap. 5). In a reimagination of the infancy narrative, *Io*

2. Isenberg, "Gospel of Philip," 140.

3. Thomassen, *Spiritual Seed*, 100, 341–42, 344; cf. Gos. Phil. 65.7–12; 69.1–4, 22–25; 71.3–15; 72.20–23; 74.16–22; 74.36–75.2; 75.25–76.5; 82.2–6; 84.20–23; 85.19–21; 85.32–86.5.

4. See esp. DeConick, "True Mysteries."

Sono Con Te (*Let It Be*, 2010) portrays several male magi arriving to see the toddler Jesus and inspect his living conditions to determine whether Mary is able to raise him properly so he can fulfill his destiny. This and other plot additions heighten the film's feminist rejection of patriarchal religion. In the rest of this chapter, we take a closer look at four specific themes, focusing on a particular film or series for each.

The Battle of Flesh and Spirit in **The Last Temptation of Christ** *(1988)*

Martin Scorsese's *The Last Temptation of Christ* (1988) provides an example of how a theme can significantly reshape the way the story of Jesus is told. The film is based on a novel by Nikos Kazantzakis (1952), and the opening caption includes a quotation from the book to establish the film's main theme:

> The dual substance of Christ—
> the yearning, so human,
> so superhuman,
> of man to attain God . . .
> has always been a deep
> inscrutable mystery to me.
> My principle anguish and source
> of all my joys and sorrows
> from my youth onward
> has been the incessant,
> merciless battle between
> the spirit and the flesh . . .
> and my soul is the arena
> where these two armies
> have clashed and met.[5]

This opening caption establishes that the film is ultimately an exploration of the human struggle between flesh and spirit. Another caption follows to signal that the film is not a straightforward retelling of the story of Jesus: "This film is not based upon the Gospels but upon this fictional exploration of the eternal spiritual conflict." Thus, the driving force of this film is not the canonical story of Jesus but the theme of the flesh-spirit tension. In line with that theme, Jesus is a reluctant Messiah who consistently wrestles with his calling, his identity,

5. The film's quote comes from the English translation of Kazantzakis's novel (*The Last Temptation of Christ*, 1), though with some minor differences, such as the film's incorporation of poetic spacing and the spelling of "principal" as "principle."

Jesus in *The Last Temptation of Christ* (1988)

the content of his message, and whether his mission is worth what he is leaving behind. Even as Jesus wrestles with his relationship with God, he assiduously tries to avoid succumbing to temptation, because he is afraid of what will happen if he sins. This Jesus is unquestionably human rather than divine, and the camerawork serves to reinforce this identity by filming him "from above." The earlier Jesus film tradition tended to film Jesus "from below."[6] The film *gives* Jesus his full humanity, even as it *takes away* his sanity.

Nevertheless, the struggle between flesh and spirit in *The Last Temptation of Christ* is not simply internal to Jesus; it is also externalized in Jesus's relationship with Judas, with the suggestion that they reflect the archetypal struggle of flesh (Judas) and spirit (Jesus). The two are portrayed as long-standing friends even before Jesus's ministry begins. Yet the way that Jesus uses his vocation as a carpenter to make crosses for Rome disturbs Judas, who is associated with the Zealots, creating tension in their relationship.

This entanglement with Rome foreshadows Jesus's death on a cross. In fact, the presence of crosses becomes something of a trope in retellings of

6. Walsh, *Reading the Gospels in the Dark*, 6.

Kalem Company

The boy Jesus carrying a beam of wood and making the shape of a cross with his shadow in *From the Manger to the Cross* (1912)

the Jesus story. Sometimes crosses function as harbingers as Jesus's family witnesses crucifixions,[7] while at other times crosses are directly connected to the family business of carpentry (cf. Mark 6:3)—for example, when Jesus unknowingly forms the shape of a cross with his shadow as he carries a chunk of wood into the family workshop in *From the Manger to the Cross* (1912).[8] In a few Jesus films, Joseph is recruited to construct crosses for Rome: He is forced to make crosses in *La Sacra Famiglia* (*The Holy Family*, 2006), and he refuses to do so in *Jesús, María y José* (*Jesus, Mary and Joseph*, 1972).[9] In both films, the situation prompts young Jesus to create toy crosses for himself out of wood and nails.[10] *The Last Temptation of Christ* significantly extends

7. E.g., while traveling to Bethlehem (*Per Amore, Solo per Amore* [*For Love, Only for Love*, 1993]; *Marie de Nazareth* [*Mary of Nazareth*, 1995]) or when returning from Egypt (*The Greatest Story Ever Told* [1965]; *Un Bambino di Nome Gesù* [*A Child Called Jesus*, 1987]).

8. Cf. also Jesus's shadow as he teaches in the temple in *Christus* (1916).

9. Although lacking the component of Roman oppression, Joseph also makes crosses in *The Thorn* (*The Greatest Story Overtold* / *The Divine Mr. J*, 1971).

10. In a few ancient Gospels, Jesus and Joseph work on carpentry projects together (Inf. Gos. Thom. 13; Gos. Phil. 73.8–19), and in Gospel of Philip, Joseph even makes the very cross used for Jesus's crucifixion.

this minor trope by having Jesus use his carpentry skills to build crosses like the one that will someday end his own life—a metaphor designed to highlight the self-destructive power of the flesh.

Confused and reluctant Messiahs also appeared on-screen before *The Last Temptation of Christ*. In *Son of Man* (1969),[11] a film that shares affinities with *The Last Temptation of Christ*, Jesus's reluctance and confusion is introduced during his wilderness temptation, with Jesus thrashing about and screaming, "Is it me?" before frantically asserting, "It is me! It is me!" Jesus's posture of wrestling with his calling never goes away in this film; his ramblings grow increasingly esoteric, and his impatience with his disciples builds. In one scene, while Jesus is with his disciples and surrounded by several crosses, he claims that one cross is actually "a tree" that "God put . . . into the soil." He berates the disciples for not understanding his meaning, and they leave him. Then Jesus speaks directly to the cross: "You should have stayed a tree, and I should have stayed a carpenter." When he is crucified, he utters a single poignant saying from the cross about God forsaking him (Mark 15:34), after which *Son of Man* cuts to credits as Jesus hangs dead on the cross, never having come to terms with what God called him to do.

The Last Temptation of Christ explores themes similar to those of *Son of Man* but adds complexity to the motif of Jesus's reluctance. This complexity is especially apparent as Jesus navigates his calling vis-à-vis his "fleshly" desire to be married and have a family—a mounting tension that leads to the titular "last temptation." In the clearest expression of this tension, Jesus decides against pursuing a romantic relationship with Mary Magdalene, which apparently drives her into sex work (cf. chap. 4) and contributes to Jesus's deep sense of regret about following a calling he barely understands. Later, Jesus asks for Mary's forgiveness, inverting the pattern of most Jesus films, where it is Mary who needs Jesus's forgiveness.[12]

The evolution of Jesus's teaching across three phases in the film provides another indication of his ambivalence, as well as the tension between flesh and spirit. In the first phase, Jesus's teaching focuses exclusively on love and peace. In the second, he becomes enamored with rhetorically wielding "the axe" that John the Baptist has spoken about (cf. Matt. 3:10), producing a much harsher and challenging message. During the third phase, Jesus comes to realize, in light of Isaiah 53, that he must die to save souls. As Jesus's message changes, so does Judas's support for him. Judas has no interest in Jesus's message of peace, but he responds with unflinching loyalty to Jesus as he moves to the

11. Brian from *Monty Python's Life of Brian* (1979) is also a reluctant Messiah.

12. Reinhartz, *Jesus of Hollywood*, 147. More to this point, Jesus even wipes Mary Magdalene's feet in a separate scene.

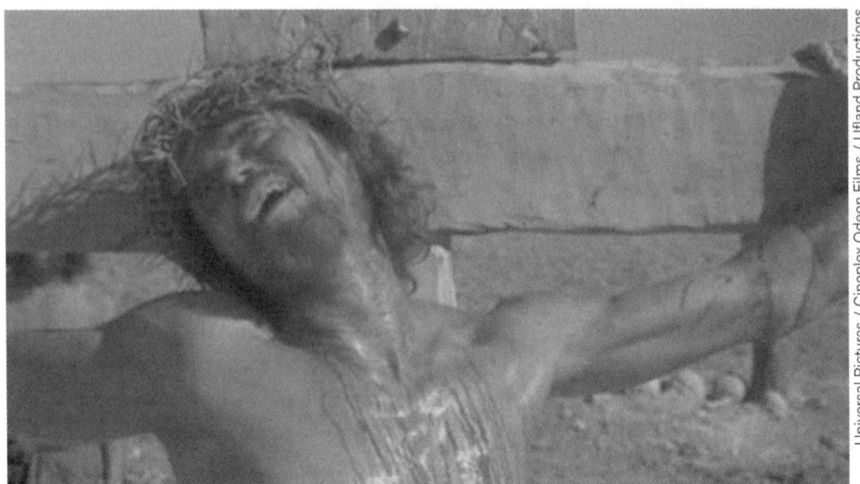

Jesus uttering the words "It is accomplished" after resisting the temptation to leave the cross and start a family in *The Last Temptation of Christ* (1988)

(second) harsh phase, even calling Jesus "Adonai" (Lord). When Jesus finally decides that he must die, Judas reflects a "fleshly" perspective by rejecting the idea that saving souls has any value. Yet for the plan to work, Jesus needs Judas to betray him, which he grudgingly agrees to do.

As Jesus is crucified, his "last temptation" begins. As he hangs on the cross, having just cried out about being forsaken, he experiences a vision in which he is escorted from the cross by Satan disguised as a guardian angel. From there, he goes on to marry Mary Magdalene. When she dies shortly thereafter, Jesus starts a family with both Mary and Martha of Bethany. The visionary experience culminates decades later with the destruction of Jerusalem (70 CE). Jesus, frail and on his deathbed, is visited by Judas, Peter, Nathaniel, and John, who each rebuke him (especially Judas) for abandoning the revolution that has led to this catastrophic event. Feeling intense guilt and shame, Jesus finally resists these tempting visions and decides he wants to be God's Son and obey God's mission to die. In that moment of clarity, Jesus realizes he is still on the cross and that he has thwarted Satan a final time. Triumphantly he twice declares, "It is accomplished," and the film comes to a close.

The Last Temptation of Christ, with no attempt at reverence (despite Scorsese's Catholic background), imagines Jesus as an anxious man attempting to discern God's calling for him. Jesus's spirit triumphs over his flesh, however, as he resists succumbing to the temptation to pursue love and family over the cross. Thus, the film ends on a confident and hopeful note, quite unlike *Son of Man*, despite their shared interest in the theme of messianic ambivalence.

The Self-Emptying of Jesus in Jesus *(1999)*

The film *Jesus* (1999) portrays a very happy and very human Jesus (cf. chap. 5). Emphasis on Jesus's humanity, however, does not undermine his divinity as it does in *The Last Temptation of Christ* (1988). In fact, *Jesus* (1999) seems designed as a response to Scorsese's film with respect to its depiction of Jesus and his experience of temptation. For instance, Jesus is initially portrayed as a family man, living at home and pursuing a romantic relationship with Mary of Bethany, evoking *The Last Temptation of Christ*.[13] But Jesus's desire to have his own family dissipates after the death of his father, Joseph, which ignites a sense of purpose within Jesus.[14] Instead of familial temptations, Jesus has visionary temptations on a *cosmic* scale (cf. chap. 8), likely a reaction to the notion that Jesus would be tempted by domestic considerations. Even though *Jesus* (1999) seems intended to offer a more balanced version of Jesus's humanity and divinity, there are indications that the film is operating with an adoptionistic and kenotic portrait of Jesus's divinity, offering a christological theme that is unique among Jesus films.

Adoptionism, the idea that Jesus was not divine before being adopted by God and granted divine power (e.g., at his baptism), had some adherents in the early centuries of the church but falls short of trinitarian theology. Adoptionism is suggested in the film's depiction of Jesus's baptism. John the Baptist tells Jesus he will only baptize him if Jesus *confesses his sin* and dedicates his life to God. Jesus does not speak but places his hand on John's arm, and the scene cuts to Jesus receiving baptism, suggesting that he has met the condition of confession. When Jesus receives the "water for repentance," we hear a crack of thunder and see a lighting effect that transfigures Jesus, suggesting that he has now been imbued with divine qualities (his "adoption" to the divine).[15]

13. Walsh, *Reading the Gospels in the Dark*, 7.

14. *The Chosen* (2017–present) also makes Joseph's death a key moment in the development of Jesus's sense of purpose (cf. the horse's bridle from the exodus—handed down to Jesus in season 3, episode 3, "Physician Heal Thyself," 2022]—which Jesus uses for the triumphal entry in season 4, episode 8, "Humble," 2024). Other films that depict Joseph's death include, e.g., *Reina de Reinas: La Virgen María* (*Queen of Queens: The Virgin Mary*, 1948); *Un Bambino di Nome Gesù* (*A Child Called Jesus*, 1987); *Per Amore, Solo per Amore* (*For Love, Only for Love*, 1993); *Giuseppe di Nazareth* (*Joseph of Nazareth*, 2000); *Maria, Figlia del Suo Figlio* (*Maria, Daughter of Her Son*, 2000); *La Sacra Famiglia* (*The Holy Family*, 2006); *Joseph and Mary* (2016). A few films imagine Joseph is still alive during Jesus's ministry (e.g., *Color of the Cross* [2006]; *Su Re* [*The King*, 2012]; *The Book of Clarence* [2023]) and even after his resurrection (e.g., *Color of the Cross 2: The Resurrection* [2008]; *Barabbas* [2019]). *Mary and Joseph: A Story of Faith* (1979) pictures him as someone sympathetic to revolutionary movements and the instigator of the Zealots before Jesus's birth; cf. *Giuseppe di Nazareth* (*Joseph of Nazareth*, 2000), where Joseph's brothers are Zealots.

15. Similarly, in *Mary, Mother of Jesus* (1999), Jesus tells Mary after they are both baptized that he feels "different" with "new powers inside" him.

Lube / Lux Vide / Beta Film

Jesus's baptism (top) and the start of Jesus's temptation (bottom), when he empties himself of his divinity, in *Jesus* (1999)

The baptism scene is followed by Jesus's wilderness temptations, where the film suggests that Jesus now empties himself of his divinity—his adoption is almost immediately followed by his kenosis or emptying. Taken from the Greek *kenoō* in Philippians 2:5–11, kenosis is the theological concept that the Son emptied himself of certain divine prerogatives when he took on humanity at the incarnation (not at the temptation, as depicted in *Jesus* [1999]). As the temptation scene begins, Satan appears to Jesus as a woman in a red dress and says, "You must be like them in every way" (i.e., completely human; see Heb. 2:14–18). Satan then tells Jesus to abandon his "shield" and "the protection of the power that abides" in him and moreover to "empty" himself both of his "divinity" and "of the Father." "Only in this way," Satan asserts, "can we challenge each other," suggesting that the legitimacy of Jesus's temptation, and indeed his suffering, is predicated on this kenosis, this emptying. As Jesus does this, the earth cracks and quakes as Jesus screams in agony.

Other scenes in *Jesus* (1999) serve to support its unique combination of kenosis and adoptionism. When Jesus interacts with the Syrophoenician woman (cf. Mark 7:24–30), he comes to the realization that his mission should include gentiles; he is portrayed as changing his mind and course. And when he approaches Gethsemane (where he receives one last intense visionary temptation from Satan), Jesus declares that he must face what is coming "as a man," evoking his earlier kenosis. In the aftermath of *The Last Temptation of Christ* (1988), *Jesus* (1999) seems intent on depicting a different kind of human Jesus. The film's distinctive way of narrating Jesus's baptism and temptation, with adoptionist and kenotic themes, creates a unique portrait of a human Jesus.

Jesus as the Forerunner in Mesih (Jesus, the Spirit of God, *2010)*

Mesih (*Jesus, the Spirit of God*, 2010) is a thirteen-part Iranian miniseries on the life of Jesus from a Muslim perspective, originally produced as a feature-length film in 2007. It is based on the Qur'an and the Gospel of Barnabas, a medieval Gospel that harmonizes the four canonical Gospels with Islamic theology. Dependence on this later Gospel is intimated early in *Mesih* (2010) when Jesus calls Barnabas to be his first disciple. (The canonical Gospels never mention him.) The director of *Mesih*, Nader Talebzadeh, made the 2007 film version, in part, to offer a different portrait of Jesus in the wake of the global popularity of Mel Gibson's *The Passion of the Christ* (2004).[16] In both the film and the expanded series (with the latter being our focus), Jesus is not the Son of God but rather the forerunner of Muhammad, the prophet to come.

As a prophet sent to prepare the way for Muhammad, Jesus laments the spread of false teachings about him. People have misjudged the significance of his miracles, wrongly claiming that he is the Son of God, or even God himself, and elevating him beyond his status as a prophet. Instead, Jesus is simply "the son of Mary" (cf. Mark 6:3).[17] In the series, Jesus's sermons consistently stress the importance of the prophets and the centrality of monotheism, which, from a Muslim perspective, cannot include a human figure participating in

16. Cf. Malone, *Screen Jesus*, 296.

17. In the Iranian film from 2000 and the series from 2002, both named *Maryam Moghadas* (*Saint Mary*), there is no Joseph figure involved in Jesus's birth narrative, as the Qur'an also teaches (Maryam 19:22–26).

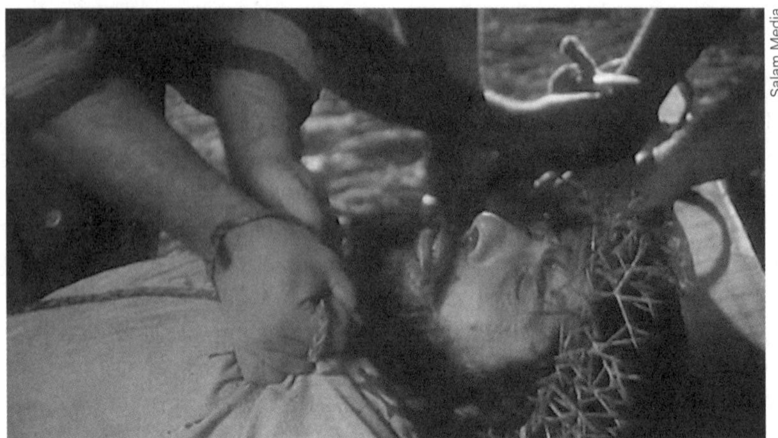

Judas (top) is crucified in the place of Jesus in part 13 of *Mesih* (*Jesus, the Spirit of God*, 2010) as Jesus (bottom) looks on during his direct ascension to heaven.

the divine identity. Jesus assures Barnabas that the final prophet (Muhammad) will come and make everything clear, despite present misunderstandings about Jesus. Moreover, on the day of judgment, Jesus himself will punish those who have believed false things about him.

The most notable change to the story of Jesus in *Mesih* (2010) is that he does not die for sinners, since he does not die at all. Instead, in keeping with the Gospel of Barnabas, Judas is crucified in Jesus's place (Gos. Barn. 217).[18] Judas is a duplicitous character in *Mesih* (see chap. 6), and God punishes him by making him take on the appearance of Jesus. As Jesus ascends into

18. Some early Christian texts also claim that Jesus was not truly crucified; cf., e.g., Acts John 97–98 and the Coptic Apocalypse of Peter (NHC 7.3).

heaven, Judas becomes a decoy for Jesus, condemned to die by crucifixion.[19] Intriguingly, both the film and the series technically have two separate endings: In one Jesus is crucified, as in the canonical Gospels, while in the other he is not, as the Gospel of Barnabas narrates. *Mesih* positions this choice as "a neutral stance" in the series version—an ecumenical concession designed to respect the Christian perspective that Jesus was crucified. Yet whatever ending is "chosen," the series and the film clearly portray Jesus as only the forerunner to Muhammad and not God's Son. Additionally, the alternate ending in which Jesus is crucified does not include a resurrection sequence, and so it will likely not satisfy Christian viewers.

As its theme of Jesus as forerunner demonstrates, *Mesih* (2010) reflects concerns of Muslims from centuries after the time of Jesus. Such interests are evident in several other decisions the series makes. First, in Jesus's discussion with the Samaritan woman about a new "location" for true worship (cf. John 4:21–23), Jesus asserts that God will choose a new place, alluding to Mecca.[20] Second, in several discussions about whether the Abrahamic covenant extends through Isaac or Ishmael, Jesus firmly decides in favor of Ishmael. Third, when Jesus raises Lazarus from the dead, he also raises Noah's son Shem, the father of all Semitic people. ("Semitic" is derived from "Shem.") In this role, Shem is able to clarify that Jesus's miraculous powers, even the power to raise Lazarus, show him to be *the last great prophet sent specifically to Israel* and not the Son of God. Fourth and finally, the series portrays the apostle Paul as straightforwardly villainous and menacing, in line with critical comments in the Gospel of Barnabas about how Paul was deceived about Jesus's true identity (cf. the historical conflicts between Paul and Barnabas reflected in Acts 15:36–41; Gal. 2:10–14). In one scene, Paul ("Saul" in the series) discusses the topic of messianic revolt against Rome with a Zealot, who claims the Messiah's goal should be to overthrow Rome. Paul responds with a question about whether the Messiah would then turn to conquer the whole world. The camera then lingers on Paul's face, as if to suggest that the legacy of his missionary efforts is one of violence, including the crusades against Islam. These themes in *Mesih* (2010) illustrate how films often import from their "second horizon" (see chap. 8) back into the horizon of the Jesus story. The later Islamic context of the filmmakers is apparent in their retelling of the Jesus story, just as all Jesus films, some more and some less, show their second horizon.

19. This dynamic adds an intriguing dimension to the characterization of Pilate (cf. chap. 6), since he realizes that it's not actually Jesus.

20. Elsewhere in *Mesih*'s (2010) version of the Olivet Discourse, where Jesus prophesies the destruction of Jerusalem and the temple, Jesus alludes to the Dome of the Rock, mentioning the place of worship that will be established there by the prophet to come.

Getting Used to Different in **The Chosen** *(2017–present)*

The Chosen (2017–present) provides the final and most extensive opportunity to explore a theme. This serial (streaming) show warrants special attention given the sheer number of hours it has already published, its global popularity, and that its primary theme provides a hermeneutical key for the entire series. A tagline for *The Chosen* is "Get used to different"—a line that appears in the show's official merchandise. In the show, these words are first spoken by Jesus to Peter (season 1, episode 7, "Invitations," 2019), and they are later repeated by Peter to Andrew (season 2, episode 7, "Reckoning," 2021). "Get used to different" reflects the show's contrast between the Jewish religion or faith and what Jesus does in his ministry. Jesus does something new.

The centrality of the theme is readily apparent in the opening of each episode. The animated title sequence depicts a school of gray fish swimming in a single direction when a lone teal fish swimming the opposite way appears. Then, one by one, gray fish morph to teal and turn around to head in the opposite direction. The final shot of this opening sequence reveals thirteen teal fish among a host of gray fish, with these thirteen representing Jesus and his twelve disciples.

Even as *The Chosen* highlights the "different" thing Jesus is doing in relation to first-century Judaism, the show also, perhaps more than any other cinematic story of Jesus, attempts to situate Jesus thoroughly in his Jewish context. For example, Jesus and his disciples pray traditional prayers; they observe the Sabbath and various Jewish holidays, including festivals that the Gospels do not mention (e.g., Rosh Hashanah, Purim); they kiss the mezuzah on doorposts as they enter and depart homes; and they retell moments of

5&2 Studio / Loaves and Fishes Production / Out of Order Studios

The opening title sequence of each episode of *The Chosen* concludes with this shot of thirteen fish swimming against the flow.

5&2 Studio / Loaves and Fishes Production / Out of Order Studios

Early representation of Jesus's male disciples wearing kippahs during Shabbat in *The Chosen* (season 1, episode 2, "Shabbat," 2019)

Israel's history to one another, including stories about the Maccabean revolt, which don't appear in the Protestant canon (cf. season 4, episode 6, "Dedication," 2024). In season 1, they wear kippahs (or yarmulkes) on the Sabbath, following the practice of Jewish men wearing head coverings (cf. season1, episode 2, "Shabbat," 2019).[21]

A Different Approach to the Jewish Law?

Despite the presence of these Jewish contextual features, *The Chosen* focuses keenly on Jesus's distinctiveness in relation to Jewish religion, particularly to the Jewish law or Torah.[22] Generally speaking, Jesus downplays the importance of Torah observance in this series. For example, he speaks directly to a lack of interest in "rules" coming from the law when John the Baptist is upset about Herod being in an incestuous relationship (season 2, episode 5, "Spirit," 2021):

John the Baptist: It is right there in the book of Moses: "If a man takes his brother's wife, it is impurity. He has uncovered his brother's nakedness and they shall be childless."

Jesus: I understand it's against the law of Moses, but I'm here for bigger purposes than the breaking of rules.

21. This practice goes away without explanation as the series continues, which might simply be an aesthetic choice not dissimilar to the way that students at Hogwarts in the *Harry Potter* films wear hoods only in the first film.

22. "Torah" is the Hebrew word for "instruction" and is used in reference to the Mosaic law. It tends to carry less baggage than the English word "law." For this reason, we use it frequently in this section.

John: You minimize incest?

Jesus: Of course not.

John: What of the laws of Moses will be minimized?

Jesus: All of this will be addressed. I'm not ready to get into the specifics.

John: You appear to be not ready to get into the specifics of a lot of things.

Jesus's ambivalent sentiments about the law are also reflected in the words of Philip in another episode. There, Matthew expresses confusion about why Jesus chose him, since as a tax collector he did not prioritize the study of religion. Philip consoles Matthew by saying, "For what I understand, Jesus doesn't love everything about religion" (season 2, episode 2, "I Saw You," 2021).

The Chosen also represents ambivalence about the Jewish law in Jesus's various confrontations with the Jewish leaders as they dispute the appropriate manner of Torah observance. For example, Jesus creates controversy with the leadership when he heals a man on the Sabbath (from the account in John 5). The man has been waiting by the Pool of Siloam to be healed by its waters when Jesus tells him to pick up his mat and walk (season 2, episode 4, "The Perfect Opportunity," 2021). The disciples turn to discuss the situation together. Matthew wonders which law forbids picking up a mat on the Sabbath, but John explains that it is not the law but *oral tradition* that prohibits it. With this clarification, *The Chosen* signals that Jesus is engaging a legal dispute rather than rejecting Sabbath laws outright. Nevertheless, when Matthew asks Jesus why he would heal the man on the Sabbath with full awareness that a dispute with Jewish leaders would follow, Jesus says, "Sometimes you gotta stir up the water." At the very least, Jesus's response emphasizes his role as a provocateur who goes against Jewish tradition on legal matters. Jesus as provocateur or renegade does not fit well with the canonical Gospels, which portray him as obeying the Torah even as he disputes with Jewish leaders, such as the Pharisees, about what that obedience should look like in specific cases (e.g., Matt. 5:17; 12:7; 15:1–9; 23:23).

The law is also characterized as oppressive, or at least onerous, in *The Chosen*. Around a campfire, the disciples confess to breaking food laws (season 2, episode 3, "Matthew 4:24," 2021). Thomas admits that he once ate meat and cheese and then got sick and never violated a "food rule" again (cf. Exod. 23:19). Thaddeus reciprocates by saying, "I tried pork once," and then notes that he really liked it. Thomas, in turn, affirms that he loves the law and being Jewish but concedes that it can also be "exhausting." In another conversation, John tells his brother, "Big James," that he almost joined the Zealots but decided against it because of the rigorous morning exercises Zee (Simon the Zealot) is required to do each day. John concludes that the 613 commandments contained in Scripture are enough to worry about (season 2, episode 6, "Unlawful," 2021). In later episodes, Big James and John disregard some of those 613 laws—for example, when they sneak a few bites of cinnamon cake when they're supposed to be removing all leavened bread before Passover (season 4, episode 8, "Humble," 2024).[23]

In line with *The Chosen*'s ambivalence toward the Jewish law, the show depicts Jesus making bold claims about his relationship to the Torah. In response to accusations that he is undermining the law after he reads from Isaiah in the synagogue (cf. Luke 4:16–21), Jesus declares, "I am the law of Moses" (season 3, episode 3, "Physician, Heal Yourself," 2022). Jesus's claim here, which has no New Testament precedent, is set in contrast to the declaration of Rabbi Shmuel, in opposition to Jesus, that "the law is God" (season 1, episode 8, "I Am He," 2019). It may be that Jesus's claim to be the Torah means (for the show's creators) that he can either keep it or dismiss it.

A Different Approach to Ritual Purity?

In *The Chosen*, Jesus and his disciples' most pronounced area of ambivalence toward the law involves regulations about ritual purity.[24] In ancient Judaism, "ritual purity" referred to a temporary state of purity required for a person to enter holy space (usually the temple). In that context, one lost the status of ritual purity by contracting impurity from specific sources: corpses, genital emissions (semen or blood), or various skin diseases like eczema (see Lev. 11–15). As this list demonstrates, ritual purity was not about sin but rather about mundane matters of everyday life: skin irritation, sexual activity, menstruation, giving birth, and burying the dead. Contracting ritual impurity was a regular occurrence, and the means for alleviating the impurity were clearly laid out in the Torah and not difficult to fulfill. For most instances of impurity, all that was needed was *time* and *water*, such as immersing oneself in a mikvah (i.e., a ritual washing pool) and waiting until evening (cf. Lev. 15:16).[25]

23. A similar sentiment of growing ambivalence to the law is exhibited by certain Jewish leaders in *The Chosen*, including Nicodemus, Jairus, and Rabbi Yussif.

24. See, e.g., Furstenberg, *Purity and Identity*. As the topic pertains to the Gospels, see especially Thiessen, *Jesus and the Forces of Death*.

25. Although some actions that lead to ritual impurity, like giving birth, take longer to address and require a concluding sacrifice (cf. Lev. 12:1–8), none of these requirements would have been considered onerous. See Levine, "Putting Jesus Where He Belongs," 168.

Despite these realities about Jewish ritual purity, common misunderstandings in Christian interpretations of the New Testament persist, including the notion that Jesus did away with ritual practices. As such, *The Chosen*'s theme of "getting used to different" is often aimed at Jewish purity laws.

When it comes to skin conditions that cause ritual impurity, *The Chosen* represents the Gospels' references to the Greek word *lepra* as "leprosy" (as do most English translations), with the assumption that it's a physical contagion. The series is by no means unique here, as can be seen in the leper colony in *Jesus Christ Superstar* (1973) and most notably in *Ben-Hur* (1959). Yet in Judaism, the problem with this and other skin conditions is that they make one *ritually impure* (not physically contagious).[26] *The Chosen* seems frequently to miss the connection between skin diseases and ritual impurity. In season 1, the disciples are startled when they encounter a leper, shouting, "Cover your mouth" and "Don't breathe his air," as if the point is the contagious nature of the disease and not impurity (season 1, episode 6, "Indescribable Compassion," 2019).[27]

Furthermore, even though Leviticus identifies the particular sources of impurity (i.e., skin diseases, corpses, and genital emissions), *The Chosen* seemingly expands this list to include spit and bloody wounds.[28] In season 4, after Jesus heals a man born blind by spitting in the dirt to create mud for his eyes (cf. John 9), he is met with hostility by the Jewish leaders,[29] not simply for performing this miracle on the Sabbath (as in John 9:16) but for using "filth" and not "honor[ing] purity laws" (season 4, episode 3, "Moon to Blood," 2024). Jesus critiques their focus on "cleanliness"[30] and their "obsession with what is clean and unclean," but spit is not one of the sources of impurity.[31]

26. On skin conditions that cause impurity, see Thiessen, *Jesus and the Forces of Death*, 43–68.

27. Even though *The Chosen*'s Jesus reinforces the Torah's teachings by instructing the man to show himself to a priest (cf. Mark 1:44), by making *lepra* a physically contagious disease, Jesus's prescription reflects a disconnect about how skin conditions relate to impurity. Similarly, in season 2 (episode 1, "Thunder," 2021), the disciples mention that lepers from a nearby colony won't come into the Samaritan town of Sychar since both Samaritan and Jewish purity laws require them to stay four cubits away, suggesting a concern for purity (cf. Lev. Rab. 16:3), but one that is muddled by the physically contagious *lepra* from season 1.

28. Impurity from demons (which the Gospels address; cf. Thiessen, *Jesus and the Forces of Death*, 123–48) is also suggested when the Jewish leaders wonder if Jesus's "false teaching" is the result of demon possession, leading a Sadducee to reactively affirm that, if so, Jesus is "unclean" and should be removed from the temple (season 4, episode 6, "Dedication," 2024).

29. Jesus intentionally baits the leaders, since "that'll make this more fun"—in keeping with his portrayal as a provocateur.

30. The term "cleanliness" is a sign that *The Chosen* mixes hygiene and ritual purity.

31. Spit is only unclean from someone already unclean from a seminal discharge (Lev. 15:8). Thus, it is unlikely that spit was routinely understood as causing impurity. Furstenberg (*Purity*

5&2 Studio / Loaves and Fishes Production / Out of Order Studios

John (far left) wields a knife and Little James (far right) covers his face when a leper comes to their camp in *The Chosen* (season 1, episode 6, "Indescribable Compassion," 2019).

Bloody wounds are also treated as a cause of ritual impurity in *The Chosen*. In the show's pilot, "The Shepherd" (2017),[32] a young shepherd boy tries to supply a spotless lamb for a merchant, but the lamb he brings has a blemish. As a thematic connection, the boy himself walks with a limp and has a bloody wound on his arm. He is told he cannot enter the synagogue because it is "a holy place." Yet not even someone with a skin condition (let alone a more temporary wound) would have been excluded from the synagogue according to the (later) Mishnah (cf. m. Neg. 13.12). By the conclusion of this episode, the shepherd finds himself at the manger on the night of Jesus's birth with his wound wrapped in the same swaddling cloth used for Jesus. Later, when asked whether he was able to find a spotless lamb, he simply smiles as the episode concludes. This story reinforces that in the place of a strict and exclusive religion, the shepherd is fully embraced within the emerging Jesus story, which sets aside purity laws (even fabricated ones).

The pair of episodes from season 3 titled "Clean" (episode 4, "Clean, Part 1," 2023; episode 5, "Clean, Part 2," 2023) illuminate most clearly *The Chosen*'s perspective on sources of ritual impurity and Jesus's relationship to purity. In these two episodes, the show dramatizes the stories of Jairus's

and Identity, 214) notes that later rabbis added further specifics (perhaps less relevant for the first century)—e.g., that spit from a gentile was defiling (m. Neg. 3.1; m. Nid. 7.3; m. Zavim 2.1; m. Mikv. 8.4) and that stepping on saliva could defile (m. Tehar. 5.8; m. Sheqal. 8.1; t. Tehar. 4.5).

32. Cf. the expanded version, *Christmas with "The Chosen": Holy Night* (2023), which edits "The Shepherd" (2017) to include another one of their short specials called *Christmas with "The Chosen": The Messengers* (2021).

daughter and the bleeding woman from Mark 5:21–43. *The Chosen* focuses keenly on menstrual and corpse impurity in these episodes,[33] weaving in two additional storylines to amplify this emphasis: a miscarriage suffered by Eden, Simon Peter's wife, and a broken cistern in Capernaum that can no longer provide water for ritual immersions.

In the two "Clean" episodes, the Jewish crowds and the Pharisees, not Jesus, are concerned about purity. In part 1, Veronica, the woman who is bleeding, is introduced as she washes her bloody garments in the river, away from society.[34] As she returns to Capernaum, a man interacts with her and then notices her bleeding. He berates her and complains that he will have to travel out to the Sea of Galilee to immerse himself because of the broken cistern. This reaction is extreme and seems to moralize ritual impurity (i.e., portray it as almost sinful for Veronica to be in public). And since this scene occurs in Capernaum not Jerusalem, the man is far from the temple and at no risk of entering sacred space in a state of impurity. Later on, after Jesus heals Veronica and raises Jairus's daughter, the Pharisees interrogate Jesus about his physical contact with them and insist that he, along with anyone he then has touched, "carry out the rituals of purification." Jesus then asks the three disciples with him, "Who among you touched either me or the woman who was formerly bleeding? Raise your hands." All three raise their hands, and so together they walk toward the sea, where Veronica has been washing. When she sees them, she asks whether the priest sent them because she had made them unclean. Jesus responds, "He thinks he did. We just wanted to go for a swim." Simon Peter quips, "Joke's on him" as Jesus laughs, and they all carry on splashing about in the water. Jesus's reaction here can be interpreted as a rejection of the ritual purity system, while in Mark 5 it is likely that Jesus was addressing sources of impurity *because the system continued to matter*.[35]

Purity concerns seem to be dismissed at other points in these twin episodes as well. The first "Clean" episode opens in a synagogue with a rabbi reading from Leviticus 15:7–10, a passage about ritual washings for those with genital discharges. Big James and John are there with their father, Zebedee, and they are anything but inspired by the droning manner of the reading. Zebedee says, "This isn't exactly one of Torah's best. Years from now, no one will

33. Technically, Leviticus distinguishes between a menstruant (*niddah*) and a woman with abnormal discharge (*zavah*).

34. Veronica is the name given to the woman who, according to tradition, wiped Jesus's bloody face with a towel during his passion (see chap. 1). Thus, her introduction here foreshadows her role on Good Friday.

35. Furstenberg, *Purity and Identity*, 57–58; Thiessen, *Jesus and the Forces of Death*, 69–96. For a reading of Jesus as attentive to primary, though not secondary, purity concerns, see Brown and Roberts, *Matthew*, 511–13.

claim, 'Oh, yes, I was there for the pronouncement on washing.'" With this initial scene, the audience is conditioned to view ritual purity as singularly dull and unimportant.

Another moment that suggests a disregard for purity pertains to surfaces. In a conversation between Simon and Gaius, a Roman centurion (*primi*), Gaius pulls out a pocket flask and offers Simon a drink as they sit near the broken cistern at night ("Clean, Part 1"). Setting aside the anachronisms (with flasks, pockets, and spirits many centuries away from development), Simon recoils at the offer, and a revealing bit of dialogue follows:

Simon: No, I . . . I can't drink from a vessel that's . . .
Gaius: Oh, you . . . Jews. Your rules make your lives very complicated.
Simon: Us Jews?
Gaius: Yeah.
Simon: Well, Jesus will undo some of that. He reminds us what we live for.

Although Simon does not indicate what will be undone by Jesus or how, the line sufficiently communicates, at least to Christian audiences, that Jesus has come to get rid of Jewish laws that are too restrictive[36] and that make, as Gaius puts it, their "lives very complicated."[37] In the context of the two episodes, matters of ritual purity are certainly included.[38]

The Chosen's attitude toward ritual purity laws is largely, though not uniformly, cavalier.[39] It reflects a position that Jewish ritual purity was never a matter of substance (it wasn't *real*) but merely a kind of word game or symbol (pointing to spiritual realities).[40] Christians holding an ambivalent or

36. This is also suggested by the inclusion of the parable of the wineskins (season 3, episode 5, "Clean, Part 2," 2023), following Matthew's placement (Matt. 9:14–17), suggesting that Jesus discards the old wineskins of the law and purity regulations.

37. Cf. the Greek man who similarly says, "Your laws about food and purity are laughable" (season 3, episode 8, "Sustenance," 2023).

38. This is suggested by Simon's reference to the vessel from which he would presumably contract impurity. Cf. when the Samaritan woman asks Jesus, "Aren't I unclean to you? Won't you be defiled by this vessel?" (season 1, episode 8, "I Am He," 2019).

39. *The Chosen* acknowledges ritual purity with respect to, e.g., (1) stone vessels being impervious to ritual impurity (season 1, episode 5, "The Wedding Gift," 2019), (2) genital emissions in sexual intercourse leading to impurity (season 2, episode 6, "Unlawful," 2021), (3) ritual immersion after Eden's miscarriage (season 3, episode 8, "Sustenance," 2023), and (4) pure oil being the only kind of oil permitted in the temple (season 4, episode 6, "Dedication," 2024; cf. b. Shabb. 21b).

40. *The Chosen* operates with a nominalist and nonessentialist view of purity. Cf. Thiessen, *Jesus and the Forces of Death*, 39.

negative perspective on the law would likely be uncomfortable with a Jesus who is much more Jewish in his practices than they are in their own religious practices. To return to *The Chosen*'s motto ("Get used to different"), Jesus's Jewishness vis-à-vis the Torah and purity in the Gospels seems to be a kind of *difference* that they themselves would not be willing to *get used to*. We consider this a missed opportunity. As Steven Greydanus asserts about Jesus films more broadly, "Too many Jesus films that find a potentially novel point of view that could disrupt viewer assumptions and move them to consider Jesus or his world in a new light fail to challenge viewers because the filmmakers settle for the parts of Jesus's message or example that they are most comfortable with. A Jesus we are comfortable with is a Jesus who has nothing to teach us."[41] When it comes to its treatment of Torah and purity, *The Chosen* portrays Jesus as a maverick, and even a lawbreaker at times. Yet for most Christian viewers (and for the filmmakers) this would not clash with their own views. In this sense, *The Chosen* presents the (Christian) status quo to its target audience. As a result, *The Chosen* is most thematically resonant for viewers already "used to different."

Conclusion

Themes are inherent in storytelling. With each fresh telling of the Jesus story, new themes are incorporated, or themes already present are further emphasized and adapted. The result is a unique retelling, a new story about Jesus. In this chapter, we have explored distinctive themes in *The Last Temptation of Christ* (1988), *Jesus* (1999), *Mesih* (*Jesus, the Spirit of God*, 2010), and *The Chosen* (2017–present). All Jesus films or shows have their distinctive themes, as do the Gospels, both canonical and noncanonical, that paved the way for modern cinematic Jesus stories. And if themes are inherent in storytelling, we will be prone to insert new themes or to heighten existing ones in the Jesus story that plays in our own heads. In all likelihood, we have "thematized" our own Jesus story by drawing on themes from our lives and experiences. The way that personal contexts inescapably implicate themselves in retellings of the Jesus story is what we refer to as the influence of "the second horizon." This topic is the subject of chapter 8.

41. Greydanus, "Through Other Eyes," 86.

8

The Two Horizons of Jesus Stories

When we encounter a story about the past, it can often transport us through time and space, with our imaginations as guides. While the story's retelling can mediate the past to us, it can do so only through its narrator, who is just as culturally and historically situated as the past itself. The relationship between a story set in the past and the storyteller's own perspective of it in their setting makes up what we call "the two horizons." The first horizon belongs to the original story, and the second horizon is "the interpreter's own horizon,"[1] so "the second horizon" can refer to any interpretation of a past text (like the Gospels). But for our purposes in this chapter, we will narrow the definition of "second horizon" to refer to the perspective of the filmmaker or director of a Jesus film as they interpret the Gospels to retell the Jesus story.[2]

A few examples from the world of theater can serve to illustrate the basic principle. The play *The Crucible* (1953), written by Arthur Miller, is a story about the Salem Witch Trials of the late seventeenth century in the Massachusetts Bay Colony (its first horizon), but Miller wrote the play to address a second horizon—the "witch hunts" conducted by US Senator Joseph McCarthy,

1. Thistleton, *Two Horizons*, xix; cf. also Bartholomew, *Introducing Biblical Hermeneutics*, 420–21; Vanhoozer, *Is There a Meaning*, 28, 108. The language of "two horizons" derives from Gadamer's concept of the fusion of horizons in reading and interpretation (*Truth and Method*).

2. "The second horizon" could also refer to the interpretive perspective of any viewer of a Jesus film or reader of a Gospel. But to avoid complication, we will restrict our use of "the second horizon" to designate the contextualized POV of a film/filmmaker.

who, in the fervor of the Cold War with the Soviet Union, was eager to label his congressional opponents as Communists. The Broadway musical *Hamilton* (2015) by Lin-Manuel Miranda focuses on America's founding fathers, and specifically Alexander Hamilton's contributions (its first horizon). Yet the story is purposefully retold so that the viewer is reminded of the second horizon: The founding fathers are represented by people of color and the songs are influenced by hip-hop and rap music, which are typically associated with Black and Hispanic cultures. The second horizon reminds the viewer that the founding fathers were themselves immigrants to America and as such are the founders of *all Americans*, regardless of race or ethnicity.

In this chapter, we identify numerous ways the two horizons tend to relate to each other across Jesus films. These patterns often reveal why filmmakers are interested in retelling Jesus's story.[3] This dynamic can also alert us to our own social locations and the cultural contexts we bring to reading the Gospels. Before turning to film analysis in this chapter, we look briefly at canonical and noncanonical Gospels, since the existence of two horizons is not merely a modern phenomenon found in TV or film. Ancient retellings of the Jesus story themselves had second horizons. This is the case even though the temporal gulf between the literary Gospels and the life of Jesus was not nearly as vast as the gulf between the contemporary world and the Gospels themselves.

The Second Horizon in the Gospels

Readers of the Gospels can notice how the second horizon of the evangelists already affects their narrations of the life of Jesus. A good example comes in Matthew's reference to the temple tax (Matt. 17:24–27). This tax—a half-shekel used to support the tabernacle or temple (Exod. 30:13–16)—was well established by the first century and at that time was valued at two drachmas (Matt. 17:24). Matthew alone includes both the account of those who collected the temple tax asking Peter whether Jesus was in the habit of paying it and the conversation that follows between Peter and Jesus about this tax. What is relevant for our purposes is that during Jesus's lifetime this tax was used to support the temple in Jerusalem (the first horizon of the Jesus story). Yet by the time Matthew was writing, which was likely after the fall of the temple in 70 CE, this tax had been absorbed into the Roman *fiscus Judaicus*—a Roman tax that supported Roman interests (the second horizon). This account, then, has a distinctly different impact on Matthew's readers within

3. Stern, Jefford, and DeBona (*Savior on the Silver Screen*) refer to this "second horizon" as their "third lens" of investigation for analyzing Jesus films.

the second horizon—after Rome's destruction of the temple—than it had in the first horizon (ca. 30 CE).[4]

The staggering nature of the events of 70 CE in the second horizon of the evangelists has also influenced their accounts of Jesus's famous speech about the temple's destruction (the Olivet Discourse; cf. Matt. 24; Mark 13; Luke 21). As Mark narrates Jesus's words that the "abomination of desolation" will be "standing where it does not belong," he inserts parenthetically, "Let the reader understand" (Mark 13:14). This phrase ties Jesus's words in the first horizon to the experiences of Mark's original readers in the second horizon during or just after the Jewish War (66–71 CE). Matthew overtly connects this abomination to "the holy place" (i.e., the temple; Matt. 24:15), and in Luke, Jesus explicitly refers to Jerusalem being surrounded by armies (Luke 21:20), highlighting the fulfillment of Jesus's words in their second horizon.

A final example comes from the Gospel of John. J. Louis Martyn argues that the Gospel of John is best read as a two-stage drama, with both stages playing out simultaneously in the retelling of the life of Jesus.[5] The first stage or time frame focuses on the life of Christ and his ministry. The second stage engages the life of the Johannine community living some decades later as they endure opposition for their commitment to Jesus. So, for example, when we read in John about growing tensions between Jesus and the Jewish authorities and specific threats of being expelled from the synagogue (cf. 9:22; 12:42; 16:2), we should not merely recognize a tension present in Jesus's ministry. For Martyn, this tension mirrors the experiences of John's community near the turn of the century. Whether or not there was a single, specific Johannine community, part of what distinguishes the Synoptics from John is the latter's more obvious overlapping of the two horizons in his retelling of the Jesus story.

The Second Horizon in Noncanonical Retellings

Each of the noncanonical Gospels that we have analyzed in this book possesses a second horizon, with some being more obvious than others. An illustration of the influence of second horizons on retellings of the Jesus story comes from a source we have yet to discuss: the Toledoth Yeshu. Rather than reflecting a single text or story, the Toledoth refers to multiple Jewish traditions that parody the life of Jesus and were passed on as folklore and legends from late antiquity and the medieval era. Since the tales originate and are shaped in

4. Carter, "Paying the Tax to Rome."
5. Martyn, *History and Theology in the Fourth Gospel.*

various contexts, they have not a single second horizon but many. A number of significant threads appear throughout these various and often divergent traditions. One is the Toledoth claim that Jesus was conceived illegitimately from a Roman soldier named Panthera (cf. Origen, *Cels.* 1.32) and that his miracles were the result of sorcery, specifically from stealing out of the temple the divine name, which Jesus used as a magical spell.

Another thread involves the figure of Helena, who seems to be a composite character informed by the second horizon. Scholars have traditionally organized the Toledoth material into three groupings based largely on the figure presented as the political authority in the story: Pilate, Helena, or Herod.[6] In the grouping of the Toledoth Yeshu focused on Helena, both first and second horizons are engaged. Within the first horizon, there was a Queen Helena of Adiabene around the time of Jesus, referenced by historians like Josephus (cf., e.g., *Ant.* 20.2.1–20.5.2 [20.17–101]). Yet the description of Helena in the Toledoth has obvious resemblance to another Helena, the mother of Constantine, the emperor who converted to Christianity after being sympathetic to Judaism and who sanctioned Christianity within the Roman Empire.[7] The way Constantine's mother informs the character of Helena in the Toledoth reflects how the horizon of Jews living in a Christian empire shaped their folktales about Jesus.

Another feature that ties the Toledoth Yeshu to the later horizon of the rise of Christianity involves its allusions to the story of Esther. Specifically, some allusions connect Jesus to Haman (the antagonist in the Esther narrative)—both are known for being hanged or crucified. The connection reflects a later polemical context in which the threat posed to Judaism by Christianity is on par with the threat of Haman to the Jews in Esther's story.[8]

The Second Horizon in Jesus Films

As these ancient examples demonstrate, the second horizon is always operative. Yet the two horizons concept is especially helpful for analyzing modern retellings to discern how they reshape the Jesus story, sometimes significantly. In modern cinematic retellings, the second horizon is far different from the first horizon (Jesus's first-century context). An interesting hermeneutical question is whether a Jesus film acknowledges in some way its second horizon. Some

6. Scholarship on the Toledoth is complex due to the divergent traditions and the different languages that preserve them.

7. See, e.g., Hasan-Rokem, "Polymorphic Helena."

8. Gribetz, "Hanged and Crucified."

filmmakers explicitly lay bare their second horizon (their contemporary situation), while others either try to hide their own horizon or fail to recognize its role. In what follows, we analyze prominent ways the second horizon influences how the Jesus story is told in cinema. We have identified eight distinct ways the two horizons can relate to each other in film.

1. Importing from the second horizon
2. Juxtaposing the two horizons
3. Anticipating the second horizon
4. Transposing the first horizon
5. Overlapping the two horizons
6. Imitating the first horizon
7. Incorporating the second horizon
8. Neglecting the second horizon

These categories are heuristic to assist in identifying hermeneutical commonalities across the breadth of Jesus films; the list does not exhaust all possibilities, and not every Jesus film fits neatly into a single category.

1. Importing from the Second Horizon

The idea here is that the Jesus story of the first horizon is retold by *importing* theology or other concerns from the second horizon. In one sense, every Jesus film could be included in this category. Yet some films quite clearly import doctrines or practices that arose well after the time of Jesus. Distinctive examples include Latter-day Saint (Mormon) theological motifs in *The Life of Jesus Christ* (2013) and Islamic themes in *Mesih* (*Jesus, the Spirit of God*, 2010; cf. chap. 7).[9] *Color of the Cross* (2006) and *Color of the Cross 2: The Resurrection* (2008) provide examples of social concerns imported into the Jesus story to address contemporary racism (cf. chap. 5). In most Jesus films, however, Catholic or evangelical theology provides an underlying current, something especially evident in *The Passion of the Christ* (2004) and *Jesus* (1979) (both discussed under no. 8 below).

9. The composite film *The Life of Jesus Christ* (2013), which is focused on the canonical Gospels, imports Latter-day Saint doctrine and practice in at least two places: When John baptizes Jesus, he quotes Mosiah 18:13 from the Book of Mormon, and when Jesus sends out the twelve, he confers the priesthood of Melchizedek to them. For other Latter-day Saint Jesus films, see, e.g., season 4 of *Book of Mormon Videos*, on 3 Nephi (2022–23); *The Testaments of One Fold and One Shepherd* (2000).

5&2 Studio / Loaves and Fishes Production / Out of Order Studios

Jesus touches and consoles Little James in *The Chosen* (season 3, episode 2, "Two by Two," 2023) after explaining why he won't offer him physical healing in this life.

To provide an example of evangelical theology shaping the second horizon, we turn again to *The Chosen* (2017–present).[10] We have already examined how its portrayal of Jesus's relationship to the law follows contemporary Christian (and specifically evangelical Protestant) theology (cf. chap. 7). Another feature of importation, one that stands out because it is unparalleled in Jesus films, involves Jesus's healing practices. In *The Chosen*, Jesus by no means heals everyone who comes to him with their maladies. For example, he does not heal "Little James" (James the son of Alphaeus), who has an undisclosed physical disability that likely aligns with the real-life actor's cerebral palsy (season 3, episode 2, "Two by Two," 2022); he does not prevent the miscarriage of Eden (Peter's wife) (season 3, episode 5, "Clean, Part 2," 2023); and he doesn't revive Ramah, Thomas's romantic interest, when she is stabbed in front of him (season 4, episode 3, "Moon to Blood," 2024). On the level of the first horizon, this decision makes little sense from the testimony of the canonical Gospels (although cf. Mark 6:5–6). We propose that this storytelling move is used to explain why, in the second horizon, (evangelical) Christians do not routinely (if ever) witness miraculous healings, despite their prayers. *The Chosen* adjusts the Gospels' depiction of Jesus as a wonder-worker to normalize the experiences of (at least Western) Christians, by *importing* this modern concern into the first horizon.

10. Cf. also *Forty-Seven Days with Jesus* (2024), where a grandfather retells a Jesus story at intervals during a family holiday, drawing from his notebook containing a harmonized and theologically loaded account of Jesus's final week and the forty days post-resurrection (cf. Acts 1:3), with references to the Council of Nicaea, the "Christ hymn" of Phil. 2, and more.

Handmade Films / Python (Monty) Pictures

Brian's graffiti is made more extensive when a Roman soldier insists he continue until he gets the Latin conjugation right in *Monty Python's Life of Brian* (1979).

While most films and series (including *The Chosen*) do not explicitly signal the importation of their horizon into the Jesus story, *Monty Python's Life of Brian* (1979) clearly and creatively communicates its horizon to the viewer. The film is set in the first century, and the story revolves around an ordinary fellow named Brian who consistently finds himself in the wrong place at the wrong time, closely adjacent to Jesus (who appears only once in the film, during the Sermon on the Mount). The film begins, for example, with the traditional magi arriving accidentally for the birth of Brian, whose father we later learn was a Roman centurion (which alludes to the Panthera tradition from the Toledoth Yeshu). Repeated happenstance events lead many to suppose that Brian might be the long-awaited Messiah, and he inadvertently accrues a large following. One way this film highlights its second horizon is by importing other Jesus films into the storyline, poking fun at them in the process (e.g., *Jesus of Nazareth* [1977]; *King of Kings* [1961]).[11] The film also imports elements from its second horizon through a title sequence that resembles a James Bond opening,[12] a strange spaceship scene owing to the

11. *Life of Brian* even filmed in Tunisia, using some of the same sets as *Jesus of Nazareth* (1977). See Telford, "*Monty Python's Life of Brian*," 10. A recent parody of the Jesus film genre, from a "metamodern perspective," is *Community*'s "Messianic Myths and Ancient Peoples" (season 2, episode 5, 2010). See Mills, "Metamodern Jesus."

12. Tatum, *Jesus at the Movies*, 153.

popularity of *Star Wars* (1977) at the time,[13] and a Roman soldier correcting Brian's Latin graffiti with an impromptu lesson in conjugation, parodying British schooling.[14] These contemporary elements woven into the film's first-century storyline signal to viewers that they are in on the joke—the satirizing of both first and second horizons.[15] The film is a parody, reflecting a cynicism toward the Christianity of its time through lowbrow British comedy. As Walsh and Staley conclude, "only the laugh is sacred" in this film.[16]

2. Juxtaposing the Two Horizons

Our second category involves the intentional *juxtaposition* of multiple storylines set in different time periods, with parallel events being mutually interpretive. Two clear examples are *Intolerance* (1916) and *Blade af Satans Bog* (*Leaves from Satan's Book*, 1920). Each film follows four storylines across history, weaving through them a common thematic thread. *Intolerance* alternates time frames to highlight how intolerance has inevitably led to violence while love has always forged a better way (as in the Jesus story). *Blade af Satans Bog* tells stories of Satan's influence on human history chronologically (beginning with Judas). In each film, the final storyline is roughly contemporaneous with the time of the film's production, revealing the central aims of the filmmakers within their second horizons: women's social reform movements in early twentieth-century America (*Intolerance*) and Finland in 1918 (*Blade af Satans Bog*). The inclusion of a contemporary storyline in each case makes clear that the filmmakers are drawing from their second horizons for the Jesus story through juxtaposition.

The Jesus storyline factors only minimally in *Intolerance*, yet it provides an important anchor for interpreting the film's message, especially for the storyline about the women's reform movements. In the film, one such movement (the Uplifter movement) imposes rigid abstinence laws on women and represents the twentieth-century temperance movement. Through juxtaposition, *Intolerance* interprets the Uplifters as "modern Pharisees," with the Pharisees of the Jesus storyline referred to on a title card as "equally intolerant hypocrites of another age." Yet connecting the Uplifters to Pharisees is rooted in a caricature of first-century Pharisees rather than an accurate portrait of this Jewish sect (see chap. 6).[17]

13. Tatum, *Jesus at the Movies*, 152.

14. Telford, "*Monty Python's Life of Brian*," 14.

15. The film does attend to realities of the first horizon that many Jesus films miss—e.g., its depiction of numerous Jewish factions and messianic pretenders in the first-century world. For an appraisal by biblical scholars, see Taylor, *Jesus and Brian*.

16. Walsh and Staley, *Jesus, the Gospels, and Cinematic Imagination*, 188.

17. See Reinhartz, "Pharisees on Film," 348–51.

It is notable that the few scenes from Jesus's ministry included in *Intolerance* are "scandalous" in some way. In each, the Pharisees respond with intolerance to Jesus (1) turning water into wine at Cana, (2) eating and drinking with tax collectors and sex workers and so gaining a reputation for being a drunkard and a glutton, and (3) refusing to condemn the woman caught in adultery. These episodes from the first horizon would have scandalized the Uplifters as well as the women's temperance movement they represent. Director D. W. Griffith's second horizon clearly influenced his selection of these scenes for his retelling of the ministry of Jesus, whom the film identifies on one title card as "the greatest enemy of intolerance." What's more, none of these episodes from the Gospels have much explanatory value for the crucifixion, which immediately follows them.[18] Through the film's unique retelling of the Jesus story, with its juxtaposed storylines, we are left to assume the values of the Uplifters led to Jesus's crucifixion. Griffith seems unaware of how the film's second horizon makes the juxtaposition of events in the first horizon highly implausible.

3. Anticipating the Second Horizon

Jesus films that *anticipate the second horizon* suggest overtly or implicitly that the first horizon points forward to the future time of the storyteller. *The King of Kings* (1927) provides an early example; it concludes with a shot of an American city landscape and the resurrected Jesus looking down with arms outstretched as "Lo I am with you always" appears on the screen (Matt. 28:20, based on KJV). *Last Days in the Desert* (2015) also anticipates its second horizon. It concludes with a couple pulling up in their car to take pictures at the place where Jesus was tempted (cf. chap. 3), anticipating second-horizon practices of pilgrimages and of commemorating traditional sites associated with biblical stories. The film *Mater Dei* (*Mother of God*, 1950) highlights how Mary's life *anticipates* her ongoing role in the life of the church through prayer and sacraments (from a Catholic perspective), as signposted by Jesus's words from the cross to the Beloved Disciple, "Woman, here is your son"; "Here is your mother" (John 19:26–27), and as displayed in the second half of the film, which focuses on contemporary Catholic practices. In *The Greatest Story Ever Told* (1965), Jewish leaders console themselves after Jesus's resurrection, and one says, "In any case, the whole thing will

18. As noted by Reinhartz (*Jesus of Hollywood*, 206), some of this is due to the editing that occurred after the film received pushback from Jewish groups like B'nai B'rith, which felt that an earlier version of the film was antisemitic. As a result, the thirty cuts to the Jesus story were dropped to seven.

DeMille Pictures Corporation

Final shot from the ending of *The King of Kings* (1927), a modern cityscape in the foreground

be forgotten in a week," which ironically anticipates the second horizon of global Christianity (something already signaled by the film's opening shots in a Christian cathedral).[19]

Jesus (1999) provides a well-developed example of anticipation, as it shows how the Jesus story points forward to subsequent events, particularly to historical evils that have been perpetrated in Jesus's name. The film opens with scenes of war and violence, including glimpses of the Crusades and soldiers during World War II calling out to Jesus as they are dying in battle. Viewers learn as Jesus awakens with a start that this short opening montage was his nightmare. These historical evils are reprised across the film during scenes of Satanic temptation. As Jesus is tempted in the wilderness, he sees visions of violence and modern-day poverty and famine. When Satan offers him the kingdoms of the earth (cf. Matt. 4:8–10), he takes Jesus to outer space to look on the planet, reflecting a second-horizon, post-Copernican perspective.[20]

19. As pointed out by Reinhartz, *Jesus of Hollywood*, 112.

20. Looking at the earth from space in the temptation also occurs in *The Revolutionary* (1995).

Lube / Lux Vide / Beta Film

The contemporary version of Jesus embracing a group of little children at the end of *Jesus* (1999)

These temptations intensify in Gethsemane,[21] where Satan shows Jesus the Crusades and witch hunts done in his name and declares, "This is what you're dying for." Yet Satan also says, "You can stop it tonight," implying that Jesus could avoid the cross and so stop these evils before they happen. In the face of this presentation of the problem of evil, Jesus remains committed to his fate and indicates that, unless people are free, they will be unable to choose God's love. After Jesus's resurrection, the film concludes as the actor who plays Jesus (now with short hair) walks around a scenic Mediterranean harbor in the twentieth century. A crowd of multinational children rush to Jesus and hug him, and he walks away with them, laughing. Given the film's emphasis on historical evils, the ending suggests that the children's free response and love is worth the evil that occurred. *Jesus* (1999) considers the ancient story of Jesus as it anticipates the film's own second horizon, focusing on the hindsight of world history and Christianity's difficult place within it.

4. Transposing the First Horizon

In this category, the story in the first horizon is *transposed* to the second horizon as if it were occurring in that horizon for the first time. The question invigorating these films is, What if the Jesus story happened today? In *Cotton Patch Gospel* (1988), a harmonized version of the Gospels is comedically

21. Satan also appears in Gethsemane in, e.g., *Santhi Sandesam* (*Message of Peace*, 2004) and *The Passion of the Christ* (2004); cf. *The Savior* (2014).

retold in an American Southern vernacular, as if the story were occurring in Georgia. *The Judas Project* (1993) similarly imagines Jesus coming for the first time to America during the 1990s.[22] The two most prominent examples of transposition in Jesus films, though, are *Godspell* (1973) and *Jezile* (*Son of Man*, 2006).

Godspell is a Jesus story transposed to 1970s New York City and set primarily in Central Park. The name Godspell offers a wordplay: It derives from the Old English word for "Gospel" and also signals the enchantment ("spell") that temporarily overtakes the film's characters.[23] As a magical John the Baptist traverses Manhattan blowing a shofar and singing "Prepare Ye (the Way of the Lord)," he places several people under that spell, drawing them into a day of clowning around and pantomiming with Jesus, acting out his parables in skits. As the film begins, Manhattan is populous and busy, with each character immersed in their mundane life in the concrete jungle. Yet once they fall under the "God spell," no one else is in sight in the entire city. The spell breaks, however, after Jesus's execution. As the disciples carry his body through Manhattan, singing again "Prepare Ye," the intense activity of Manhattan resumes. In *Godspell* there is no resurrection appearance, but the film seems to imply that these "disciples" will return to their routine lives inspired by their experiences with Jesus—a kind of resurrection motif more palatable within the second horizon of the 1970s. This interpretation seems forecasted in the musical's opening as Jesus describes the person who will follow him: "I will make him gardener for his own re-creation." *Godspell* straddles the tension between an urbane and even skeptical perspective on religion and a critique of fast-paced urban life—a life certainly not preferable to the film's hippie activities taking place in Central Park. *Godspell*, in this regard, highlights the compatibility of the Jesus movement with the "'flower power' movement's more natural forces and lifestyle."[24]

The South African film *Jezile* (*Son of Man*, 2006) explores a modern arrival of Jesus by transposing the Jesus story into an alternate version of Africa: "Kingdom of Judea, Afrika." Some of Jesus's teachings in the film are inspired by an African activist who opposed apartheid, Stephen Bantu Biko,[25] and the *ubuntu* theology of reconciliation associated with Desmond Tutu.[26] In *Jezile*,

22. The Netflix series *Messiah* (2020) imagines the contemporary appearance of an enigmatic messianic figure. However, the show does not presume that the first horizon never occurred, since the Messiah figure is interpreted as the return of Christ or of Isa by Christians and Muslims, respectively.

23. Walsh and Staley, *Jesus, the Gospels, and Cinematic Imagination*, 122.

24. Bakker, "Jesus in a Modern Contemporary Context," 161.

25. Zwick, "*Son of Man*," 245; Mokoena, "Steve Biko Christ-figure."

26. Middleton and Plate, "'Who Do You See That I Am?,'" 21.

Spire Films

Jesus triumphantly throws his fist in the air while ascending the side of a hill surrounded by angelic figures in *Jezile* (*Son of Man*, 2006).

the themes of the Jesus story are applied to the modern African setting of colonial oppression—a running motif that comes to a head in the film's final moments. Jesus is beaten, shot, left for dead in a ditch, and later buried. When his followers find his body, he is exhumed and held by his mother in the back of a pickup truck, mimicking the form of the *Pietà*, before his body is lifted up on a cross for all to see. Mary then leads a defiant song and dance, singing about how the land is covered in darkness as the oppressive colonizers look on. Sometime later, Jesus is reburied, after which he suddenly appears alive again and ascends a dirt hill surrounded by child angels. Together they gesture in triumph as they climb upward. The film concludes with a caption from Genesis 1:26 about all humanity being created in God's image. As the credits roll, images of African people appear on-screen, further highlighting the sociohistorical location of the film's second horizon. *Jezile*'s depiction of the resurrection of Jesus becomes a symbol for the resurrection of the people of Africa.[27]

5. Overlapping the Two Horizons

The two horizons overlap in some Jesus films, making both horizons visible at the same time. In this category, a semblance of verisimilitude confirms that the story is set in the ancient past. Yet also present are unambiguously

27. As Walsh and Staley (*Jesus, the Gospels, and Cinematic Imagination*, 302) suggest, the English title *Son of Man* likely supports this symbolism.

anachronistic elements from the second horizon. Both horizons operate simultaneously.

Perhaps the earliest example is *La Voie Lactée* (*The Milky Way*, 1969). The film is a parody that lampoons the perceived absurdity of debates about religious dogma. It follows two men traveling by foot on a well-known pilgrimage route—Camino de Santiago—from Paris, France, to Santiago, Spain. Along the way, they find themselves intersecting with people from across history debating minutiae of Christian doctrine. The film weaves together different storylines from across church history, including the life of Jesus, with the two horizons visibly overlapping rather than being simply juxtaposed (as in, e.g., *Intolerance* [1916]).[28]

A more subtle example of overlapping horizons appears in Pier Paolo Pasolini's *Il Vangelo Secondo Matteo* (*The Gospel According to St. Matthew*, 1964). Pasolini's film, an example of a "visual translation" (cf. chap. 1), overlaps the first horizon with his second horizon, with no real concern for historicity as such. We see this in three primary ways. First, the film was made in Matera in Southern Italy, with the second horizon of mid-twentieth-century Italy always present. Second, the film is an expression of the Italian neorealist film movement, which characteristically uses nonprofessionals and non-elites as actors to better represent the lived circumstances of the people depicted. This style is conveyed beautifully through a recurring fixation on people's faces and the retention of the actors' own dialects and accents in the film.[29] Third, the film incorporates the African American spiritual "Sometimes I Feel Like a Motherless Child" to introduce the slaughter of the innocents, a choice seemingly designed to evoke the US civil rights movement, which was taking place while the movie was being filmed. *Il Vangelo Secondo Matteo* appears to be stressing the significance of the Jesus story's first horizon for the poor and marginalized fighting for an end to oppression in the second horizon, in keeping with Pasolini's Marxist perspective.

The filmmakers behind *Das Neue Evangelium* (*The New Gospel*, 2020), were inspired by and emulated aspects of Pasolini's film. They filmed in Matera and chose nonprofessionals as actors to address the contemporary injustices experienced by African migrant agricultural workers in the city. The film is mostly documentary interspersed with elements of a Jesus film,

28. Other examples of overt overlapping horizons include *The Thorn* (*The Greatest Story Overtold / The Divine Mr. J*, 1971), with its mixing of "ancient" costuming and contemporary sets and props, and *Pilatus und Andere: Ein Film für Karfreitag* (*Pilate and Others*, 1972), a German adaptation of *The Master and Margarita* (1940/1967) based on the Pilate storyline that recurs across that novel.

29. Baugh, "Three Revolutionary Gospel Films," 143.

Fruitmarket Kultur and Medien / Langfilm / IIPM

Migrant workers stomping tomatoes in the supermarket to evoke the cleansing of the temple sequence from the Gospels in *Das Neue Evangelium* (*The New Gospel*, 2020)

including "behind the scenes" moments between takes. *Das Neue Evangelium* overtly draws its inspiration from Pasolini as the filmmakers discuss his film, watch clips from *Il Vangelo Secondo Matteo*, and even cast Enrique Irazoqui (who played Jesus in Pasolini's film) in the role of John the Baptist. Some scenes in the Jesus film embedded within the documentary are particularly suffused with the complexities of the plight of the agricultural workers. During the temple cleansing, for example, Jesus and his disciples, dressed in "ancient" garb, throw tomatoes from trucks and smash tomatoes in a modern supermarket. The Jesus story helps address the present context, with more of contemporary Matera and its modern social problems visible than in Pasolini's film.

Jesus Christ Superstar (1973) provides a striking example of the two horizons overlapping, both visually and ideologically. The film opens with shots of the hills and valleys of Israel along with ancient ruins, laying bare topographical and architectural witnesses to the events of the first horizon. A bus arrives in the desert, and the actors about to perform *Jesus Christ Superstar* unload props and costumes. The costuming is iconic 1970s fashion, and at times the overlapping of the past and the present is jarring. Roman soldiers wear pink tank tops and brandish machine guns, while other characters, like Jesus, wear approximations of first-century tunics. The landscape and costuming visually bring together the two horizons in overlapping fashion.

An ideological overlap of horizons is central to *Jesus Christ Superstar*. Judas is given a key role in the musical (cf. chap. 6), portrayed as concerned that Jesus approves of people's adulation of him as a "Superstar."[30] Judas

30. Walsh and Staley (*Jesus, the Gospels, and Cinematic Imagination*, 138–40) contend that "Superstar" is the 1970s translation of "Messiah."

The contrast between the costuming for the Roman soldiers and for Jesus in *Jesus Christ Superstar* (1973)

provides the musical's POV,[31] with his skepticism about Jesus and his followers presumably commended by its writers and producers. Indeed, they may have viewed the Jesus followers of the 1970s and had reason to be cynical. Nothing encapsulates the cynicism of *Jesus Christ Superstar* toward second-horizon Christians more powerfully than the scene of Simon Zealotes and his entourage singing about Jesus's greatness ("Simon Zealotes"). The lyrics convey a simplistic version of faith focused on fanfare, and Christ devotion is portrayed as selfish and superficial. Jesus responds ("Poor Jerusalem") by declaring that no one understands the true nature of power and glory or that true life can only come, paradoxically, through dying. This counterintuitive message that to follow Jesus means death (cf. Matt. 16:24–26) is so unintelligible that the camera lingers on a perplexed Simon with his head tilted to the side in confusion.

When Jesus is condemned to die, he turns to see a vindicated Judas dressed in white descending from above (what Reinhartz calls his "resurrection").[32] As Judas sings triumphantly, accompanied by an entourage of angelic "Soul Sisters," he asks Jesus a series of questions, wondering whether Jesus believes what people have been claiming about him and whether his imminent death

31. Walsh and Staley, *Jesus, the Gospels, and Cinematic Imagination*, 136.
32. Reinhartz, *Jesus of Hollywood*, 169.

Final shots of *Jesus Christ Superstar* (1973) as Jesus is left on the cross while the sun is setting on the horizon(s)

is worth the fanfare. With a nod to the second horizon, Judas sings that Jesus should have come "today" to reach a wider audience, given the lack of "mass communication" then ("Superstar"). Judas continues to play the role of *doubter*, and in his vindicated state he has gained the insight that, if the goal was to spread his fame and message, Jesus chose the wrong era to be a "Superstar." The vindication of Judas in *Jesus Christ Superstar* is thus the vindication of the skeptic who finds reason to doubt Jesus because of his celebrity. The film concludes with the crucifixion as everyone packs up and gets back on the bus. Everyone, that is, except Jesus, who remains on the cross as the bus drives away under the setting sun. As the credits silently roll, Jesus is left behind in the world of the first horizon as the bus returns to the 1970s.

6. Imitating the First Horizon

In this category, the characters or storyline of the second horizon imitates the first horizon in one of two ways. The first involves allusions and echoes to the story of Jesus. Really, any film with a Christ figure—someone resembling Christ, usually through a sacrificial death—would fit in this category (e.g., *The Matrix* [1999]; *Harry Potter and the Deathly Hallows: Part 2* [2011]). In Jesus films, such parallels are more extensive, with the second horizon involving a modernized version of the first horizon story. For instance, *Je Vous Salue, Marie* (*Hail Mary*, 1985) tells the story of a young woman navigating pregnancy in the 1980s; allusions to traditions about the Virgin Mary shape the story. Another example, *The Gospel of Us* (2012), is a highly stylized and edited recording of a live three-day nontraditional passion play ("The

Passion of Port Talbot" from Easter 2011) performed in various locations in Port Talbot, Wales.[33] The play is set intentionally *within* the contemporary second horizon and focuses on the history and future of the town, using elements from the first horizon's life of Jesus to tell Port Talbot's own story of overcoming economic hardship and governmental neglect.

The second way imitation of the first horizon occurs is when the process of retelling the ancient story transforms those who retell it. This reflection of *life imitating art* most often occurs in films that include a passion play, a Christmas pageant, or even their own Jesus film. The characters who play actors performing in the embedded Jesus story experience transformation through their parts in that story.[34] For example, in *Mary* (2005) an actress playing the role of Mary Magdalene in an embedded film about the Gnostic Gospels decides, as a result of that experience, to move to Jerusalem and recruit disciples around herself.

A common formational impact in these kinds of Jesus films involves a character's moral shift stemming from involvement in an embedded Jesus story. For instance, in *The Best Christmas Pageant Ever* (1983 and 2024), based on Barbara Robinson's novel (1971), the Herdman children, who are "absolutely the worst children in the history of the world," come to see themselves reflected in the poor conditions of Mary and Joseph. Similarly, Raul, a criminal leader in *Cristo 70* (1969), begrudgingly agrees to participate in a local passion play while laying low in a small town after a plane heist. Through his participation, Raul becomes increasingly conscientious about matters of faith. In the end, he is betrayed by a member of his gang, who stabs him as he is being raised up on the cross (within the play) just as the police are arriving to arrest them. Another example highlights transformations of actors in their real life. *Lamentations of Judas* (2020) embeds portions of a Jesus film within a documentary about Angolan ex-combatants hired to betray Black South Africans and fight against them during apartheid. The film intersperses story elements from the life of Jesus with interviews of these ex-combatants, who play the disciples, the crowds, and the Roman soldiers in the embedded Jesus film.[35] The filmmakers ask the interviewees to reflect on their respective parts in the reenactment of the Jesus story and on their previous occupations as mercenaries. A few of the men, who had viewed what they were doing as merely following orders to earn a living, began to feel

33. Cf. the BBC Wales documentary series *Passion in Port Talbot* (2011).

34. Although *The Prince of Peace* (1959) doesn't explore how performing The Lawton Passion Play (cf. *The Lawton Story* [1949]) shaped those involved, it begins by introducing the townspeople from Lawton, Oklahoma, and so hints in this direction.

35. Accordingly, this film also fits the category of overlapping the two horizons.

remorse when asked whether the Roman soldiers' treatment of Jesus could be similarly characterized.

Some Jesus films showcase an *imitation of experiences* between a character who acts in an embedded Jesus story and the part they play. For example, an actor playing the thief on the cross dies in the storyline of Pasolini's *La Ricotta* (1963), having been neglected and ridiculed by the cast and crew (as part of a critique of Christianity's complicity with classism). In the case of *Celui Qui Doit Mourir* (*He Who Must Die*, 1957), viewers never see the passion play, but the establishment of the roles played by the townspeople has a direct effect on the dramatic tension that ensues and shapes character relationships. Additionally, in *La Última Cena* (*The Last Supper*, 1976) a Cuban slaveholder chooses to have a meal with twelve of his slaves on Maundy Thursday to reenact the Last Supper, with the intention of teaching them Christian theology. This event ends up inspiring a revolt, led by a Judas-like slave who betrays the slaveholder (who assumes the position of Jesus at the meal), with events transpiring in a weekend of violence that resonates with ironic connections to Good Friday and Easter Sunday.

Jésus de Montréal (*Jesus of Montreal*, 1989) is perhaps the best example of *imitation of experiences* in Jesus films. It tells the story of a man named Daniel tasked with writing a new passion play for a Catholic church in 1980s Montreal. Much of the film's critique focuses on the corruption of the Catholic Church in Quebec, personified chiefly by the vile priest Father Leclerc and entertainment lawyer Richard Cardinal (note the surname's association).[36] Daniel meets secretly with a theology professor to bring the latest scholarship into the play, even though that scholarship is at cross-purposes with some elements of Catholic dogma.[37] Throughout the film, *proximity* to the story of Jesus transforms those involved in its retelling. Nearly every interaction in the film's second horizon involves some allusion to an event in the life of Jesus and his disciples. And the actors cast to play the disciples in the play resemble the original disciples of Jesus (notably Peter, Mary Magdalene, and Thomas). As the movie progresses, the actors in the passion play develop (further) into their archetypal representations.

In *Jésus de Montréal*, the cipher for the religious tension in the Gospels is the purity of theater acting. Mass-produced media is pitted against the pure form of acting on the small stage. Given this frame, the Gospel accounts of Satan tempting Jesus with the prospect of inheriting all the earth's kingdoms

36. Reinhartz, *Jesus of Hollywood*, 35–36, 190; cf. Reinhartz, "Pharisees on Film," 357–59.

37. E.g., traditions about Jesus's parentage from Panthera, as in the Toledoth Yeshu (see above). In many respects this film functions on the metalevel, since it is a Jesus film concerned with how to visualize the Jesus story.

Max Films Productions / Gérard Mital Productions / National Film Board of Canada (NFB)

Daniel being offered a film contract by a business executive in *Jésus de Montréal* (*Jesus of Montreal*, 1989)

shift to Daniel being offered a major film contract. Jesus's temple cleansing transposes to a scene of Daniel reacting destructively during the recording of a commercial to protest exploitative consumerism. Betrayal is conveyed by Daniel's friend Pascal going mainstream with his acting career, subtly depicted by Pascal's appearance on a film poster in the subway.[38]

Daniel's character imitates the person of Jesus most clearly at the film's end. During the play's final performance, Daniel falls from the cross and hits his head, which results in a brain injury. He is taken to (the Catholic) St. Mark's Hospital, which has no room for him. Daniel and those with him take a set of escalators down to the subway (representing a descent into hell),[39] where he gives an incoherent speech with apocalyptic material taken directly from Jesus's Olivet Discourse (e.g., Mark 13) before passing out. Daniel is then taken to the Jewish hospital, where he succumbs to his injuries. When his organs are harvested for donation, the doctor says, "Give us his body"—words with clear eucharistic overtones[40]—as Daniel lays on the hospital bed in a crucifix posture. The doctor mentions that Daniel's type O blood is a "godsend." These images imitate and reinterpret Jesus's healing miracles and

38. Pascal's headshot evokes the beheading of John the Baptist (cf. an agent saying about Pascal, "I want his head"). But given how the film upholds the purity of theater, Pascal's mainstream acting career suggests that he has betrayed that vision and so also plays the role of Judas (cf. *Godspell* [1973], where one character fills the roles of both Judas and John the Baptist). The ambiguity is briefly suggested in Stern et al., *Savior on the Silver Screen*, 313.

39. Tatum, *Jesus at the Movies*, 206.

40. Walsh and Staley, *Jesus, the Gospels, and Cinematic Imagination*, 232.

death while providing a more palatable image of "resurrection" for the film's second horizon of late 1980s Montreal.

7. Incorporating the Second Horizon

This classification refers to the incorporation of the second horizon into the first horizon so that the former becomes part of the latter. *Assassin 33 A.D.* (2020)[41] incorporates the second horizon into the Jesus story by way of time travel. The film follows a few precocious scientists recruited to help a secret Islamic terrorist group called Lab-19. This organization, led by a former refugee named Ahmed, initially hopes that the scientists will help transfer matter from one place to another. Ram, the lead scientist, realizes that if the amount of time needed to move something from point A to point B is not factored in, the process will transfer matter to the past—time travel. Preferring this innovation to matter transfer, the terrorists determine to travel through time to kill Jesus to prevent the disciples from spreading "the resurrection myth" and so keep Christianity from ever existing.

The storyline fractures into multiple timelines and alternate realities as different past events are changed (à la *Butterfly Effect* [2004]). In one timeline Jesus is executed in Gethsemane at gunpoint, and in another a couple of scientists and mercenaries end up becoming characters from the Gospel passion narratives, including the thieves on the cross, Simon of Cyrene, the young man who runs away naked in Gethsemane (cf. Mark 14:51–52), and the angels at the empty tomb. When one of the scientists named Simon, who will become Simon of Cyrene, tries to warn Jesus in Gethsemane about the threat, Simon tells him that being shot might be preferable to the cross. Jesus asks Simon how he knows what's ahead, and Simon responds, "I've seen your movie. We got it on bootleg."[42] Somehow, Simon's words help Jesus. "I know what is going to happen to me," Jesus says, "and if you had finished my movie, you would know that I'll be back." After Jesus walks away, Simon considers his words and then exclaims, "*I'll be back?* That ain't your movie!" This (resurrection) allusion to the *Terminator* franchise is bolstered by other shared features—both stories involve time travel deployed to kill a messianic figure with the initials J. C. (i.e., John Connor and Jesus Christ), and Lab-19 eventually takes over the planet much like *Terminator*'s Skynet. *Assassin 33 A.D.* ends with a stinger: Ram has time traveled thirty years into the future after Lab-19 has used Jesus's DNA to create the anti-Christ.

41. This is the only film we place in the category, although *La Voie Lactée* (*The Milky Way*, 1969) could also be an example of incorporation.

42. If only we could know which film Simon is referring to; since the modern setting is 2029, it might be a film that came out after we finished our book!

Although *Assassin 33 A.D.* (2020) may feel like a parody, the film does not identify itself as such. The film is earnest in its effort to create a faith-based film, in which many of the unbelieving and doubting characters come to faith by the end of the movie. It also sincerely presents itself as clever, even though it fails on this count. Most problematically, it is deeply Islamophobic and anti-refugee. After its debut, the film was severely criticized and so the filmmakers released a director's cut (*Black Easter* [2021]) with several significant edits and an excessive voice-over narration to simplify the story and minimize the xenophobia of the film's second horizon.

8. Neglecting the Second Horizon

A final category for understanding the relationship of the two horizons arises when a filmmaker neglects to acknowledge fully the influence of the second horizon on the first. To be clear, films that neglect their second horizon still have one. Although many filmmakers seem less inclined to recognize the impact of their own horizon on their retelling of the Jesus story, we discuss in some detail *Jesus* (1979) and *The Passion of the Christ* (2004). We have already identified both films as examples of importation (no. 1 above), as they import later developments in evangelical and Catholic theology, respectively. Yet they present their retellings of Jesus's story seemingly without much, if any, recognition of their own influences—the cultural Zeitgeist and their own theological presuppositions.

Jesus (1979)

Jesus (1979) and its later editions (notably, *The Jesus Film* [2001]) have been viewed by more people than any other Jesus film, and it can even contend for the title of the most watched film of any genre.[43] It was produced by Cru (formerly Campus Crusade for Christ) and used primarily as an apologetic and evangelistic tool around the world.

Jesus (1979) claims to be a straightforward presentation of the Gospel of Luke. Indeed, one caption in the film identifies it as "a documentary taken from the Gospel of St. Luke." Additionally, John Heyman, a producer of *Jesus* (1979), apparently did not want to include any credits at the film's end because, in his view, the film brought viewers into Luke's Gospel "without interpretation."[44] Yet the film reflects its cultural moment from the start, as

43. Page, *100 Bible Films*, 124.

44. Walsh and Staley, *Jesus, the Gospels, and Cinematic Imagination*, 206. On first glance, the 1979 film seems to include only the most chastened of liberties—the only time Jesus's speech is not taken from the Bible is when he says "hello" to children.

its opening title sequence imitates the text crawl made famous by *Star Wars* (1977).[45] Additionally, the use of voice-over narration provides commentary from a *particular POV*—for example, when the narrator asks viewers to consider whether Jesus is "more than a prophet" or affirms that on entering Jerusalem Jesus "knew he was going to be killed for the sins of mankind." Even more striking, *Jesus* (1979) is actually an edited version of a much longer "visual translation" of Luke called *The New Media Bible: The Gospel According to St. Luke* (1979), which relied on narration of the KJV. The result of the editorial and streamlining work to produce a more digestible version is a *highly edited version of Luke*, with multiple scenes *reordered*, many scenes entirely *omitted* (more than four hundred verses),[46] and several elements *added* from other Gospels.[47]

Moreover, *Jesus* (1979) was rereleased multiple times with various additional elements, resulting in a version that began circulating in 2001 titled *The Jesus Film*. This film is framed by biblical prophecy and an evangelical salvation message. Through this framing narrative, *The Jesus Film* reveals a distinctly American evangelical interpretation of the Old Testament and its relation to Jesus. The opening narrative frame begins with Adam and Eve's sin and the need for a sacrifice to appease God, and it adds the story of the binding of Isaac (Gen. 22). Material from Isaiah and other prophets is included to prophetically anticipate Christ. The Lukan Jesus story within *The Jesus Film* provides the solution to the plight of Adam and Eve and the search for a fitting sacrifice. Yet Luke, of all the Gospels, has the least developed atonement theology.[48]

In the concluding editorial frame, the narrator connects the dots for the viewer by asserting that Jesus was like the ram that was sacrificed in Isaac's place (though no Gospel explicitly cites Gen. 22).[49] The narrator also confirms that Jesus is the one whom the prophets anticipated. The viewer is then given a "Romans road" style of evangelistic appeal, with the narrator leading the viewer in repeating the "sinner's prayer." The issue with *The Jesus Film* is not that the Gospel of Luke is reframed via evangelical theology but that the theology presented is rooted in a specific 1970s evangelical and individualistic

45. Walsh, "Reading the Gospel(s) in the Dark," 106.

46. For a complete list of omissions, see Walsh and Staley, *Jesus, the Gospels, and Cinematic Imagination*, 198–200.

47. *Jesus* (1979) reveals harmonizing tendencies, but a notable example comes at the end, when Jesus declares the Great Commission from Matthew (28:18–20) while ascending to heaven as in Luke (24:51).

48. E.g., Luke omits verses from Mark that focus on the atoning significance of Jesus's death, such as Mark 10:45. For an overview, see Brown, "Jesus Messiah as Isaiah's Servant," 63–64.

49. Although on Matthew, see, e.g., Huizenga, *New Testament*.

version of the gospel—something like, Jesus died for me so I can go to heaven. What concerns us about *Jesus* (1979) and its later expansions is not that these films have a second horizon within American evangelicalism but that the makers of these films seem painfully unaware of the reality of that horizon in their claims to give us the Bible "without interpretation."

The Passion of the Christ (2004)

Mel Gibson's *The Passion of the Christ* (2004), the highest-grossing Jesus film to date, is another example of a film that tends to ignore its second horizon. The pope at the time, John Paul II, allegedly said after a private screening of the film, "It is as it was,"[50] sanctioning the movie as reaching the height of verisimilitude in representing the horror of Jesus's crucifixion within the ancient horizon. Gibson made similar claims himself, comparing the film to time travel and "watching the events unfold exactly as they occurred."[51] Gibson even declared, "We've done the research. I'm telling the story as the Bible tells it. I think the story, as it really happened, speaks for itself. The Gospel is a complete script, and that's what we're filming."[52]

The Passion of the Christ does not acknowledge fully its second horizon, in terms of either the theology that informs it or the filmmaking techniques that shape it. Illuminating its theological assumptions, the film opens with a caption of Isaiah 53:5: "He was wounded for our transgressions, crushed for our iniquities; by His wounds we are healed." As Walsh and Staley note, this verse provides the biblical "justification for the film's graphic violence" that ensues.[53] Yet despite this opening scriptural caption, the film relies on material that goes beyond Scripture.[54] First, no evangelist cites Isaiah 53:5 with reference to the crucifixion. Across the entire New Testament, only 1 Peter contains the phrase "by his wounds you have been healed" (1 Pet. 2:24).[55] More importantly, *The Passion of the Christ* is deeply indebted to sources and traditions much later than the Gospels, including the visions of Anne Catherine Emmerich (1774–1824),[56] the Catholic traditions of the Via Dolorosa and the stations of the cross,[57] and medieval reflection on Jesus's "secret passion."[58]

50. Page, *100 Bible Films*, 165.
51. Page, *100 Bible Films*, 165.
52. As cited in Cohen, *Christ Killers*, 249.
53. Walsh and Staley, *Jesus, the Gospels, and Cinematic Imagination*, 281.
54. Walsh and Staley, *Jesus, the Gospels, and Cinematic Imagination*, 280.
55. See Brown, "Jesus Messiah as Isaiah's Servant," 64–66.
56. Published as *The Dolorous Passion of Our Lord Jesus Christ* (1833). See Webb, "*The Passion*."
57. Guðmundsdóttir, "*The Passion of the Christ* (2004)," 203.
58. Cohen, *Christ Killers*, 250; cf. 194–202.

Icon Productions

The Satan figure from *The Passion of the Christ* (2004)

Gibson's filmmaking techniques also illuminate his aims, which move far beyond the canonical Gospels. He uses various cinematic tropes that set the film apart from other Jesus films and move beyond the evidence of the Gospels. Minor keys pervade the musical score, and the first shots of the film, which are set in Gethsemane, are given a dark and eerie feel accentuated by the "blue wash" applied to the cinematography.[59] There is a full moon, and a creepy snake slithers around. Indeed, throughout the film demonic figures lurk about. Judas is nearly attacked by a monster, and demonic-looking children taunt him. An androgynous Satan character and a baby-like demon watch Jesus as he is tortured by sadistic men with blood spattering all over their faces. A bird picks out the eye of the crucified unrepentant thief. Taken together, these features and images could lead one to conclude that *The Passion of the Christ* is a horror film.[60] Ostensibly the film's purpose is to give viewers an appreciation for the intense suffering Jesus endured, with anecdotal evidence

59. Walsh and Staley, *Jesus, the Gospels, and Cinematic Imagination*, 288–89.

60. This is not said to preclude the possibility that the film participates in other genres (cf. Judd, *Modern Genre Theory*). Further corroboration comes from the planned sequel, *The Resurrection of the Christ* (forthcoming), which will reportedly include Jesus's descent into

suggesting that this is one of the film's effects. Yet interpreting *The Passion of the Christ* from the perspective of its tropes and filmmaking techniques makes the horror film identification seem inescapable. Rather than depicting what Jesus's experience was like according to the Gospels, the film depicts Mel Gibson's visual interpretation of Jesus's experience.

This is where the matter of the unacknowledged second horizon gets particularly troubling. The horror movies prominent in the mid-2000s—films like *Saw* (2004) and *Hostel* (2005)—have been dubbed "torture porn" for their violent depictions of gore and of intense, painful violence.[61] Film critic Roger Ebert even stated that if *The Passion of the Christ* were not religious, it would have received an NC-17 rating.[62] In light of the film's second horizon, it is intriguing to consider the forces in the mid-2000s that might have made moviegoing audiences seek out films amplifying torture. We think it possible that the public discourse about the ethics and efficiency of torture practices tied to interrogations in the aftermath of 9/11 played a role in this cinematic development. Even if not a direct influence, the unacknowledged second horizon of *The Passion of the Christ* resembles the Zeitgeist of the mid-2000s.

Conclusion

This chapter has demonstrated that the phenomenon of the two horizons is an inevitable reality of retelling the story of Jesus, whether it happens mere decades after Jesus's lifetime or two millennia later. We have suggested eight categories for understanding how a film's second horizon (its maker's or director's perspective) can influence the retelling of the first. As located human beings, we cannot avoid bringing our contexts and concerns to the process of retelling Jesus's story (i.e., we also have contextual perspectives). As we visualize the Jesus story when reading or viewing, the directors in our heads have only our prior experiences and understandings to work with for our story building, which is often as full of anachronisms as the films we watch. Adele Reinhartz contends that "the Jesus of the biopics reflects our own societies and cultures more than he illuminates the historical Jesus whose story the movies purport to tell."[63] No one can produce a retelling that dispenses with

hell before his resurrection (the "harrowing of hell"). Setting the sequel in hell surely suggests a horror film franchise.

61. *The Passion of the Christ*'s violence is not technically "pornographic," as some have accused (cf. *South Park*, season 8, episode 3, "The Passion of the Jew," 2004), since the viewer is not made to crave more, as Mark Goodacre rightly points out (see "Power of *The Passion*," 34–35).

62. Walsh and Staley, *Jesus, the Gospels, and Cinematic Imagination*, 289–90.

63. Reinhartz, *Jesus of Hollywood*, 10.

the second horizon. To be sure, some of the Jesus films make their horizon overt and explicit, and others do so implicitly but with self-awareness. Yet films with hidden horizons are no more "objective" than the rest. Every Jesus film has a second horizon, and as conscientious viewers we are invited to notice and analyze that hermeneutical horizon. When we do, we can reflect in rich ways on what retelling the Jesus story *might do* in discrete contexts. And we can reflect on how retelling the Jesus story within those diverse spaces might also cause us to return to the earliest stories with new questions, renewed appreciation, and fresh insights.

Conclusion

Perspective matters, and as the saying goes, *it's all a matter of perspective*. Imagine that you have downloaded and begun watching a newly released Jesus film; let's call it *The Authentic Story of Jesus*. The storyline begins with a group of six servants from the court of an Eastern kingdom visiting Jesus's family in a Bethlehem house, where we see Jesus toddling around. These servants are well dressed and look official but are clearly not royalty (e.g., no crowns). Instead, they communicate that they have come from royal courts only as *representatives* of Eastern royalty, and they bring gifts from their masters. Additionally, there are four men and two women in this group of magi. What is your reaction? You might be thinking, *This is hardly an* authentic *Jesus story. There weren't six magi, and there certainly weren't any women in the group. It's the "wise* men,*" after all! And, where's the manger, and why is Jesus portrayed as a toddler walking about?*

What may be surprising is that Matthew—the only Gospel that tells this part of the nativity story—gives us no details that conjure up three wise men, a manger, and a baby Jesus (cf. Matt. 2:1–12). Church tradition has shaped how most of us picture the magi in Matthew's Gospel. As we noted in chapter 1, the image of *three* "wise men"—Melchior, Gaspar, and Balthazzar, originating from three different parts of the world—is a sixth-century CE tradition (cf. Armenian Infancy Gospel), and yet each Christmas season, images and songs reinforce this visualization (e.g., "We three kings of Orient are . . .").

Now Matthew does identify "magi" (*magoi*) who come from the East but does not specify their number (or their genders, for that matter).[1] And on the

1. Matthew's use of *magoi* ("magi") may focus on a specific group with specific roles (i.e., sages or priests), which could constrain the term to refer to a male-only role, but the plural

topic of royalty, the earliest readers of Matthew may have heard the story and expected to hear of the world's kings celebrating the arrival of the Messiah, as we read about in Psalm 72:10–11, a text Matthew alludes to (cf. Matt. 2:11). Instead Matthew writes of *magoi*—who were most likely servants to kings, causing his audience to wonder, "Where are the kings?"[2] Additionally, given that the only temporal markers in the passage indicate that magi seek out Jesus after his birth and that Herod determines to kill all children (or boys) ages two and under, we could easily visualize Jesus at the time of the magi's visit as a young toddler instead of an infant in a manger (with the detail of a "manger" found in Luke's Gospel). In fact, Matthew mentions that the family is lodged in a "house" (2:11). We—all of us—fill in gaps and harmonize details to create a more complete Jesus story. Jesus films (and other such retellings) simply illuminate that we do so, while also making clear the features of our own particular rendering of that story.

The Themes We Have Traced

We have found the hermeneutical questions about the Jesus story as it is told and retold to be fascinating issues for exploration, and these questions have occupied a central place in *The Greatest Story Ever Retold*. While addressing these questions, we have provided a sampling of the many ways the story of Jesus has been recast over the centuries, whether in early Gospels or in modern film.

Two central themes have guided our analysis across the book. First, all Jesus films—and in fact, all retellings of the Jesus story—are *interpretive retellings*. And this is not a bad thing. The interpretive nature of retelling the Jesus story is not a problem to be solved; it is a reality to be acknowledged. Knowing this truth encourages us to lean into the hermeneutics of Gospels and Jesus films. We should be sure to raise our hermeneutical antenna as we read ancient Gospels (whether canonical or noncanonical) and when we view modern Jesus films.

A second theme of the book is that our own responses to Jesus films hint that we have already visualized the Jesus story in our mind's eye if we have been readers or hearers of the Gospels. In this way, all of us are inevitably directors of a Jesus story. As we focus attention on that story, we interpret and direct our

masculine term could, theoretically, be generic. In Greek, a plural masculine term for a group can include both men and women. Indeed, to communicate a mixed group, the masculine plural form must be used. For example, see Matthew's use of the masculine plural for "crowds" (*ochloi*; 14:19) that he explicitly notes includes men, women, and children (14:21). There may be a historical argument for understanding *magoi* as men, but not a linguistic one. Cf. BDAG, 608.

2. Powell, *Chasing the Eastern Star*, 147; cf. 136–47.

own "film" via innumerable decisions about staging, casting, costuming, set design, camera angles, and more. This, too, is not a bad thing. It does, however, invite us to notice and account for our own hermeneutical (interpretive) lenses.

By being attuned to these realities—the hermeneutical perspectives in Gospels and films, as well as our own implicit visualizations of the Jesus story—we are able to consider them in conversation with one another. We can be more thoughtful readers and viewers, asking a variety of questions. For example, how does our own "implied director" shape our responses to any particular Jesus film (or early Gospel)? And can a Jesus film help us understand the Gospels better by illuminating fresh interpretive possibilities and by guiding us to ask different, and sometimes better, questions?[3] We believe that grappling with these hermeneutical realities allows us to have a keener grasp on the process of reading the Gospels. At least, we have found this to be true for our own engagement with Gospels, films, and our own internal "directors."

In addition to these central themes, we have traced across the book some of the intriguing patterns in the retellings of the Jesus story—from the four canonical Gospels, to literary Gospels of the early centuries, to modern Jesus films. We have examined tendencies toward harmonization (chap. 2) and filling in narrative gaps (chap. 3) and numerous impulses related to characterization (chaps. 4–6), including focusing on, expanding, and refashioning individuals in the Gospels, sometimes "filling in" contours of characters who have relatively minor roles in the canonical Gospels. We have also considered how Jesus films thematize the Jesus story, sometimes highlighting motifs already present in the Gospels and other times introducing new or surprising themes into the story (chap. 7).

We have also addressed the complex questions of evaluating the faithfulness of Jesus films to the canonical Gospels (chap. 1), as well as the ways a Jesus film inevitably showcases on some level its own context and concerns—its "second horizon" (chap. 8). In the end, we wonder if it might be fruitful to consider not so much the question of whether a Jesus film succeeds at being "faithful" to the Gospels but the alternate questions of what a Jesus film sets out to accomplish and whether it achieves those purposes.

Our Hopes

Writing this book together, we have attempted to analyze the phenomenon of retelling the Jesus story in a *storied way*. At every turn, we have retold

3. In this sense, we could think of a Jesus film as a kind of commentary on the Gospels. Asking if and how Jesus films might illuminate the biblical text is what Larry Krietzer refers to as "reversing the hermeneutical flow" (see this language throughout *Gospel Images in Fiction and Film*).

vignettes from the stories of ancient Gospels and modern films so that our readers can sample many, many Jesus films and their ancient counterparts. Indeed, we hope we have whetted your appetite for viewing some of the two hundred films and series that we have cataloged. No Jesus film gets everything right, and some Jesus films can be more frustrating than compelling. Yet there is something meaningful about the plethora of Jesus films and how most reflect, in their best moments, something good, true, and beautiful about Jesus. Taken together in their plurality, these films reinforce how Jesus transcends our ability to comprehend and represent him fully. Not even two hundred films (or series) are able to do justice to a figure like Jesus, who has made a deep and highly personal impact over the centuries on a countless number of people across the globe. Were it possible to film them all, we suppose that the world itself could not contain the movies that would be produced.

If you choose to invest time in reading and viewing Jesus stories and films, we hope you will do what researching this book has caused us to do: to more thoughtfully engage these Jesus stories and to do so with a clearer understanding of how our own internal director's viewpoint affects our evaluations of Jesus films. This brings us to a final hope for this book. For those who come from a place of faith, it can be easy while watching a Jesus film to make quick judgments—pro or con. By bringing our own internal director into view, we are able to step back and consider the decisions made by a filmmaker that raise certain emotions in us: satisfaction and inspiration on the one hand, or confusion and even frustration on the other. We hope that by engaging this book you might find yourself watching a Jesus film with sustained curiosity rather than quick evaluation. We hope that, when the lights go down in the theater, you can see more clearly the vision of *the film's* director because you've already gotten to know *your own*.

Appendix of Films Cited

This is not a comprehensive list of Jesus films. Rather it includes the over two hundred films, shorts, television or streaming shows, miniseries, and cartoons cited in this book, arranged chronologically.

The Horitz Passion Play. Directed by Walter W. Freeman. Klaw and Erlanger, 1897.

La Passion du Christ (*The Passion of Christ*). Directed by Albert Kirchner. Maison de la Bonne Presse, 1897.

La Passion (*The Passion*). Directed by George Hatot. Auguste and Louis Lumière, 1898.

The Passion Play of Oberammergau. Directed by Henry C. Vincent. Eden Musée, 1898.

La Vie et Passion de Notre Seigneur Jésus-Christ (*The Life and Passion of Our Lord Jesus Christ*). Directed by Lucien Nonguet and Ferdinand Zecca. Pathé Frères, 1902–5.

La Vie du Christ, or *La Naissance, La Vie et La Mort du Christ* (*The Birth, the Life and the Death of Christ*). Directed by Alice Guy. Société des Etablissements L. Gaumont, 1906.

Ben Hur. Directed by Sydney Olcott and Frank Oakes Rose. Kalem Company, 1907.

La Vie et Passion de Notre Seigneur Jésus-Christ (*The Life and Passion of Our Lord Jesus Christ*). Directed by Ferdinand Zecca. Pathé Frères, 1907.

The Miracles of Jesus. Director uncredited. Mogull Film Company of New York, 1910.

From the Manger to the Cross. Directed by Sydney Olcott. Kalem Company, 1912.

The Star of Bethlehem. Directed by Lawrence Marston. Thanhouser Film Corporation, 1912.

Quo Vadis? Directed by Enrico Guazzoni. Società Italiana Cines, 1913.

The Shadow of Nazareth. Directed by Arthur Maude. Venus Features, 1913.

The Birth of a Nation. Directed by D. W. Griffith. David W. Griffith Corp.; Epoch Producing Corporation, 1915.

Christus. Directed by Giulio Antamoro. Società Italiana Cines, 1916.

Civilization. Directed by Reginald Barker, Thomas H. Ince, Raymond B. West, Walter Edwards, David Hartford, Jay Hunt, and J. Parker Read Jr. Thomas H. Ince Corporation, 1916.

Intolerance. Directed by D. W. Griffith. D. W. Griffith Productions, 1916.

Salomé. Directed by J. Gordon Edwards. Fox Film Corporation, 1918.

Blade af Satans Bog (*Leaves from Satan's Book*). Directed by Carl Theodor Dreyer. Nordisk Film, 1920.

Der Galiläer (*The Galilean*). Directed by Dimitri Buchowetzki. Express-Films Co. GmbH, 1921.

I.N.R.I. (*Crown of Thorns*). Directed by Robert Wiene. Neumann-Filmproduktion, 1923.

Quo Vadis? Directed by Gabriellino D'Annunzio and Georg Jacoby. Unione Cinematografica Italiana, 1924.

Ben-Hur: A Tale of the Christ. Directed by Fred Niblo, Charles Brabin, and Christy Cabanne. Metro-Goldwyn-Mayer, 1925.

The King of Kings. Directed by Cecil B. DeMille. DeMille Pictures Corporation, 1927.

Golgotha: Ecce Homo (*Behold the Man*). Directed by Julien Duvivier. Ichtys Film, 1935.

Jesús de Nazareth (*Jesus of Nazareth*). Directed by José Díaz Morales. Pereda Films, 1942.

María Magdalena, Pecadora de Magdala (*Mary Magdalene, Sinner of Magdala*). Directed by Miguel Contreras Torres. Hispano Continental Films, 1946.

Reina de Reinas: La Virgen María (*Queen of Queens: The Virgin Mary*). Directed by Miguel Contreras Torres. Hispano Continental Films, 1948.

The Lawton Story. Directed by William Beaudine and Harold Daniels. Hallmark Productions, 1949.

The Pilgrimage Play. Directed by Frank R. Strayer. Roland Reed Productions, 1949.

Mater Dei (*Mother of God*). Directed by Emilio Cordero. Incar; Parva, 1950.

The Living Christ Series. 12 parts. Directed by John T. Coyle. Cathedral Films; J. K. F. Productions, 1951.

Quo Vadis. Directed by Mervyn LeRoy and Anthony Mann. Metro-Goldwyn-Mayer, 1951.

El Mártir del Calvario (*The Martyr of Calvary*). Directed by Miguel Morayta. Oro Films, 1952.

The Nativity. Directed by Franklin J. Schaffner. Arranged by Andrew Alan. Produced by Fletcher Markle. *Westinghouse Studio One*, season 5, episode 13. Aired December 22, 1952, on CBS.

Barabbas. Directed by Alf Sjöberg. Sandrews, 1953.

I Beheld His Glory. Directed by John T. Coyle. Cathedral Films, 1953.

The Robe. Directed by Henry Koster. Twentieth Century Fox, 1953.

Salome. Directed by William Dieterle. The Beckworth Corporation, 1953.

Day of Triumph. Directed by John T. Coyle and Irving Pichel. Century Films, 1954.

El Beso de Judas (Judas' Kiss). Directed by Rafael Gil. Aspa Producciones Cinematográficas, 1954.

The Prodigal. Directed by Richard Thorpe. Metro-Goldwyn-Mayer, 1955.

The Star of Bethlehem. Directed by Vivian Milroy, Lotte Reiniger, and Jan Sadlo. Cathedral Films; Primrose Productions, 1956.

Celui Qui Doit Mourir (He Who Must Die). Directed by Jules Dassin. Indusfilms; Prima Film; Cinétel, 1957.

The Life of Christ. 15 parts, *Mysteries of the Rosary* series. Directed by Joseph Breen and Fernando Palacios. Father Peyton's Family Theater, 1957. Also known as three films: *The Savior* (1959), *The Redeemer* (1959), *The Master* (1959).

The Power of the Resurrection. Directed by Harold Schuster. Family Films, 1958.

The Sword and the Cross. Directed by Carlo Ludovico Bragaglia. Liber Film, 1958.

Ben-Hur. Directed by William Wyler. Metro-Goldwyn-Mayer, 1959.

The Big Fisherman. Directed by Frank Borzage. Centurion, 1959.

Herod the Great. Directed by Victor Tourjansky. Vic Film; Faro Film; Explorer Film '58, 1959.

The Prince of Peace. Directed by William Beaudine and Harold Daniels. K. Gordon Murray, 1959.

Barabbas. Directed by Richard Fleischer. Columbia Pictures; Dino De Laurentiis Company, 1961.

King of Kings. Directed by Nicholas Ray. Samuel Bronston Productions, 1961.

Ponzio Pilato (Pontius Pilate). Directed by Gian Paolo Callegari and Irving Rapper. Glomer Film; Lux Compagnie Cinématographique de France, 1962.

La Ricotta. Directed by Pier Paolo Pasolini. Arco Film, 1963.

Snapaka Yohannan (John the Baptist). Directed by P. Subramaniam. Neela, 1963.

Il Vangelo Secondo Matteo (The Gospel According to St. Matthew). Directed by Pier Paolo Pasolini. Arco Film; Lux Compagnie Cinématographique de France, 1964.

The Greatest Story Ever Told. Directed by George Stevens. George Stevens Productions, 1965.

El Proceso de Cristo (The Trial of Christ). Directed by Julio Bracho. Estudios América, 1966.

The Little Drummer Boy. Directed by Jules Bass, Arthur Rankin Jr., and Takeo Nakamura. Rankin/Bass Productions, 1968.

Cristo 70. Directed by Alejandro Galindo. Foga Films; Constelación; Twentieth Century Fox, 1969.

La Voie Lactée (*The Milky Way*). Directed by Luis Buñuel. Greenwich Film Productions; Fraia Film, 1969.

Son of Man. Directed by Gareth Davies. *The Wednesday Play*, season 8, episode 25. Aired April 16, 1969, on BBC.

Jesús, el Niño Dios (*Jesus, the Child of God*). Directed by Miguel Zacarías. Panorama Films, 1971.

Jesús, Nuestro Señor (*Jesus, Our Lord*). Directed by Miguel Zacarías. Panorama Films; Producciones Zacarías S. A., 1971.

The Thorn (*The Greatest Story Overtold / The Divine Mr. J*). Directed by Peter McWilliams. Framemonger Productions, 1971.

Jesús, María y José (*Jesus, Mary and Joseph*). Directed by Miguel Zacarías. Panorama Films; Producciones Zacarías S. A., 1972.

The Master and Margaret. Directed by Aleksandar Petrović. Dunav Film; Euro International Films, 1972.

Pilatus und Andere: Ein Film für Karfreitag (*Pilate and Others*). Directed by Andrzej Wajda. Zweites Deutsches Fernsehen, 1972.

Godspell. Directed by David Greene. Columbia Pictures, 1973.

The Gospel Road: A Story of Jesus. Directed by Robert Elfstrom. Twentieth Century Fox, 1973.

Jesus. Directed by P. A. Thomas. Shaji Movies, 1973.

Jesus Christ Superstar. Directed by Norman Jewison. Universal Pictures, 1973.

Il Messia (*The Messiah*). Directed by Roberto Rossellini. Orizzonte 2000; Procinex; France 3, 1975.

Thomasleeha (*Saint Thomas*). Directed by P. A. Thomas. Thomas Family Trust, 1975.

La Última Cena (*The Last Supper*). Directed by Tomás Gutiérrez Alea. Instituto Cubano del Arte e Industria Cinematográficos, 1976.

The Passover Plot. Directed by Michael Campus. Atlas Film; Coast Industries; Golan-Globus Productions, 1976.

Jesus of Nazareth. 4 parts. Directed by Franco Zeffirelli. ITC Films; RAI Radiotelevisione Italiana, 1977.

Karunamayudu (*Ocean of Mercy*). Directed by A. Bhimsingh. Dayspring International, 1978.

Jesus. Directed by Peter Sykes and John Krish. Inspirational Films; The Genesis Project; The Jesus Film Project, 1979.

Mary and Joseph: A Story of Faith. Directed by Eric Till. Lorimar Productions; CiP-Europaische Treuhand AG; CTV Television Network, 1979.

Monty Python's Life of Brian. Directed by Terry Jones. HandMade Films; Python (Monty) Pictures, 1979.

The New Media Bible: The Gospel According to St. Luke. Directed by Peter Sykes and John Krish. The Genesis Project, 1979.

The Day Christ Died. Directed by James Cellan Jones. 20th Century Fox Television, 1980.

The Best Christmas Pageant Ever. Directed by George Schaefer. Comworld Productions; Schaefer/Karpf Productions, 1983.

Cammina, Cammina (Keep Walking). Directed by Ermanno Olmi. RAI Radiotelevisione Italiana, 1983.

The Fourth Wise Man. Directed by Michael Ray Rhodes. Paulist Productions, 1985.

Je Vous Salue, Marie (Hail Mary). Directed by Jean-Luc Godard. Sara Films; Pégase Films; JLG Films, 1985.

Quo Vadis? 6 parts. Directed by Franco Rossi. Rai 1; Leone Film Group; France 2, 1985.

Secondo Ponzio Pilato (According to Pontius Pilate). Directed by Luigi Magni. Massfilm; Reteitalia, 1987.

Un Bambino di Nome Gesù (A Child Called Jesus). Directed by Franco Rossi. Reteitalia; Leone Film Group; Media Com, 1987.

Cotton Patch Gospel. Directed by Michael Meece and Russell Treyz. Written by Clarence Jordon and Russell Treyz. Music and Lyrics by Harry Chapin. The Dramatic Publishing Company, 1988.

The Last Temptation of Christ. Directed by Martin Scorsese. Universal Pictures; Cineplex Odeon Films; Ufland Productions, 1988.

Jésus de Montréal (Jesus of Montreal). Directed by Denys Arcand. Max Films Productions; Gérard Mital Productions; National Film Board of Canada, 1989.

Incident in Judaea. Directed by Paul Bryers. Channel 4, 1991.

"A Dramatic Presentation of the Gospel of Mark." Performance by David Rhoads, 1992. Posted January 24, 2022, by Phil Ruge-Jones. YouTube, 1 hr., 48 min., 42 sec. https://www.youtube.com/watch?v=P7pgHV4pMo0.

The Gospel According to Matthew. Directed by Regardt van den Bergh. Visual Bible; Visual International, 1993.

The Judas Project. Directed by James H. Barden. Judas Project, 1993.

Per Amore, Solo per Amore (For Love, Only for Love). Directed by Giovanni Veronesi. Filmauro, 1993.

The Master and Margarita. Directed by Yuri Kara. Tvorcheskaya Assotsiatsiya Mezhdunarodnykh Programm, 1994.

The Visual Bible: Acts. Directed by Regardt van den Bergh. Visual Bible; Visual International, 1994.

Marie de Nazareth (Mary of Nazareth). Directed by Jean Delannoy. Belvision; Comité Français de Radio-Télévision; Films Azur, 1995.

The Revolutionary. Directed by Robert Marcarelli. Trinity Broadcasting Network, 1995.

Kristo. Directed by Ben Yalung. Cine Suerte, 1996.

Dogma. Directed by Kevin Smith. View Askew Productions, 1999.

Jesus. 2 parts. Directed by Roger Young. Lube; Lux Vide; Beta Film, 1999.

Mary, Mother of Jesus. Directed by Kevin Connor. Happy Crew Company; Hallmark Entertainment; The Shriver Family Film Company, 1999.

Giuseppe di Nazareth (*Joseph of Nazareth*). Directed by Raffaele Mertes and Elisabetta Marchetti. MediaTrade; Lux Vide, 2000.

Maria, Figlia del Suo Figlio (*Mary, Daughter of Her Son*). Directed by Fabrizio Costa. Canale 5; Titanus, 2000.

Maria Magdalena (*Mary Magdalene*). Directed by Raffaele Mertes. Epsilon TV Production; Lux Vide, 2000.

Maryam Moghadas (*Saint Mary*). Directed by Shahriar Bahrani. I.R.I.B. Channel 1, 2000.

The Miracle Maker. Directed by Derek W. Hayes and Stanislav Sokolov. British Broadcasting Corporation; British Screen Productions; Cartwn Cymru, 2000.

The Testaments of One Fold and One Shepherd. Directed by Kieth Merrill. Church of Jesus Christ of Latter-Day Saints, 2000.

The Cross. Directed by Lance Tracy. Emerald Cove Productions; KNN Productions, 2001.

Gli Amici di Gesú: Giuda (*The Friends of Jesus: Judas*). Directed by Raffaele Mertes. Epsilon TV Production; Lux Vide, 2001.

Gli Amici di Gesú: Tommaso (*The Friends of Jesus: Thomas*). Directed by Raffaele Mertes. Epsilon TV Production; Lux Vide, 2001.

The Jesus Film. Directed by Peter Sykes and John Krish. Inspirational Films; The Genesis Project; The Jesus Film Project, 2001.

Maryam Moghadas (*Saint Mary*). 11 parts. Directed by Shahriar Bahrani. I.R.I.B. Channel 1, 2002.

Ben-Hur. Directed by William R. Kowalchuk Jr. Goodtimes Entertainment; Agamemnon Films; Tundra Productions, 2003.

The Gospel of John. Directed by Philip Saville. Visual Bible International; Gospel of John Ltd.; Toronto Film Studios, 2003.

Judas. Directed by Charles Robert Carner. Fatima Productions; Paramount Network Television; Paulist Productions, 2004.

The Passion of the Christ. Directed by Mel Gibson. Icon Productions, 2004.

"The Passion of the Jew." *South Park*, season 8, episode 3. Directed by Trey Parker. Written by Trey Parker, Matt Stone, and Brian Graden. Aired March 31, 2004, on Comedy Central.

Santhi Sandesam (*Message of Peace*). Directed by P. Chandrasekhara Reddy. Padmalaya Studios, 2004.

Mary. Directed by Abel Ferrara. Wild Bunch; Associated Film; Central Films, 2005.

Master i Margarita (*The Master and Margarita*). 10 episodes. Directed by Vladimir Bortko. Goskino; Rossiya 1, 2005.

Color of the Cross. Directed by Jean-Claude La Marre. Nu-Lite Entertainment, 2006.

The Da Vinci Code. Directed by Ron Howard. Columbia Pictures; Imagine Entertainment; Skylark Productions, 2006.

Jezile (*Son of Man*). Directed by Mark Dornford-May. Spier Films, 2006.

La Sacra Famiglia (*The Holy Family*). Directed by Raffaele Mertes. Fidia Film; R.T.I.; Zaman Productions, 2006.

Mulla Kireetam (*Crown of Thorns*). Directed by N. S. Raja Reddy. Kyoshi Studios, 2006.

The Nativity Story. Directed by Catherine Hardwicke. New Line Cinema; Sound for Film; Temple Hill Entertainment, 2006.

Magdalena: Released from Shame. Directed by Charlie Jordan Brookins. Inspirational Films, 2007.

Mesih (*Jesus, the Spirit of God*). Directed by Nader Talebzadeh. I.R.I.B. Channel 1, 2007.

Color of the Cross 2: The Resurrection. Directed by Jean-Claude La Marre. Nu-Lite Entertainment; Blackwood Films, 2008.

El Cant dels Ocells (*Birdsong*). Directed by Albert Serra. Andergraun Films; Eddie Saeta S.A.; Televisió de Catalunya, 2008.

The Passion. 6 episodes. Directed by Michael Offer. British Broadcasting Corporation; Deep Indigo Productions; HBO Films, 2008.

Io Sono Con Te (*Let It Be*). Directed by Guido Chiesa. Colorado Film Production; Magda Film; Rai Cinema, 2010.

Mesih (*Jesus, the Spirit of God*). 13 parts. Directed by Nader Talebzadeh. I.R.I.B. Channel 1, 2010.

"Messianic Myths and Ancient Peoples." *Community*, season 2, episode 5. Directed by Tristram Shapeero. Written by Dan Harmon, Andrew Guest, and Dino Stamatopoulos. Aired October 21, 2010, on NBC.

The Nativity. 4 episodes. Directed by Coky Giedroyc. Red Planet Pictures; K Films; Temple Street Productions, 2010.

Passion in Port Talbot. Directed by Rupert Edwards. Prospect Cymru, 2011.

Apostle Peter and the Last Supper. Directed by Gabriel Sabloff. Pure Flix Productions; B-Still Productions, 2012.

Barabbas. Directed by Roger Young. Compagnia Leone Cinematografica; Rai Fiction; ReelzChannel, 2012.

The Gospel of Us. Directed by Dave McKean. Film Agency for Wales; National Theatre Wales; Rondo Media Production, 2012.

Maria di Nazaret (*Mary of Nazareth*). Directed by Giacomo Campiotti. Rai Fiction; Bayerischer Rundfunk; Lux Vide, 2012.

Su Re (*The King*). Directed by Giovanni Columbu. Luches Film; Pontificia Facoltá Teologica della Sardegna; Cagliari Opera House, 2012.

The Bible. 10 episodes. Directed by Crispin Reece, Christopher Spencer, and Tony Mitchell. K Films; LightWorkers Media, 2013.

The Life of Jesus Christ. Edited from fifty-five clips of "Bible Videos" produced by the Church of Jesus Christ of Latter-Day Saints, 2013. Posted September 9, 2013, by WildwoodCastle. YouTube, 2 hrs., 52 min., 3 sec. https://www.youtube.com/watch?v=o-ZcbjLBtls.

The Gospel of John. Directed by David Batty. Big Book Media; Endcrawl.com; H Films, 2014.

Jesus: The Desire of Ages. Directed by Nancy Hamilton and Desiree Orozco. Golden Eagle Films / Myers Media, 2014.

The Savior. Directed by Robert Savo. Grace Productions; Savo's Productions; The Imaginarium Films, 2014.

Son of God. Directed by Christopher Spencer. Hearst Entertainment Productions; K Films; LightWorkers Media, 2014.

The Two Thieves (*Once We Were Slaves*). Directed by Dallas Jenkins. Vision Video, 2014.

A.D.: The Bible Continues. 12 episodes. Directed by Ciaran Donnelly, Tony Mitchell, Brian Kelly, Rob Evans, and Paul Wilmshurst. United Artists Media Group; LightWorkers Media; K Films, 2015.

Full of Grace. Directed by Andrew Hyatt. Justin Bell Productions; ODB Films; ReKon Productions, 2015.

The Gospel of Luke. Directed by David Batty. Big Book Media; H Films; Toy Gun Films, 2015.

The Gospel of Mark. Directed by David Batty. Big Book Media; Toy Gun Films; H Films, 2015.

Histoire de Judas (*Story of Judas*). Directed by Rabah Ameur-Zaïmeche. Sarrazink Productions; ARTE; Arte France Cinéma, 2015.

Killing Jesus. Directed by Christopher Menaul. Bounder & Cad; Dune Films; Scott Free Productions, 2015.

La Espina de Dios (*The Thorn of God*). Directed by Óscar Parra de Carrizosa. Mystical Films, 2015.

Last Days in the Desert. Directed by Rodrigo García. Mockingbird Pictures; Division Films; Ironwood Entertainment, 2015.

Le Tout Nouveau Testament (*The Brand New Testament*). Directed by Jaco Van Dormael. Terra Incognita Films; Climax Films; Après le Déluge, 2015.

My Son, My Savior. Directed by Steve Boettcher. Studiohub, 2015.

The Apostle Peter: Redemption. Directed by Leif Bristow. Leif Films; Sugar Shack North Bay Productions, 2016.

Ben-Hur. Directed by Timur Bekmambetov. Paramount Pictures; Metro-Goldwyn-Mayer; LightWorkers Media, 2016.

Forty Nights. Directed by Jesse Low. Collective Development, 2016.

The Gospel of Matthew. Directed by David Batty. Big Book Media; Toy Gun Films; H Films, 2016.

Hail, Caesar! Directed by Joel Coen and Ethan Coen. Universal Pictures; Working Title Films; Mike Zoss Productions, 2016.

Jesus VR. Directed by Dave Hansen. Autumn Productions; Film Production Consultants; PanoGrama VR, 2016.

Joseph and Mary. Directed by Roger Christian. Leif Films; Sugar Shack North Bay Productions, 2016.

Risen. Directed by Kevin Reynolds. Affirm Films; Columbia Pictures; LD Entertainment, 2016.

The Young Messiah. Directed by Cyrus Nowrasteh. 1492 Pictures; CJ Entertainment; Hyde Park International, 2016.

Chasing the Star. Directed by Bret Miller. Collective Development, 2017.

The Chosen. Directed by Dallas Jenkins. 2017–.

"The Shepherd." Pilot episode of *The Chosen*. Directed and written by Dallas Jenkins. 5&2 Studio; Vertical Church Films, 2017.

Season 1, *The Chosen*. 8 episodes. Directed by Dallas Jenkins. Loaves &Fishes Production; Out of Order Studios; Vertical Church Films, 2019.

Season 2, *The Chosen*. 8 episodes. Directed by Dallas Jenkins. Loaves & Fishes Production; Out of Order Studios; The Chosen, LLC, 2021.

Christmas with "The Chosen": The Messengers. Directed by Dallas Jenkins, Jacob Schwarz, and Aaron Edson. Loaves & Fishes Production; Out of Order Studios; Mystery Box, 2021.

Season 3, *The Chosen*. 8 episodes. Directed by Dallas Jenkins. Loaves & Fishes Production; Out of Order Studios; The Chosen, LLC, 2022–23.

Christmas with "The Chosen": Holy Night. Directed by Dallas Jenkins, Jacob Schwarz, and Aaron Edson. Mystery Box; Loaves & Fishes Production; Out of Order Studios, 2023.

Season 4, *The Chosen*. 8 episodes. Directed by Dallas Jenkins. Loaves & Fishes Production; Out of Order Studios; The Chosen, LLC, 2024.

The Shack. Directed by Stuart Hazeldine. Summit Entertainment; TIK Films; Netter Productions, 2017.

The Star. Directed by Timothy Reckart. Affirm Films; Sony Pictures Animation; Walden Media, 2017.

Mary Magdalene. Directed by Garth Davis. See-Saw Films; Porchlight Films; Universal Pictures International Production, 2018.

7 Miracles. Directed by Rodrigo Cerqueira and Marco Spagnoli. Film Production Consultants; PanoGrama VR; Sun Films, 2018.

Barabbas. Directed by Evgeniy Emelin. Artworks Film Production Company, 2019.

The Christ Slayer. Directed by Nathaniel Nose. Collective Development, 2019.

Jesús de Nazaret: El Hijo de Dios (*Jesus of Nazareth*). Directed by Rafa Lara. Beverly Hills Entertainment, 2019.

Assassin 33 A.D. Directed by Jim Carroll. Timed Out Productions, 2020.

Das Neue Evangelium (*The New Gospel*). Directed by Milo Rau. Fruitmarket Kultur und Medien; Langfilm; IIPM, 2020.

40: The Temptation of Christ. Directed by Douglas James Vail. FaithWorks Pictures, 2020.

Lamentations of Judas. Directed by Boris Gerrets. KV Films; Les Films d'lci; Witfilm, 2020.

Messiah. 10 episodes. Directed by James McTeigue and Kate Woods. Industry Entertainment, 2020.

The Penitent Thief. Directed by Lucas Miles and Jon Blaze. 4:13 Films; Miles Media, 2020.

Black Easter. Directed by Jim Carroll. Timed Out Productions, 2021.

Book of Mormon Videos, season 4 (3 Nephi). 9 episodes. Directed by Blair Treu. The Church of Jesus Christ of Latter-Day Saints, 2022–23.

The Book of Clarence. Directed by The Bullitts (Jeymes Samuel). Legendary Entertainment; Legendary Studios; TriStar Pictures, 2023.

Journey to Bethlehem. Directed by Adam Anders. Affirm Films; Anders Media; Monarch Media, 2023.

The Best Christmas Pageant Ever. Directed by Dallas Jenkins. Lionsgate; Media Capital Technologies; Kingdom Story Company, 2024.

Forty-Seven Days with Jesus. Directed by Emilio Palame and David Gutel. Reel Big Studios; Vero Entertainment, 2024.

Jesus: A Deaf Missions Film. Directed by Joseph Josselyn. Deaf Missions; GUM Vision Studio, 2024.

"John the Baptist." *Martin Scorsese Presents: The Saints*, season 1, episode 2. Directed by Matti Leshem. Lionsgate Alternative Television, 2024.

Mary. Directed by D. J. Caruso. Aloe Entertainment; Creativity Media; FitzHenry Films, 2024.

The Resurrection of the Christ. Directed by Mel Gibson. Icon Productions; Lionsgate, forthcoming.

Bibliography

Adams, Sean A. *Greek Genres and Jewish Authors: Negotiating Literary Culture in the Greco-Roman Era*. Waco: Baylor University Press, 2020.

Adler, Yonatan. *The Origins of Judaism: An Archaeological-Historical Reappraisal*. The Anchor Yale Bible Reference Library. New Haven: Yale University Press, 2022.

Ascough, Richard S. "Jesus: Real to Reel." *Word and World* 29, no. 2 (2009): 179–86.

Bakker, Freek L. *The Challenge of the Silver Screen: An Analysis of the Cinematic Portraits of Jesus, Rama, Buddha, and Muhammad*. Leiden: Brill, 2009.

———. "Jesus in a Modern Contemporary Context." In Walsh, *T&T Clark Handbook of Jesus and Film*, 153–64.

Barker, James W. "The Narrative Chronology of Tatian's Diatessaron." *New Testament Studies* 66 (2020): 288–98.

———. *Tatian's Diatessaron: Composition, Redaction, Recension, and Reception*. Oxford Early Christian Studies. Oxford: Oxford University Press, 2021.

———. *Writing and Rewriting the Gospels: John and the Synoptics*. Grand Rapids: Eerdmans, 2025.

Bartholomew, Craig G. *Introducing Biblical Hermeneutics: A Comprehensive Framework for Hearing God in Scripture*. Grand Rapids: Baker Academic, 2015.

Baugh, Lloyd. *Imaging the Divine: Jesus and Christ-Figures in Film*. New York: Sheed and Ward, 1997.

———. "Three Revolutionary Gospel Films: By the People, with the People, and for the People." In Walsh, *T&T Clark Handbook of Jesus and Film*, 141–51.

Becker, Eve-Marie, Helen K. Bond, and Catrin H. Williams, eds. *John's Transformation of Mark*. London: Bloomsbury T&T Clark, 2021.

Bennema, Cornelis. *A Theory of Character in New Testament Narrative*. Minneapolis: Fortress, 2014.

Blanton, Thomas R. "Did Jewish Women Circumcise Male Infants in Antiquity? A Reassessment of the Evidence." *Journal of the Jesus Movement in its Jewish Setting* 10 (2023): 38–66.

Boillat, Alain, and Valentine Robert. "*La Vie et Passion de Notre Seigneur Jésus-Christ* (Pathé-Frères, 1902–05): Tableau Variation in the Early Cinema." In Shepherd, *Silents of Jesus in the Cinema*, 24–59.

Bond, Helen K. *Caiaphas: Friend of Rome and Judge of Jesus?* Louisville: Westminster John Knox, 2004.

———. *The First Biography of Jesus: Genre and Meaning in Mark's Gospel*. Grand Rapids: Eerdmans, 2020.

———. *Pontius Pilate in History and Interpretation*. Society for New Testament Studies Monograph Series 100. Cambridge: Cambridge University Press, 1998.

Bowen, Amber, and John Anthony Dunne, eds. *Theology and Black Mirror*. Theology, Religion, and Pop Culture. Lanham, MD: Lexington Books / Minneapolis: Fortress Academic, 2022.

Brakke, David. *The Gospel of Judas: A New Translation with Introduction and Commentary*. The Anchor Yale Bible Commentaries. New Haven: Yale University Press, 2022.

Brown, Jeannine K. "Creation's Renewal in the Gospel of John." *Catholic Biblical Quarterly* 72, no. 2 (2010): 275–90.

———. *The Gospels as Stories: A Narrative Approach to Matthew, Mark, Luke, and John*. Grand Rapids: Baker Academic, 2020.

———. "Interpreting Gentile Women in Matthew: Misrepresentation, Misappropriation, and a Missed Chance." *Journal of Gospels and Acts Research* 6 (2022): 7–24.

———. "Jesus Messiah as Isaiah's Servant of the Lord: New Testament Explorations." *Journal of the Evangelical Theological Society* 63, no. 1 (2020): 49–68.

———. "Reconstructing the Historical Pharisees: Does Matthew's Gospel Have Anything to Contribute?" In *Jesus, Skepticism and the Problem of History: Criteria and Context in the Study of Christian Origin*, edited by Darrell L. Bock and J. Ed Komoszewski, 164–82. Grand Rapids: Zondervan Academic, 2019.

———. *Scripture as Communication: Introducing Biblical Hermeneutics*. 2nd ed. Grand Rapids: Baker Academic, 2021.

Brown, Jeannine K., and Kyle Roberts. *Matthew*. Two Horizons New Testament Commentary. Grand Rapids: Eerdmans, 2018.

Burke, Tony. *The Syriac Tradition of the Infancy Gospel of Thomas: A Critical Edition and English Translation*. Gorgias Eastern Christian Studies 48. Piscataway, NJ: Gorgias, 2017.

Burnette-Bletsch, Rhonda. "The Bible and Its Cinematic Adaptations: A Consideration of Filmic Exegesis." *Journal of the Bible and Its Reception* 1, no. 1 (2014): 129–60.

———, ed. *The Bible in Motion: A Handbook of the Bible and Its Reception in Film*. 2 vols. Berlin: de Gruyter, 2016.

———. "'Tis Pity She's (Still) a Whore: Mary Magdalene in *The Chosen*." *Journal for the Study of the Historical Jesus* 20 (2022): 192–201.

Burridge, Richard A. *What Are the Gospels? A Comparison with Graeco-Roman Biography*. 25th anniv. ed. Waco: Baylor University Press, 2020.

Carlson, Stephen C. "The Accommodations of Joseph and Mary in Bethlehem: Κατάλυμα in Luke 2.7." *New Testament Studies* 56 (2010): 326–42.

Carter, Warren. *Matthew and the Margins: A Sociopolitical and Religious Reading*. Bible and Liberation. Maryknoll, NY: Orbis Books, 2001.

———. "Paying the Tax to Rome as Subversive Praxis: Matthew 17.24–27." *Journal for the Study of the New Testament* 76 (1999): 3–31.

———. *Pontius Pilate: Portraits of a Roman Governor*. Interfaces. Collegeville, MN: Liturgical Press, 2003.

Chartrand-Burke, Tony. "The Infancy Gospel of Thomas." In *The Non-Canonical Gospels*, edited by Paul Foster, 126–38. T&T Clark Biblical Studies. London: Bloomsbury, 2008.

Chattaway, Peter T. "Jesus in the Movies." *Bible Review* 14, no. 1 (1998): 28–35, 45–46.

Cohen, Jeremy. *Christ Killers: The Jews and the Passion from the Bible to the Big Screen*. Oxford: Oxford University Press, 2007.

Corley, Kathleen E., and Robert L. Webb, eds. *Jesus and Mel Gibson's "The Passion of the Christ": The Film, The Gospels and the Claims of History*. London: Continuum, 2004.

Culpepper, R. Alan. "Nicodemus: The Travail of New Birth." In Hunt et al., *Character Studies in the Fourth Gospel*, 249–59.

Dancygier, Barbara. *The Language of Stories: A Cognitive Approach*. Cambridge: Cambridge University Press, 2012.

de Bruin, Tom. *Fan Fiction and Early Christian Writings: Apocrypha, Pseudepigrapha, and Canon*. Scriptural Traces: Critical Perspectives on the Reception and Influence of the Bible 33 / Library of New Testament Studies 673. London: Bloomsbury T&T Clark, 2024.

DeConick, April D. "The True Mysteries: Sacramentalism in the 'Gospel of Philip.'" *Vigilae Christianae* 55 (2001): 225–61.

Doughty, Ruth, and Christine Etherington-Wright. *Understanding Film Theory*. 2nd ed. London: Bloomsbury Academic, 2017.

Dunne, John Anthony. *Esther and Her Elusive God: How a Secular Story Functions as Scripture*. Eugene, OR: Wipf & Stock, 2014.

———. *The Mountains Shall Drip Sweet Wine: A Biblical Theology of Alcohol*. Biblical Theology for Life. Grand Rapids: Zondervan Academic, 2025.

Dunne, John Anthony, and Kris Song, eds. *Theology, Religion, and Twin Peaks.* Theology, Religion, and Pop Culture. London: Bloomsbury, forthcoming.

Ehrman, Bart D. *The New Testament and Other Early Christian Writings: A Reader.* 2nd ed. Oxford: Oxford University Press, 2004.

Elder, Nicholas A. *Gospel Media: Reading, Writing, and Circulating Jesus Traditions.* Grand Rapids: Eerdmans, 2024.

Elliott, J. K. *Apocryphal New Testament: A Collection of Apocryphal Christian Literature in an English Translation.* Oxford: Oxford University Press, 2005.

Erlank, Natasha. "'Brought into Manhood': Christianity and Male Initiation in South Africa in the Early 20th Century." *Journal of South African Studies* 43, no. 2 (2017): 251–65.

Esteves, Junno Arocho. "Pope Francis Raises Memorial of St. Mary Magdalene to a Feast Day." *America: A Jesuit Review*, June 10, 2016. https://www.americamagazine.org/faith/2016/06/10/pope-francis-raises-memorial-st-mary-magdalene-feast-day.

Forster, E. M. "Flat and Round Characters." In *Essentials of the Theory of Fiction*, edited by Michael J. Hoffman and Patrick D. Murphy, 35–41. 3rd ed. Durham, NC: Duke University Press, 2005.

Foster, Paul. *The Gospel of Peter: Introduction, Critical Edition and Commentary.* Texts and Editions for New Testament Study 4. Leiden: Brill, 2010.

———. "The Gospel of Philip." In *The Non-Canonical Gospels*, edited by Paul Foster, 68–83. T&T Clark Biblical Studies. London: Bloomsbury, 2008.

———. "Passion Traditions in the *Gospel of Peter*." In *Gelitten—Gestorben—Auferstanden: Passions- und Ostertraditionen im antiken Christentum*, edited by Andreas Merkt, Tobias Nicklas, and Joseph Verheyden, 47–68. WUNT II/273. Tübingen: Mohr Siebeck, 2010.

———. "The Protevangelium of James." In *The Non-Canonical Gospels*, edited by Paul Foster, 110–25. T&T Clark Biblical Studies. London: Bloomsbury, 2008.

France, R. T. *The Gospel of Matthew.* New International Commentary on the New Testament. Grand Rapids: Eerdmans, 2007.

Friesen, Dwight H. "*La Vie et Passion de Notre Seigneur Jésus-Christ* (Pathé-Frères, 1907): The Preservation and Transformation of Zecca's Passion." In Shepherd, *Silents of Jesus in the Cinema*, 78–97.

Furstenberg, Yair. *Purity and Identity in Ancient Judaism: From the Temple to the Mishnah.* Translated by Sara Tova Brody. Bloomington: University of Indiana Press, 2023.

Gadamer, Hans-Georg. *Truth and Method.* 2nd rev. ed. New York: Crossroad, 1991.

Garcia, Robert K., Paul Gondreau, Patrick Gray, and Douglas S. Huffman, eds. *Watching "The Chosen": History, Faith, and Biblical Interpretation.* Grand Rapids: Eerdmans, 2025.

Garland, David E. *A Theology of Mark's Gospel*. Biblical Theology of the New Testament. Grand Rapids: Zondervan, 2015.

Gathercole, Simon James. *The Gospel of Thomas: Introduction and Commentary*. Leiden: Brill, 2014.

Gleaves, G. Scott. *Did Jesus Speak Greek? The Emerging Evidence of Greek Dominance in First-Century Palestine*. Eugene, OR: Pickwick, 2015.

Goodacre, Mark. "Do You Think You're What They Say You Are? Reflections on Jesus Christ Superstar." *Journal of Religion and Film* 3, no. 2 (1999): 1–22.

———. "The Power of *The Passion*: Reacting and Over-Reacting to Gibson's Artistic Vision." In Corley and Webb, *Jesus and Mel Gibson's "The Passion of the Christ,"* 28–44.

———. "The Synoptic Jesus and the Celluloid Christ: Solving the Synoptic Problem Through Film." *Journal for the Study of the New Testament* 80 (2000): 31–43.

———. *The Synoptic Problem: A Way Through the Maze*. Understanding the Bible and Its World. London: T&T Clark, 2001.

Gorman, Michael J. *Elements of Biblical Exegesis: A Basic Guide for Students and Ministers*. 3rd ed. Grand Rapids: Baker Academic, 2020.

Green, Joel. *Conversion in Luke-Acts: Divine Action, Human Cognition, and the People of God*. Grand Rapids: Baker Academic, 2015.

Greydanus, Steven D. "Through Other Eyes: Point of View and Defamiliarization in Jesus Films." In Walsh, *T&T Clark Handbook of Jesus and Film*, 76–87.

Gribetz, Sarit Kattan. "Hanged and Crucified: The Book of Esther and *Toledot Yeshu*." In *Toledot Yeshu ("The Life Story of Jesus") Revisited: A Princeton Conference*, edited by Peter Schäfer, Michael Meerson, and Yaacov Deutsch, 159–80. TSAJ 143. Tübingen: Mohr Siebeck, 2011.

Guðmundsdóttir, Arnfríndur. "*The Passion of the Christ* (2004)." In *Bible and Cinema: Fifty Key Films*, edited by Adele Reinhartz, 202–6. Taylor & Francis, 2012.

Hasan-Rokem, Galit. "Polymorphic Helena: *Toledot Yeshu* as a Palimpsest of Religious Narratives and Identities." In *Toledot Yeshu ("The Life Story of Jesus") Revisited: A Princeton Conference*, edited by Peter Schäfer, Michael Meerson, and Yaacov Deutsch, 247–82. TSAJ 143. Tübingen: Mohr Siebeck, 2011.

Hebron, Carol A. *Judas Iscariot: Damned or Redeemed; A Critical Examination of the Portrayal of Judas in Jesus Films (1902–2014)*. Scriptural Traces: Critical Perspectives on the Reception and Influence of the Bible 9. London: T&T Clark, 2016.

Henderson, Timothy P. *The Gospel of Peter and Early Christian Apologetics*. WUNT II/301. Tübingen: Mohr Siebeck 2011.

Hock, Ronald F. *The Infancy Gospels of James and Thomas*. The Scholars Bible. Santa Rosa, CA: Polebridge, 1995.

Hornik, Heidi J., Ian Boxall, and Bobbi Dykema, eds. Introduction to *The Art of Biblical Interpretation: Visual Portrayals of Scriptural Narratives*, 1–9. Atlanta: SBL Press, 2021.

Huckabee, Tyler. "Never Forget That 'VeggieTales' Weren't Allowed to Show Jesus as a Vegetable." *Relevant*, June 9, 2021. https://relevantmagazine.com/culture/never-forget-that-veggietales-werent-allowed-to-show-jesus-as-a-vegetable/.

Huizenga, Leroy A. *The New Testament: Tradition and Intertextuality in the Gospel of Matthew*. Supplements to Novum Testamentum 131. Leiden: Brill, 2009.

Hunt, Steven A., D. Francois Tolmie, and Ruben Zimmerman, eds. *Character Studies in the Fourth Gospel: Narrative Approaches to Seventy Figures in John*. Grand Rapids: Eerdmans, 2016.

Isenberg, Wesley W., trans. "The Gospel of Philip (II, 3)." In *The Nag Hammadi Library*, edited by James M. Robinson, 131–51. San Francisco: Harper & Row, 1977.

Jensen, Robin Margaret. *Understanding Early Christian Art*. London: Routledge, 2000.

Judd, Andrew. *Modern Genre Theory: An Introduction for Biblical Studies*. Grand Rapids: Zondervan, 2024.

Kazantzakis, Nikos. *The Last Temptation of Christ*. Translated by P. A. Bien. New York: Simon & Schuster, 2015. First published in Greek in 1952.

King, Karen L. "The Place of the *Gospel of Philip* in the Context of Early Christian Claims About Jesus' Marital Status." *New Testament Studies* 59 (2013): 565–87.

Knust, Jennifer, and Tommy Wasserman. *To Cast the First Stone: The Transmission of a Gospel Story*. Princeton: Princeton University Press, 2018.

Kreitzer, Larry. *Gospel Images in Fiction and Film: On Reversing the Hermeneutical Flow*. Biblical Seminar 84. London: Sheffield Academic, 2002.

———. *The New Testament in Fiction and Film: On Reversing the Hermeneutical Flow*. Biblical Seminar 17. Sheffield: Sheffield Academic, 1993.

———. *The Old Testament in Fiction and Film: On Reversing the Hermeneutical Flow*. Biblical Seminar 24. Sheffield: Sheffield Academic, 1994.

———. *Pauline Images in Fiction and Film: On Reversing the Hermeneutical Flow*. Biblical Seminar 61. Sheffield: Sheffield Academic, 1999.

Levine, Amy-Jill. "Putting Jesus Where He Belongs: The Man from Nazareth in His Jewish World." *Perspectives in Religious Studies* 27 (2000): 167–78.

Malone, Peter. *Screen Jesus: Portrayals of Christ in Television and Film*. Lanham, MD: Scarecrow, 2012.

———. "'Who Do You Say That I Am?': Responses to Cinema Sequences of the Woman Taken in Adultery." In Walsh, *T&T Clark Handbook of Jesus and Film*, 31–40.

Martyn, J. Louis. *History and Theology in the Fourth Gospel*. New Testament Library. Louisville: Westminster John Knox, 1968.

McGeough, Kevin M. "The 'False Syllogism' of Archaeological Authenticity in Jesus Movies." In Walsh, *T&T Clark Handbook of Jesus and Film*, 115–25.

McGrath, James F. *Christmaker: A Life of John the Baptist*. Grand Rapids: Eerdmans, 2024.

Meier, J. P. *A Marginal Jew*. Vol. 3, *Rethinking the Historical Jesus*. Anchor Yale Bible Reference Library. New Haven: Yale University Press, 2001.

Middleton, Darren J. N., and S. Brent Plate. "'Who Do You See That I Am?': Global Perspectives on Jesus Films." *New Theology Review* (August 2011): 17–28.

Mills, Ian N. "Crucifying the Musical Christ: The Politics of Jesus' Death in 'Godspell' and 'Jesus Christ Superstar.'" *The Revealer: A Review of Religion and Media*, March 7, 2024. https://therevealer.org/crucifying-the-musical-christ/.

———. "A Metamodern Jesus: Failed Apocalypse and Post-Postmodern Religion in Dan Harmon's *Community*." In *The Routledge Handbook of the Bible and Film*, edited by Jason Buel and Shane Thompson. New York: Routledge, forthcoming.

Mokoena, Katleho K. "Steve Biko Christ-Figure: A Black Theological Christology in the *Son of Man* Film." *HTS Theological Studies* (2017): 1–8.

Mroczek, Eva. *The Literary Imagination in Jewish Antiquity*. Oxford: Oxford University Press, 2016.

Nel, Marius J. "He Who Laughs Last: Jesus and Laughter in the Synoptic and Gnostic Traditions." *HTS Teologiese Studies* 70, no. 1 (2014): 1–8.

North, Wendy E. S. *What John Knew and What John Wrote*. New York: Lexington Books / Fortress Academic, 2020.

Oatley, Keith. *Such Stuff as Dreams: The Psychology of Fiction*. West Sussex, UK: Wiley-Blackwell, 2011.

Page, Matthew. *100 Bible Films*. BFI Screen Guides. London: Bloomsbury, 2022.

Perrin, Nicholas. "Diatessaron." In *The Reception of Jesus in the First Three Centuries*. Vol. 2, *From Thomas to Tertullian: Christian Literary Receptions of Jesus in the Second and Third Centuries CE*, ed. Jens Schröter and Christine Jacobi, 141–60. London: T&T Clark, 2020.

Pietz, Jennifer Vija. *Mary Magdalene, La Malinche, and the Ethics of Interpretation*. Lanham, MD: Lexington Books / Fortress Academic, 2023.

Porter, Stanley E. "Did Jesus Ever Teach in Greek?" *Tyndale Bulletin* 44, no. 2 (1993): 199–235.

———. *When Paul Met Jesus: How an Idea Got Lost in History*. Cambridge: Cambridge University Press, 2016.

Powell, Mark Allan. *Chasing the Eastern Star: Adventures in Biblical Reader Response Criticism*. Louisville: Westminster John Knox, 2001.

Reinhartz, Adele. *Bible and Cinema: An Introduction*. Abingdon: Routledge, 2013.

———, ed. *The Bible and Cinema: Fifty Key Films*. Routledge Key Guides. London: Routledge, 2012.

———. “Jesus and Christ-Figures.” In *The Routledge Companion to Religion and Film*, edited by John Lyden, 420–39. New York: Routledge, 2011.

———. *Jesus of Hollywood*. Oxford: Oxford University Press, 2007.

———. “The Pharisees on Film.” In *The Pharisees*, edited by Joseph Sievers and Amy-Jill Levine, 344–60. Grand Rapids: Eerdmans, 2021.

Robbins, Vernon K. “New Testament Texts, Visual Material Culture, and Earliest Christian Art.” In *The Art of Visual Exegesis: Rhetoric, Texts, Images*, edited by Vernon K. Robbins, Walter S. Melion, and Roy R. Jeal, 13–54. Emory Studies in Early Christianity. Atlanta: SBL Press, 2017.

Roberts, Alexander, and James Donaldson, eds. *The Ante-Nicene Fathers: Translations of the Writings of the Fathers Down to A.D. 325*. 10 vols. New York: Scribner’s Sons, 1885–87. Reprint, Peabody, MA: Hendrickson, 1994.

Rüggemeier, Jan, and Elizabeth E. Shively. “Introduction: Towards a Cognitive Theory of New Testament Characters; Methodology, Problems, and Desiderata.” *Biblical Interpretation* 29 (2021): 403–29.

Russell, D. A. “On Reading Plutarch’s *Lives*.” *Greece and Rome* 13 (1966): 139–54.

Sabar, Ariel. *Veritas: A Harvard Professor, A Con Man and the Gospel of Jesus’s Wife*. New York: Doubleday, 2020.

Schrader, Elizabeth, and Joan E. Taylor. “The Meaning of ‘Magdalene’: A Review of the Literary Evidence.” *Journal of Biblical Literature* 140, no. 4 (2021): 751–73.

Shepherd, David J. “Introduction: The Silence/Silents of Jesus.” In Shepherd, *Silents of Jesus in the Cinema*, 24–59.

———. “*La naissance, la vie et la mort du Christ* (Gaumont, 1906): The Gospel According to Alice Guy.” In Shepherd, *Silents of Jesus in the Cinema*, 60–77.

———, ed. *The Silents of Jesus in the Cinema (1897–1927)*. Routledge Studies in Religion and Film. London: Routledge, 2016.

Skinner, Christopher W., ed. *Characters and Characterization in the Gospel of John*. London: Bloomsbury T&T Clark, 2013.

Snodgrass, Klyne R. “The Temple Incident.” In *Key Events in the Life of the Historical Jesus: A Collaborative Exploration of Context and Coherence*, edited by Darrell L. Bock and Robert L. Webb, 429–75. WUNT I/247. Tübingen: Mohr Siebeck, 2009.

Soon, Isaac T. “The Little Messiah: Jesus as τῇ ἡλικίᾳ μικρός in Luke 19:3.” *Journal of Biblical Literature* 142, no. 1 (2023): 151–70.

Staley, Jeffrey L. “The First Seventy Years of Jesus Films: A Canonical, Source-Critical History.” In Walsh, *T&T Clark Handbook of Jesus and Film*, 89–102.

Stein, Robert H. *Mark*. Baker Exegetical Commentary on the New Testament. Grand Rapids: Baker Academic, 2008.

Stern, Richard C., Clayton N. Jefford, and Guerric DeBona. *Savior on the Silver Screen*. Mahwah, NJ: Paulist Press, 1999.

Stockwell, Peter. *Cognitive Poetics: An Introduction*. 2nd ed. London: Routledge, 2020.

Strauss, Mark L. *Four Portraits, One Jesus*. 2nd ed. Grand Rapids: Zondervan Academic, 2020.

Tatum, W. Barnes. *Jesus at the Movies: A Guide to the First Hundred Years*. 2nd ed. Santa Rosa, CA: Polebridge, 2004.

Taylor, Joan E., ed. *Jesus and Brian: Exploring the Historical Jesus and His Times via "Monty Python's Life of Brian."* London: Bloomsbury T&T Clark, 2015.

———. *What Did Jesus Look Like?* London: Bloomsbury T&T Clark, 2018.

Telford, William R. "*Monty Python's Life of Brian* and the Jesus Film." In Taylor, *Jesus and Brian*, 3–18.

Terian, Abraham. *The Armenian Gospel of the Infancy*. Oxford: Oxford University Press, 2008.

Thiessen, Matthew. *Jesus and the Forces of Death: The Gospels' Portrayal of Ritual Impurity Within First-Century Judaism*. Grand Rapids: Baker Academic, 2020.

Thistleton, Anthony C. *The Two Horizons: New Testament Hermeneutics and Philosophical Description*. Grand Rapids: Eerdmans, 1980.

Thomassen, Einar. *The Spiritual Seed: The Church of the 'Valentinians.'* Nag Hammadi and Manichaean Studies. Leiden: Brill, 2006.

Tuckett, Christopher M. *The Gospel of Mary*. Oxford: Oxford University Press, 2007.

Turner, Katie. *Costuming Christ: Re-Dressing First-Century 'Jews' and 'Christians' in Passion Dramas*. Library of New Testament Studies. London: T&T Clark, forthcoming.

———. "The Representation of New Testament Figures in Passion Dramas." PhD diss., King's College London, 2018.

———. "'The Shoe Is the Sign!' Costuming *Brian* and Dressing the First Century." In Taylor, *Jesus and Brian*, 221–37.

Vanhoozer, Kevin J. *Is There a Meaning in This Text? The Bible, the Reader, and the Morality of Literary Knowledge*. Grand Rapids: Zondervan Academic, 1998.

Wainright, Elaine M. *Shall We Look for Another? A Feminist Rereading of the Matthean Jesus*. Maryknoll, NY: Orbis Books, 1998.

Wallace, Daniel B. "Mark 16:8 as the Conclusion to the Second Gospel." In *Perspectives on the Ending of Mark: Four Views*, edited by David Alan Black, 1–39. Nashville: B&H, 2008.

Walsh, Richard. "*The Birth of a Nation* (D. W. Griffith, 1915) and *Intolerance* (Triangle/Wark, 1916): Griffith's Talismanic Jesus." In Shepherd, *Silents of Jesus in the Cinema*, 179–99.

———. "Reading the Gospel(s) in the Dark: The Gospel Effect." In *T&T Clark Handbook of Jesus and Film*, 103–14.

———. *Reading the Gospels in the Dark: Portrayals of Jesus in Film*. London: Trinity Press International, 2003.

———, ed. *The T&T Clark Handbook of Jesus and Film*. London: T&T Clark, 2021.

Walsh, Richard, and Jeffrey Staley. *Jesus, the Gospels, and Cinematic Imagination: Introducing Jesus Movies, Christ Films, and the Messiah in Motion*. London: T&T Clark, 2021.

Watson, Francis. "Towards a Redaction-Critical Reading of the Diatessaron Gospel." *Early Christianity* 7 (2016): 95–112.

Webb, Robert L. "*The Passion* and the Influence of Emmerich's *The Dolorous Passion of Our Lord Jesus Christ*." In Corley and Webb, *Jesus and Mel Gibson's "The Passion of the Christ,"* 160–72.

Witherington, Ben, III. *The Gospel of Mark: A Socio-Rhetorical Commentary*. Grand Rapids: Eerdmans, 2001.

Wolterstorff, Nicholas. "Three Films About Jesus." *The Reformed Journal* (1973): 8–11.

Zwick, Reinhold. "*Son of Man* (*Jezile*) (2006)." In *Bible and Cinema: Fifty Key Films*, edited by Adele Reinhartz, 242–47. London: Taylor & Francis, 2012.

Film Index

Name Index

Scripture and Ancient Sources Index

Mark